Falastiniyyat

Nada Elia is a diasporic Palestinian scholar and activist and a founding member of the Palestinian Feminist Collective. She is the author of *Greater Than the Sum of Our Parts: Feminism, Inter/Nationalism, and Palestine* and *Palestine and Feminist Liberation.*

Falastiniyyat

A Century of Palestinian Feminisms

Nada Elia

VERSO
London • New York

First published by Verso 2026

The manufacturer's authorized representative in the EU for product safety (GPSR) is LOGOS EUROPE, 9 rue Nicolas Poussin, 17000, La Rochelle, France
contact@logoseurope.eu

1 3 5 7 9 10 8 6 4 2

Verso
UK: 6 Meard Street, London W1F 0EG
US: 207 East 32nd Street, New York, NY 10016
versobooks.com

Verso is the imprint of New Left Books

ISBN-13: 978-1-80429-705-6
ISBN-13: 978-1-80429-707-0 (US EBK)
ISBN-13: 978-1-80429-708-7 (UK EBK)

British Library Cataloguing in Publication Data
A catalogue record for this book is available from the British Library

Library of Congress Cataloging-in-Publication Data

Names: Elia, Nada author
Title: Falastiniyyat : a century of Palestinian feminisms / Nada Elia.
Description: London ; New York : Verso, 2026. | Includes bibliographical references and index.
Identifiers: LCCN 2026023965 (print) | LCCN 2026023966 (ebook) | ISBN 9781804297056 trade paperback | ISBN 9781804297070 ebook
Subjects: LCSH: Feminism—Palestine—History | Women, Palestinian Arab—Political activity | Anti-imperialist movements—Palestine
Classification: LCC HQ1728.5 .E448 2026 (print) | LCC HQ1728.5 (ebook)
LC record available at https://lccn.loc.gov/2026023965
LC ebook record available at https://lccn.loc.gov/2026023966

Typeset in Sabon by MJ & N Gavan, Truro, Cornwall
Printed and bound by CPI Group (UK) Ltd, Croydon CR0 4YY

To my mother,
Laila Hanna Mourey,
Daughter of Falasteen

Contents

Acknowledgments

I generally shy away from acknowledging individuals as I send a book to publication, because of my awareness that no list can ever be complete, as well as my concern that a friend may feel slighted by not seeing their name among those whose support I do recognize. So I will not name anyone here. But I must acknowledge my debt to the Palestinian Feminist Collective, which has been my political home for the past five years, and through which I have honed my analysis and learned valuable lessons in caring, organizing, and sustaining life and love during an accelerated genocide.

A Note on Terminology

In this book, I do not refer to al-Nakba as a moment frozen in time, which occurred on May 15, 1948. Rather, I speak of "the onset of al-Nakba" to emphasize that the displacement, dispossession, land theft, massacres, and other such crimes that characterized the foundation of Israel in 1948 are all ongoing.

Similarly, as I write about Israel's war on Gaza in the aftermath of the October 7, 2023, attacks, I write about an accelerated or intensified genocide, since Israel's genocide of the Palestinian people has been ongoing since 1948. This is according to the UN definition of the term, which states:

> Genocide means any of the following acts committed with intent to destroy, in whole or in part, a national, ethnical, racial or religious group, as such:
>
> (a) Killing members of the group;
>
> (b) Causing serious bodily or mental harm to members of the group;
>
> (c) Deliberately inflicting on the group conditions of life calculated to bring about its physical destruction in whole or in part;
>
> (d) Imposing measures intended to prevent births within the group;
>
> (e) Forcibly transferring children of the group to another group.

Since 1948, Israel has actively engaged in (a) through (d) of this definition.

Genocide deniers point to the fact that intentionality is a critical component of the definition ("intent to destroy"), but they would be hard put to argue convincingly that Israel has not always intended to destroy, at least "in part," the Palestinian people.

I use "Third World," even though the term may be historically obsolete since the collapse of the Soviet Union, because it nevertheless still holds a revolutionary meaning, expressing an aspiration toward an alternative, away from the binary of US empire and the former Soviet Bloc. The "Third World" is thus not an economic designation; rather, it is rooted in the Non-Aligned Movement, consisting primarily of recently independent states, or states still colonized by European imperial powers, which rejected the two superpower blocs. I have used "Third World feminists" to refer not only to feminists in the Third World, but to feminists in the West who embrace a gendered analysis that gives consideration to the impacts of racism, colonialism, and neocolonialism, while taking into account community organizing, Indigenous knowledge, and everyday strategies for survival. I use "Third World feminism" to refer to feminism that is about collective empowerment, rather than individual advancement within a rights-based framework.

I have used "Global North feminism" to refer to feminism that embraces the ideologies of the Global North, regardless of the racial identity of the beholders. Similarly, "colonial feminists" are feminists who embrace a colonial ideology, regardless of their own racial or ethnic background. Colonial feminists depict Palestinian women as oppressed by their own culture and in need of saving, through war and colonial intervention, but completely ignore the larger oppressive system of Israeli occupation and militarism, even though this has gendered aspects that impact the lives of women, children, and men. Prime examples include Hillary Clinton and Kamala Harris, respectively white and Black-Brown, who seem oblivious to the fact that Palestinian women are more oppressed by Israel than by Arab patriarchy.

And I use "Indigenous" to refer to the people who belong to the land, who feel they have obligations to steward the land, and who cannot fathom thriving away from the land. Many of us are dispersed around the globe, but our dream, our demand, our right, is to return to our land. Settlers believe they can own or steal land,

and that they have rights to it, rather than obligations. As Yaacov Fauci, a settler born in Brooklyn, New York, told Palestinian activist Muna el-Kurd about her family home in Sheikh Jarrah, Jerusalem: "If I don't steal it, someone else will."

Introduction

Random Acts of Feminism

I am a freedom fighter. So I will not be the victim.

—Ahed Tamimi, upon her release at age seventeen from Israeli prison for slapping an occupation soldier (*Guardian*, July 30, 2018)

I grew up in a household of women and children that, as my sisters and I matured, eventually became a household of only women. My father was frequently gone on long overseas business trips before his untimely death when I was seven. I often wonder if this is the reason the expression "women and children" strikes me as essentially flawed: It suggests that women and children are the more vulnerable members of society, rather than its resilient survivors. It infantilizes women by grouping them with children, rather than adult men. In the context of a national struggle, it strips women of agency, as if such agency can only manifest through armed revolt. In a military context, the expression "women and children"—or "womenandchildren," to use the term coined by antimilitary feminist scholar Cynthia Enloe—presumes that women and children never take up arms or participate in resistance, even as we see such actions occurring in numerous struggles around the world. And in listing casualties, it implies that men's deaths and injuries are less tragic, less mournable.

In the case of Palestine, women and youth have led, and continue to lead, some of the most transformative efforts and initiatives in our people's quest for justice—that is, our resistance first to imperialism, then to settler colonialism and apartheid. They have not been spared Israel's violence, just for being women, or children, and many have been and remain at the forefront of popular resistance to Zionism's ultimate aim of eliminating all Palestinians. While this may have become more obvious during Israel's accelerated genocidal assault on Gaza following Hamas's October 7, 2023, attacks, it had always been clear to anyone not deliberately looking away. From a number of uprisings over the past century in Palestine, it is obvious that youth, "the children," are not just among the leaders; they are the more effective, because more transformational, leaders. Unfettered by traditions and social norms they do not relate to, they engage in novel forms of organizing, seeking the complete abolition of oppressive systems, rather than their reversal. And women, in their capacity as autonomous adults, rather than merely as wives and mothers, have consistently resisted both the imperial ideology targeting their country, and the military assaults that accompanied it. They did so while providing men, as well as the youth and children, the moral, emotional, and practical support the Palestinian people need in order to persist. This was perhaps most evident on a global scale during the 1987–93 Intifada, when women organized most of the popular committees tending to the educational, nutritional, and health needs of Palestinians resisting Israel's clampdown, as youth took to the streets daily to express their rejection of Israel's decades-long oppressive rule. These defenseless children hurled rocks at armored tanks, fully aware of the hefty price they would pay for their defiant act, because they knew that risking limb and life is preferable to living without freedom and dignity.

Women's and children's agency is enacted daily in the courage of girls such as Janna Jihad, who was dubbed "the world's youngest journalist" when she started documenting Israel's crimes at a mere seven years of age. Jihad started recording Israel's attacks using her mother's cell phone, posting her recordings far and wide on social media. She has repeatedly said that her camera is her weapon of choice. Jihad is the cousin of Ahed Tamimi, the "lioness" who has confronted heavily armed Israeli soldiers determined to take over her village lands since she was a toddler. Israel imprisoned Tamimi for eight months when she was sixteen; she used the time behind bars to read up on international law, later enrolling in college planning to go to law school, so as to hold Israel accountable for its violations. "I am a freedom fighter. So I will not be the victim," she told journalists upon her release.

Palestinian children's agency was also clear in the 2022 uprising of rebellious youth standing up to Israel's might. Ibrahim al-Nabulsi, dubbed "the Lion of Nablus," was eighteen when he was brutally assassinated by the Israeli Occupation Forces. Following his martyrdom, his mother, Huda al-Nabulsi, declared, "There are hundreds of Ibrahims now. You are all Ibrahim, you are all my children." She did not mean that all young Palestinians will be martyred like her own son but, rather, that they will carry on the struggle she raised her son Ibrahim to fight. Her statement recalls that of Fatima Breijeh, a decade earlier. Breijeh, who had lost one son to Israel's violence, asserted: "I have decided to continue to resist until the last breath and to continue to urge people to resist and to teach my children to resist and to lay the foundation for this through their milk."[1] Breijeh, Nabulsi, Tamimi, and Jihad are some of the more recent Palestinian women and children challenging Israel's might, and its mighty oppression. They do not present a new social development but, rather, follow in the footsteps of generations of Palestinian women and children who have stood up to colonialism in the past century, deftly navigating their social and political circumstances as they have sought their liberation, and that of their people. And in the Diaspora, it is groups like the Palestine Youth Movement, the Palestinian Feminist Collective, and the youth-led Within Our Lifetime who are at the forefront of organizing for total liberation.

My own mother is a poor urban Jerusalemite, from Musrara, in what is now "East Jerusalem." She was born in 1932, during the British Mandate, which encouraged the adoption of European names, hence Laila, the name her parents gave her at birth, gradually gave way to "Evelyn." We do not have deeds to our home, because her family did not own property. My father is from Maskubiyyeh, but he grew up fatherless and intermittently spent weeks in the orphanage in which his mother, when unable to care for him, placed him and his sister, three years his elder. "Maskubiyyeh," the Arabic rendition of "Moscovia," once referred to the neighborhood immediately around the Russian Quarter in what is now "West Jerusalem." It is one of the oldest districts in the city, featuring a hospital, a large Russian Orthodox church, the Russian-owned Sergei's Courtyard, the Russian consulate general in Jerusalem, as well as numerous former hostels for both men and women pilgrims to the holy city. Some of these are used today as Israeli government buildings, including the Maskubiyyeh detention center, notorious for its dungeons where Palestinian prisoners are tortured by Israeli "security" forces. Today, the hospital is used as the prison dispensary.

My paternal grandmother was a young wife, mother only to my aunt, when her husband, my grandfather, decided to strike out for a better life for his family and try his fortune in the US. Neither of them knew she was pregnant with my father when he left. My grandfather sent her one postcard from "the New World," informing her he had arrived and that he would be sending for her and my aunt, the child he knew about, as soon as he found some employment and a place for them to stay. That postcard was the last communication she ever received from my grandfather. She held on to it till her dying day, a testament to her "respectable" status, a wife, a married woman, even as she gave birth as a single mother, cleaned houses, and briefly placed my aunt and father in an orphanage, because it was their best chance to be fed, clothed, and roofed.[2] I was an inquisitive child and asked endless questions before managing to gather this minimal information, not from my grandmother, who was too "ashamed" of her destitute past, but from my aunt, when she eventually became a successful business owner, albeit in the Far Diaspora, where her name, Farida, had effortlessly slipped into Frieda. How many such stories of resilient, resourceful women are there that were not recorded, precisely because these women felt "lesser" and wanted their stories hushed up?

At the time, "orphanages" raised the out-of-wedlock babies of single mothers, who delivered their infants in secrecy, generally inside the building that would have harbored them as their pregnancy became visible. Most never saw their children again, unless they were fortunate enough to secure a job on site. I have met a few of these "orphans," adults at the time I spoke to them, who truly had no knowledge of any family member whatsoever, as they were given the names of fictitious parents rather than that of their unwed mother. Orphanages also raised the children of indigent parents who could not feed their children. In Palestine, close-knit extended families took care of all their members; thus, children whose parents were dead, rather than unwed, rarely needed to go to an orphanage. They would be absorbed into the larger family, cared for by relatives. However, if a social disruption had occurred—and al-Nakba, the catastrophe that befell the Palestinian people beginning in 1948, was certainly a seismic disruption—the parent, generally a mother somehow severed from her extended family and support network, could resort to placing her child in an orphanage. Why did my aunt and father spend time in an orphanage, even though their mother was close by, never abandoned them, and eventually came to live with us? I can only assume that, like tens of thousands of Palestinians in the opening decades of the twentieth century, she was too poor to provide for her two children and thought they would be better cared for by the orphanage staff. I have a vague but persistent memory of her, sleeping in the large bedroom I shared with my sisters, telling me about the one postcard her husband had sent her. I never knew him, my paternal grandfather, just as I never knew my maternal grandfather, who was already dead in 1948, when his wife fled to Lebanon with seven young children in tow. My two grandmothers, poor, illiterate, had navigated al-Nakba and their forced exile as single mothers, strong and resourceful.

My paternal grandmother died when I was four. My father died three years later. And a few years after that, my maternal grandmother passed. With the exception of the few shreds I gathered, my grandmothers' stories, which they were reluctant to tell me, faded away with them. Though never documented, they are important. I was raised by resilient women, my mother and aunt, who themselves had been raised by resilient women. They, and the thousands of other strong, resourceful women, are Handala's many sisters, the record of whose struggles fall through the cracks caused by poverty, illiteracy, patriarchy, and imperialism. I cannot imagine that they thought of themselves as feminists, a term only a handful of educated women were familiar with at the time, even as they engaged in multiple random acts of feminism, empowering themselves in order to sustain and in turn empower their communities, as the world they were used to was crumbling all around them.

Recently, I met and befriended women who told me they had gone to school in Dar al-Tifl al-Arabi (the Arab Children's Home), the orphanage founded by Jerusalemite Hind al-Husseini in the aftermath of the Deir Yassin massacre, as she converted her upper-class family's mansion into a home for the fifty-five children whose parents and relatives had been executed in the massacre. By the time my own friends went to Dar al-Tifl, the institution had expanded, with buildings that included a nursery and kindergarten, a boarding school, and a day school with over twenty classrooms—while retaining the orphanage and focusing on the needs of the most dispossessed of the Palestinian children. Like me, my friends had lost their fathers. When their mothers could not support them, they had placed them in the boarding school, restricted by that time to "female orphans and needy girls." They have very fond memories of Dar al-Tifl, describing their time there as "the best years of our lives." Because of the vision and selfless love of Hind al-Husseini, carried on today by Hind's friend Mahira al-Dajjani and the foundation's advisory board, these women never felt abandoned as children. They knew how much their mothers loved them and wanted the best for them, and that being placed in Dar al-Tifl offered them the warm shelter and daily meals their mothers could not consistently provide them.

History, we are told, is written by the victors. History also tends to narrate the stories of the elite, the rich, the privileged. We know of Hind al-Husseini's founding Dar al-Tifl, for which we are immensely grateful. But what do we know about the hundreds of children who have grown up, as well as those who continue to be sheltered and educated in that mansion, except for the cases where some have become famous themselves?[3] There is still so much that cries out to be documented, especially in the Diaspora, where our fragmentation across continents and languages presents an even greater challenge to the task of recording our experiences. This book is my effort at *lamlama* (gathering up), as I piece together the shards of our memories and reconstitute some of the experiences of those neglected by historians.

My own childhood was neither easy nor happy, and it was certainly not safe, but it is illustrative of the diverse backgrounds and experiences of Palestinian feminist organizers. I barely knew my father, whose job took him out of the country for weeks at a time. Upon his premature death, my mother raised us, her four young daughters, as best she could. In Lebanon, where we grew up, she put herself through secretarial school so she could obtain employment to support us, and eventually took driving lessons and bought a car, so we could visit our aunts and cousins on weekends. We were poor; my mother struggled to make ends meet, and frequently failed. My aunt, her sister-in-law, helped us out, and as she rose above poverty into the middle class, she eventually paid for my college education. Neither my mother nor my aunt would have called themselves feminists, yet it is their determination to rise above their personal and political circumstances, to make a better life for my sisters and me, that allowed me to become the woman that I am.

I am now a feminist scholar based on Turtle Island, and my aim in this book is to capture some of the stories of Palestinian women organizers both in the homeland and in the North American Diaspora, to add to the mosaic of our experiences globally.

A Land-Based Identity

Palestinian women, and our sense of identity *as Palestinians*, predate Israel, just as we will outlive it. Regardless of the claim by some Zionists that the Palestinian people never existed—an absurdity proclaimed by Golda Meir in 1969, when she was Israel's prime minister, and regularly pandered since, including in 2023, by Israeli settler and Knesset Member Bezalel Smotrich—our consciousness, our sense of belonging to the land, predates the imperial and colonial boundaries drawn by Europe in the aftermath of World War II. Meir's statement about the Palestinian people, namely that "they did not exist," reveals the Eurocentrism of Zionists, who do not recognize Indigenous belonging to the land when that belonging does not take the form of a modern nation-state, or simply when it stands in the way of the settlers' desire to steal that land.[4] It is equivalent to the claim that Turtle Island, the North American continent, was up for grabs because the Indigenous peoples of this land did not have borders and flags recognized by the settlers. Throughout history, and around the globe, peoples, and nations, have existed and identified with the land before the official creation of countries. Many roamed vast distances in search of food and water, traditionally stopping at a significant topographical boundary. A river, ravine, mountain range, or the sea or ocean—that is, a natural feature—would delineate the territory that offered them their subsistence needs. Indeed, identifying one's nationality through a modern state's borders is itself a settler characteristic: The Indigenous peoples whose land straddles the US-Mexico border, which they refer to as "the imaginary line," or the US-Canada border, which they think of as the "medicine line," do not see themselves as members of two different nations. Centuries after the conquest and division of their land by European colonizers, the Indigenous peoples of Turtle Island, now in Canada, the US, and Mexico, still identify as Mohawk, Tlingit, Haida, Lipan Apache, or Tohono O'odham. The superimposition of these countries over Turtle Island, despite the violent and systemic colonial attempt at eliminating the Indigenous nations, failed to erase these land-based identities.

Similarly, despite its relentless savagery, Israel has failed to erase Palestine, the Palestinian people's attachment to our land, or our identification as Palestinian. The settler colonial idea that the Palestinians "did not exist" because Palestine was not a sovereign state is simply preposterous. The land known to its inhabitants as Falasteen was part of the Ottoman Empire for four centuries, from 1516 until the end of World War I, when the three decades of the

British Mandate began. There is ample documentation of the fact that Palestinians referred to ourselves as Palestinians, not Turks, even though we were called that by outsiders. The most influential Arabic-language newspaper under both the Ottoman Empire and the British Mandate was *Falastin*, founded in Yaffa in 1911. The newspaper was highly critical both of the British Mandate's plans to create a Jewish homeland in parts of Palestine and, later, of Zionism and Israel itself. It also published numerous editorials expressing concern for the Palestinian peasants, who at the time were the population most imminently threatened with dispossession.

With our homeland located between three continents, Palestinians understood and took into stride cultural and ethnic diversity centuries before this became a buzzword, in stark contrast to Israel's attempts to "Judaize" the area by ethnically cleansing its non-Jewish stewards. Even though most of us claim Arab cultural identity, we also consider ourselves descendant of the Indigenous peoples who had lived on the land since time immemorial, as well as the relatively more recent exogenous communities: Greeks, Turks, Russians, Armenians, and North Africans, among others. Jerusalem's old quarters, named after different communities, are an indication of that long-standing diversity. Palestinians also view ourselves as descendants from the ancient Canaanites, who lived in the area thousands of years ago. This rooted diversity is a source of pride, as it makes Palestinians heirs to numerous civilizations that have blended to create the distinctive Palestinian identity. Nor did Palestinians ever identify with a single religion: Variations of Judaism, Christianity, and Islam are all understood as the religions of the land.[5] Similarly, Bedouin and Black are equally Palestinian.[6] Palestinians did not feel threatened culturally by the Ottoman Empire, which did not attempt to transform the region as much as exploit it financially and, much later, as its military power waned, for the purpose of drafting subject citizens into the ranks of its army. Under the influence of growing European nationalism, and buoyed by the Arab intellectual and literary renaissance of the late nineteenth century, Palestinians started identifying as "Arab," itself an amorphous ethnic designation, while retaining their appreciation of their multifaceted cultural specificity as Palestinians. The idea that Palestinians did not identify as such until Zionism threatened our identity—indeed, sought to obliterate our very existence—is simply untenable: We would not feel threatened, as a people, if we did not exist *as a people*. Our resistance, historically, has not been merely to remain alive but to remain Palestinian, in Palestine.

Palestinian Indigenous Feminism

This book looks at Palestinian women, and Palestinian feminism, over the past century, since before the modern state of Israel was founded on our historic homeland. The title, *Falastiniyyat* (the plural feminine form of "Palestinian" in Arabic), refers to the pride Palestinian women have in their cultural and national identity, which they have sought and continue to seek to preserve, despite the heavy-handed imperial attempts at erasing both our traditions and our people.

Palestinian women's defiant indigeneity is perhaps best illustrated by the *dayat*—traditional midwives—whose total rejection of the Western ways the British Mandate officers tried to impose on them, in the early twentieth century, earned them the reputation of being "uppity women." These dayat insisted on doing things—literally bringing Palestinian life into being—their own way, rather than the European way, which pathologized childbirth and discredited the traditional Palestinian practices.[7] The Palestinian midwives made it clear to their would-be teachers that they were not impressed by Britain's alienating ways of having medically trained men interject themselves in this most natural feminine practice, and they persisted in what they viewed as their better ways.

Both Britain's racist dismissal of the dayat's expertise and, later, Israel's imposition of stringent restrictions on traditional Palestinian midwives reveal the colonizers' desire to control Palestinian life and Palestinian ways—from birth, literally. The poverty of rural villages meant that they often lacked basic conveniences such as running water, and Britain sought to train the dayat into Western ways, which they viewed as more sanitary. Yet, even as Mandate officers claimed they were particularly concerned with what they perceived as Palestinian society's "lack of hygiene," they did not attempt to address this by providing the infrastructure for clean water—to take but one example. Decades later, upon its 1967 occupation of the West Bank and Gaza Strip, Israel's restriction of the issuance and renewal of midwives' licenses contributed to making this traditionally female practice—an experienced, knowledgeable woman assisting another woman give birth—often illegal. As Palestinian feminist researchers have documented, Israel stopped issuing licenses to the Palestinian dayat not out of concern for the well-being of pregnant Palestinians and their newborn infants, but specifically in order to better control and document Palestinian demographics. And as it did so, Israel also made it exceedingly challenging, and sometimes impossible, for Palestinian women to reach a hospital.

Falastiniyyat: A Century of Palestinian Feminisms looks at the long road Palestinian women and feminists have walked, carving it out step by strenuous step in an increasingly hostile environment. This first necessitated fighting for national and cultural sovereignty under the British Mandate, in the early twentieth century, then resisting Israel's relentless settler colonial attacks since the onset of al-Nakba, into the present, when organizing for social and political liberation, in both the historic homeland and the global Diaspora, takes place primarily outside the framework of the nation-state and national institutions, while we jealously guard our culture and Indigenous ways.

The term "feminism" is fraught with the tensions that have long characterized many aspects of the relationships between oppressor and oppressed. Consequently, it has been variously rejected, problematized, or reclaimed by Indigenous women, Black women, Third World women, and women of color generally. The opening decades of the "women's movement" in the US, for example, reveal the deep-seated racism of its main proponents. Indeed, when the Fifteenth Amendment was adopted in 1870, following the abolition of slavery, some suffragettes aligned with racist whites who opposed giving Black men the right to vote, as they argued that white women are more deserving of this "right"—a privilege really, so long as it was not universal—than Black men. The Fifteenth Amendment states that "the right of citizens of the United States to vote shall not be denied or abridged by the United States or by any State on account of race, color, or previous condition of servitude," but "citizens" at the time was understood to refer exclusively to males. Decades later, second-wave feminists, who exposed and denounced the "feminine mystique" and elaborated on the ennui of being a college-educated middle-class housewife, failed to take into consideration that Black women did not have the leisure of longing to work outside the home: Many were domestic maids whose labor in the houses of the wealthy made it possible for these white women to pine for an outside occupation. From the right to vote, to the right to work at respectable and well-paying jobs outside the house, to the right to travel alone, privileged white women wanted a piece of the pie that white men had been enjoying for decades. But few were critically examining the ingredients of that pie, an unhealthy concoction of patriarchy, heterosexism, racism, classism, imperialism, and more. Third World feminists, on the other hand, aspired to radical change—a different pie altogether, with different ingredients, rather than a bigger piece of the same toxic one.

As the wives and daughters of colonizers outside of Europe, white women also imposed their racist views on the colonized women. White nuns committed much of the horrific abuse in the Indian residential schools, where the Indigenous spirit of young children was to be snuffed out, even as their bodies were being savaged. The racist imposition of white ways, always deemed superior, even as they completely devastated entire communities and nations, was all the more chafing when done in the name of "women's liberation," as happened with the advent of European feminism. Examples include the roundup of veiled women in Algeria and the stripping of their veils in public squares—a violation perpetrated by French women, mostly the wives of colonial officers, not by those male officers themselves. Of course, for these French colonizers, the Muslim women were to be liberated of their veils, but not of French occupation. Today, the racism of some white (would-be) feminists is most obvious in their embrace of Zionism, with its exclusionary ideology, its privileging of one community over another, and its complete dehumanization of the Palestinian people.

It is therefore not surprising that there are women of color, Arab women, Indigenous women, Black women, colonized women who hesitate to call themselves feminists, preferring alternatives that are less alienating, because they are not straddled with the colonizers' language, and baggage. They speak of "women's issues," "the women's agenda," or "social empowerment for women and girls." Yet others—including myself—feel that the ideology behind the term "feminism" is not the exclusive property of one group of people. Acutely aware that patriarchy also impacts us, and not just the women of the oppressor class, we claim the term "feminism" to describe our own vision of liberation, one that reflects our multifaceted experiences of oppression: gender, yes, but also race, class, expulsion to another land, dispossession of one's ancestral land, vilification of one's traditional ways, and more. Liberation cannot come from removing only one of the vectors of disenfranchisement, but must address all the structural systems of oppression. Third World feminisms, then, and women-of-color and Indigenous feminisms, all hinge on organizing for social and political liberation, addressing gender dynamics as well as liberation from the structural systems that impact all the members of these communities. As I was researching this book, I was comforted to see that, as early as the 1920s, Palestinian women understood that there could be no free homeland without free women, and no free women in an occupied homeland. Indeed, some formulation of that truism appears in each chapter. This understanding of "feminism" as an emancipatory worldview that aspires to full liberation, for all oppressed members of all communities, is becoming more prevalent today, even as we frequently retain our attachment to some qualifier: Third World feminism, Black feminism, Indigenous feminism, Palestinian feminism.

I view Palestinian women's activism as feminist activism, because it has long been an encompassing endeavor to liberate women, and their nation, with the understanding that liberation from only one system of oppression would not result in freedom. Nevertheless,

Palestinian women's activism, while widely acknowledged via oral history, had not been written about until recently. I am immensely grateful to Ellen Fleischmann, whose research safeguarded valuable information that was otherwise threatened with disappearance. Fleischmann offers us as thorough a record as possible, considering the paucity of written material about the topic, of Palestinian women's political activism from the beginning of the British Mandate until the onset of al-Nakba in 1948. Her historical focus is on Palestine before the creation of Israel, and she rightly acknowledges that it inevitably foregrounds the urban educated elite, whose privileged status afforded them an experience, and a written record of that experience, quite different from those of rural women, and even of poor urban women. Islah Jad has written and continues to write extensively about Palestinian women and nationalism, the diffusion of feminist organizing as a result of what she terms the "NGO-ization" of Arab/Palestinian women's movements, as well as, more recently, Palestinian women and Islamist movements.[8] Her focus is on the territories occupied in 1967. Orayb Najjar's *Portraits of Palestinian Women* traces the radicalization of West Bank women of varied backgrounds during the First Intifada.[9] A less known but equally important book is Jehan Helou's *Making Palestine's History: Women's Testimonies*, based on interviews with Palestinian women in Lebanon's refugee camps.[10] Obviously, these books all zoom in on one facet of Palestinian women's experiences. *Falastiniyyat*, on the other hand, is not focused on a specific period, country, or region. Instead, by looking at a select few key moments over the past hundred years, from the early years of the British Mandate to the present, in the homeland and the Diaspora, it provides an overview of the continuity of Palestinian women's engagement in the liberation struggle, both as women and as members of a disenfranchised people, while emphasizing our unity, despite the fragmentation imposed upon us since the onset of al-Nakba.

My hope is to show that today's Palestinian feminist activism is simply the contemporary manifestation of an impulse that has long sustained our people, rather than a recent development, or a Western influence or imposition. In chapter 1, we follow the formation of the

Arab Women's Congress in the late 1920s, with Matiel Mogannam, Tarab Abdulhadi, and Sadhij Baha Nassar clearly organizing toward feminist goals of social and political liberation, from outlawing oppressive customs such as child marriage to opposing imperial plans to establish a Jewish homeland in Palestine. In chapter 2, we follow Sitt Hind al-Husseini as she gathers up the orphans of the Deir Yassin massacre and establishes a foundation that continues to empower Palestinian women to this day. In chapter 3, we see women doing their best to preserve Palestinian culture after Israel's takeover of the rest of the homeland in 1967, amid its efforts to erase, even criminalize, Palestinian national identity. Chapter 4 takes us to Turtle Island, where growing US support for Israel after 1967 prompted Palestinians living in the Far Diaspora to organize against Western perceptions of Palestine and the Palestinian people. Chapter 5 looks at the First Intifada, which erupted in 1987 and is widely acknowledged as a youth- and women-led uprising, and a radically transformative moment in Palestine's history. The Intifada ended with the signing of the Oslo Accords, dealing a severe blow to the popular organizing and allowing for the return of the old-guard patriarchal Palestinian leadership to the Occupied Territories. In chapter 6, we look at the "Oslo years," and the efforts of Maha Abu-Dayyeh and her colleagues in the Women's Centre for Legal Aid and Counselling to seek redress for their concerns through the newly established Palestinian National Authority (also known as the Palestinian Authority). Chapter 7 explores the rise of queer activism with the formation, in 2000, of the LGBTQI+ organizations Aswat and alQaws. And chapter 8 looks at Tal'at, a grassroots feminist coalition that came together in 2019 to denounce the trickle-down effect of Israel's protracted occupation upon the Palestinian household, as well as the Palestinian Feminist Collective, a Diaspora-based group which officially launched in 2021.

Finally, I could not complete this book without discussing, in the final chapter, the reproductive genocide Israel enacted upon the Palestinian people in the aftermath of the October 7, 2023, Hamas attacks—a genocide that is an accelerated and intensified continuation of the sexual violence in which Israel has engaged since the early Zionist militias first came to Palestine. The epilogue brings us back to the critical role that Palestinian feminists have played in the struggle, sustenance, and transformation of our people as we seek liberation from various forms of oppression, from the river to the sea, as well as in our Diaspora.

Obviously, one book could not encompass all aspects of Palestinian feminisms over an entire century. What follows takes key moments in Palestinian women's history that demonstrate how the dual aspect of Palestinian women's struggle is inevitable, since their yearning for social liberation has historically been intertwined with the national liberation struggle. Many of these women understood that participating in the national liberation struggle necessitated transgressing cultural norms. There is ample evidence that women who were empowered by taking part in the anticolonial struggle were determined to reach out to their disenfranchised sisters to help improve their circumstances too. Palestinian women's feminism was not individualistic, seeking the advancement of privileged women while leaving others behind. Instead, it was collective, looking out for others. Additionally, because Palestinian women's circumstances have always been very diverse, and since Palestinian society has long been composed of an urban elite, the urban poor, and impoverished rural communities, my book tries to survey the many different aspects of Palestinian women's struggles, discussing, for instance, not only the generosity of Hind al-Husseini, who had the financial and social resources to turn her family's mansion into an orphanage, but also the resilience of the children who were sheltered there.

Since we are not yet a sovereign people, it is impossible to separate Palestinian women's activism from the national struggle for liberation. However, there is no doubt that, while the struggles of Palestinian women in the opening decades of the twentieth century were inextricably connected to the broader national struggle for liberation, their activism also challenged the internal status quo of Palestinian society and should be understood as random acts of feminism, as it not only charted new paths for these women themselves but also sought to improve the circumstances of all women, whatever their social status.

My analysis does not go back to the Ottoman Empire—not because its rule stopped short of colonial domination or hesitated to treat its subject citizens harshly, but because that rule was essentially different, eyeing the fruits of the labor of Palestinians, rather than the land that produced that fruit. The Ottoman rule was extractive colonialism, not settler colonialism. That is, under the Ottoman Empire, Palestinians cultivated the land, which was recognized as theirs, even as the Ottomans exacted a tax from their subjects. Under the British Mandate, followed by the Israeli occupation, Palestinians lost and continue to lose their lands, homes, and lives.[11] The infamous Israeli detention center, Maskubiyyeh, previously served that same purpose under the British Mandate, when British forces imprisoned and tortured both Palestinian leaders and Zionists. Many of present-day Israel's convoluted laws, privileging Zionist Jews over the Indigenous Palestinian people, are adopted from the period of British rule, which was neither just nor kind to the Palestinians.[12] Today, there is consensus that al-Nakba is not a static moment in history, May 15, 1948, but rather a process that began in May 1948 and is ongoing. Personally, I would argue that this process of disenfranchisement and dispossession began in 1917, with Britain's Balfour Declaration of support for the Zionist aspirations to establish a Jewish state on parts of Palestine.

In the Diaspora, the oppressor is Zionist ideology, which seeks to shackle our organizing and activism, just as, in the homeland, Israel's occupation soldiers control Palestinians' every move. My focus in this book, however, is on feminist activism that is transformational in terms of its impact on society, rather than strictly on women's contributions to the national liberation struggle. Thus I am more interested in examining those initiatives that were and are focused inward, seeking to improve the circumstances of marginalized and disenfranchised members of Palestinian society, rather than initiatives aimed primarily at ousting the occupier—even as the two struggles, one for social transformation, the other for national liberation, cannot be separated in the Palestinian context.

Today, it is acknowledged that fully half of the Palestinian people live in the global Diaspora, but their ties to the homeland remain strong, as evident in the fact that almost every Diaspora Palestinian knows which town or village they come from. Palestine has been transnational for over a century, as our displacement began with the forced exile of many Palestinian political leaders, and the denial of their Right of Return, under the British Mandate. Today's transformational leaders—the organizers and activists in Palestine and globally who are genuinely invested in creating a just society, rather than preserving the unjust status quo—are the youth and the feminists, just as the young and the proto-feminists of a century ago also organized to improve their society, to liberate their brothers and sisters, and to rescue and shelter the orphans by committing random acts of feminism, before that term entered their vocabulary.

I am the first to acknowledge that this book is incomplete. As I wrote the concluding paragraph of each chapter, I thought to myself that there is much more to that particular moment, person, or organization than I have suggested, let alone actually covered. In what may be viewed as an unacceptable omission, for example, I only mention, but do not discuss, the 1936–39 Great Revolt under the British Mandate. Yet women's role in that early anticolonial uprising could fill many pages. I could write an entire book about Hind al-Husseini and Dar al-Tifl al-Arabi; in fact, every woman I interviewed for that chapter told me I could not do justice to Sitt Hind in just a few pages, and obviously I did not.[13] The same could be said about Sitt Samiha Khalil, about Soraida Hussein, about Haneen Maikey. But more so, as I list the absences in this book: I should have devoted an entire chapter to the Institute of Women's Studies at Birzeit University, founded in 1994 and still thriving, producing critically needed feminist scholarship and nurturing activists whose organizing stretches well beyond academia.

I wrote this book between October 2023 and October 2025—during two years of Israel's intensified genocide of my people. I had signed my book contract in late September 2023, giving myself a year to complete the manuscript. Only days later, the October 7, 2023, Hamas attack on Israel took place, and Israel unleashed its unbridled, monstrous savagery on the besieged people who had dared to still dream of freedom. I felt like a fraud, writing about Palestinian women's agency as my sisters in Gaza were enduring reproductive genocide, and as the still-unsubstantiated allegations of rape by Hamas militants were weaponized to justify genocide, while amply documented reports of the decades-long systematic sexual abuse by Israeli soldiers of Palestinian men, women, and children did not raise eyebrows in the Global North, where I live. I could not travel to my homeland to conduct the research I had hoped to engage in. Many times, I came close to giving up on this book altogether. It is only when I shared parts of it with trusted colleagues and they told me that what I had written, incomplete as I still feel it is, is needed, that I finally let myself submit it to my publisher.

It is needed because it begins to counter our erasure by reinscribing, into the past century's Palestinian history, the many important contributions of Palestinian women. My guiding thought in writing this book has been that I am attempting a "women's history of modern Palestine." I know I have swept over years in a few paragraphs. I could never complete this work otherwise, and I thought a start was better than nothing at all.

1

Emerging: The Personal and the (Macro-)Political

This state of uncertainty derives its origin from the peculiar circumstances under which the country is now placed. It is due in no small measure to the attempts which are being made to establish a National Home for an alien race in a country which is already populated. The contribution made by the Arab women to the disclosure of the evils of such policy has not been insignificant. Their efforts to secure an undisturbed future have been continuous. They directed their endeavours to one end: to remove all causes of unrest and bloodshed, and in that they made their message quite clear.

—Matiel Mogannam, *The Arab Woman and the Palestine Problem*, 1937

Born in Lebanon in 1899 to Palestinian parents who shortly after emigrated to New York, Matiel Mogannam (née Tomey/Tohme) could have grown up to become an American housewife, trying to perfect meatloaf, green bean casserole, and apple pie. After all, the 1930s saw many Arab women in the United States doing their best to "melt down into all-American blandness," as the pioneering Arab American scholar Evelyn Shakir put it in her groundbreaking book *Bint Arab: Arab and Arab American Women in the United States*.[1] Shakir, herself the daughter of Lebanese immigrants to Boston, follows the trajectories of many of these women in New England, detailing how the early arrivals held on to their customary ways, often assuming they were only in the US for a few years, during which they would build a nest egg in anticipation of returning back home. The community of first-generation immigrants would gather around dinners of Arab-style grilled chicken served with a generous dollop of *toum*, the prized garlic paste for which every woman had her own secret recipe, followed by Turkish coffee and baklawa. Nevertheless, the opportunities offered this first generation of immigrants allowed for various departures from restrictive traditional norms, including departure from normative sexuality. Such possibilities rendered the sojourn abroad particularly appealing and were frequently a reason for its extension.[2]

As the children of first-generation immigrants grew up, however, they sought to assimilate and to blend in with their American classmates. Having been mocked for the school lunches their mothers packed for them, as adults they started their meals with "fruit cups, moved on to steak, and ended with lemon meringue pie."[3] But Matiel was destined for another life. While in college in the United States, she met Mughannam Mughannam, a Ramallah-born law student who would become her husband, and the two moved to Palestine in the mid-1920s, where she soon blossomed into a pioneering feminist organizer and astute political analyst. Outraged at Britain's imperial designs for her homeland, Matiel started hosting political meetings at her home, which equally discontent women attended from Jerusalem, Nablus, Ramallah, and beyond. Many evenings, Mogannam's home, or that of her close friend and ally Tarab Abdulhadi, would be abuzz with women organizing around numerous issues ranging from ending child marriage to ensuring rural girls' education to the release of political prisoners, as they planned protests, formed delegations to meet with British officers, and drew lists of demands for Palestinian independence, seamlessly merging nationalist fervor with feminist aspirations.

The 1920s were a time of great turmoil in Palestine. Britain and France had secretly signed the Sykes-Picot Agreement in 1916, defining their mutually agreed spheres of influence in the Arab World following the anticipated collapse of the Ottoman Empire. The treaty allocated Palestine, Jordan, and parts of Iraq to Britain. In 1917, Britain issued the infamous "Balfour Declaration," offering European Zionist Jews a "national home" in Palestine. While the term "national home" itself had no precedent in international law, early Zionist writings clearly articulated settler colonial ambitions, laying out the plans for creating a Jewish-majority state in parts of Palestine. The British Mandate, which officially began in April 1920, was thus bound to be treacherous because of Britain's conflicting commitments. This was because, as the mandatory power, it was meant to provide administrative advice and assistance to the Palestinian people until they became sovereign. At the same time, however, it was facilitating the creation of a Jewish "national home" in Palestine. Despite the rampant antisemitism of Europe's leading politicians, and in part to accommodate it, Britain was more committed to establishing the Jewish "national home" outside of Europe than it was to facilitating Palestinian sovereignty. Certainly, the concept of a new settler colonial state, namely Israel, in lands Britain controlled was neither novel nor abhorrent to the European imperial power.

The early Zionist thinkers were cognizant of that affinity, and relied on it. Writing in his 1923 essay "The Iron Wall," Vladimir Jabotinsky, perhaps the second most influential early Zionist after Theodor Herzl, expounds on his conviction that the Palestinian people will reject the colonization of their land, adding that the Zionists will need Britain's support in their endeavor. "My readers have a general idea of the history of colonisation in other countries," Jabotinsky writes, adding:

> I suggest that they consider all the precedents with which they are acquainted, and see whether there is one solitary instance of any colonisation being carried on with the consent of the native population. There is no such precedent. The native populations, civilised or uncivilised, have always stubbornly resisted the colonists, irrespective of whether they were civilised or savage ... *Zionist colonisation must either stop, or else proceed regardless of the native population.* Which means that it can proceed and develop only under the protection of a power that is independent of the native population—behind an iron wall, which the native population cannot breach.

He then states his reliance on Britain:

> That is our Arab policy; not what we should be, but what it actually is, whether we admit it or not. What need, otherwise, of the Balfour Declaration? Or of the Mandate? Their value to us is that outside Power has undertaken to create in the country such conditions of administration and security that if the native population should desire to hinder our work, they will find it impossible.[4]

Indeed, the Palestinians were staunchly opposed both to the Zionist plans, and to Britain's support of these plans. This support manifested in extreme repression of Palestinian resistance: Palestinians found with even the most rudimentary rifles were jailed, while the Zionist militias accumulated weapons with impunity. Popular Palestinian leaders were arrested, jailed, exiled, or killed. "Hundreds of men were sent to prison, hundreds of homes unmercifully destroyed, hundreds of children became orphans, without parents to whom they could turn for care and affection," Mogannam writes.[5]

As resentment over their planned dispossession grew, the Great Revolt erupted in rural areas, where the people felt more immediately threatened. There, women were just as involved as the men, albeit differently, in ways that exploited the racism of the British officers, who assumed they would be passive. Many sold their jewelry to help pay for weapons. Bullets were so hard to come by that if any were found that did not fit into the rifles the Palestinians had, women would whittle them down accordingly, using pestles, vegetable corers, or whatever kitchen utensils did the job. Others smuggled ammunition under their dresses, or inside food packages they would deliver to their neighbors. Women hanging laundry would break out in song, sending coded messages about the arrival of British officers to the village. Others would be ready with large cauldrons of boiling water that they poured onto the advancing officers from a higher vantage point.[6] At its height, the Great Revolt of 1936–39 was so large that Britain had to station more British soldiers in relatively small Palestine than in all of the

Indian subcontinent, transferring "counterinsurgency" officers from there to the Palestinian countryside.

The situation across Palestine was, Mogannam describes, so "deplorable," the overall atmosphere so "depressed," that women overcame "traditional restrictions" as they felt compelled to take public political action to stymie their national dispossession. The entire country was in upheaval. As the situation grew more restive, Mogannam and Abdulhadi, along with other members of Palestine's elite families (including the Khalidi, al-Husseini, Shehadeh, Nashashibi, and more) were instrumental in organizing the October 26, 1929, Arab Women's Congress of Palestine, itself the culmination of the many years of women organizing in numerous cities across the country. The Arab Women's Congress meeting was attended by over 200. Its objectives were similar to those of an earlier association, the "Arab Ladies Society," formed in 1919, namely

> the development of the social and economic affairs of the Arab woman in Palestine, to endeavour to secure the extension of educational facilities for girls, to use every possible and lawful means to elevate the status of women, to promote national industries, to assist national institutions, and support any national body in any enterprise which may be beneficial to the country, whether economically, socially, or politically.[7]

The scope of that earlier society, however, had been limited to Jerusalem. Another women's association that predates the Arab Women's Congress, and which is noted as the first Palestinian women's group to hold protests and demonstrations against the Balfour Declaration, is the Arab Women's Union, formed in 1921. Its scope was also geographically limited, this time to Nablus. The 1929 Arab Women's Congress, then, was different in that it was the first nationwide Palestinian women's group that concerned itself with both social and political matters. Mogannam's generation thus represents the first wave of Palestinian feminist organizing, an organic movement seeking independence from both Western imperialism and the homegrown traditional restrictions on a woman's full potential. The 1929 Arab Women's Congress, which met in Jerusalem, concluded with the election of the Arab Women's Executive Council, tasked with delivering the women's demands to the British Mandate officers.[8]

Shortly after the 1929 congress, women's societies affiliated with it were established in Akka, Nazareth, Yaffa, Ramallah, Tulkarm, Safed, and other towns and cities. Mogannam was Christian, Abdulhadi Muslim, and the women took pride in being nonsectarian, placing the nation above religion; sometimes they spoke at each other's place of worship, Mogannam in the courtyard of a mosque, Abdulhadi in front of a church. Within just a few years, the active engagement of Palestinian women from across the country in the national struggle made it clear they saw themselves as full participants in determining their homeland's future. As Mogannam put it in her book,

> If until now the Arab woman of Palestine has preferred to work unobserved it is because she felt that the time was not yet ripe for her to emerge from her home. But events of late prompted her to step forward with a determined effort to do her share in the upbuilding of the Arab Palestine and to work side by side with the man towards the attainment of its objective.[9]

The fact that Arabs composed "about 75 percent" of Palestine's population when Mogannam was writing her 1937 book is itself a result of the significant influx of European Jews to Palestine since Britain had started facilitating their immigration to our country following the Balfour Declaration. Prior to that, Palestinian Jews made up less than 10 percent of the population. Jewish immigration was initially calculated to allow for gradual absorption into the Palestinian population, and to meet the needs of that population. The plan was for Britain to determine how many dentists, pharmacists, optometrists, and other such specialized professions Palestine needed, and to allow a certain number of immigrant families in, each year, to meet these demands. This calculated immigration, however, was soon abandoned as Adolf Hitler came to power in Germany, necessitating the flight of Europe's Jews, who were being turned away by other European countries, as well as by the US.

While women's protests in the cities garnered much attention, rejection of Great Britain's designs for Palestine had started in the villages, where the *fellahat*, or rural women, were most active in their objection to these imperial plans. In fact, as mentioned above, the Great Revolt of 1936–39 was first and foremost a countryside revolt in which a majority of peasants participated, which only later spread to the cities. Rural women defiantly challenged various measures imposed upon them by the British, sometimes by simply refusing to acknowledge and engage with British rules, plans, or organizations. The *dayat* who rejected Western medicine immediately come to mind, but other Palestinian women also declined invitations to join advisory groups created by the British to tend to village infrastructure needs, because such groups also catered to Zionist settlers. They boycotted British goods and made sure no Palestinian family sold land to Zionist settlers: Noncompliance is a powerful form of resistance. At other times, they actively fought these rules and oppressive measures by warning their fellow villagers of the arrival of British troops through the aforementioned coded songs, by hiding fighters in their private rooms, by smuggling weapons and ammunition in food baskets, and even by bearing arms to defend their land. It is no coincidence that the majority of Palestinian women who were jailed by the British Mandate officers were fellahat, not urbanites. Their stories are finally being surfaced today, even though it remains difficult to write much about them—precisely because their challenge to imperialism most frequently took the form of avoiding engagement with the colonizer unless absolutely necessary.

Because of her own circumstances as a Western-educated urban woman, Mogannam gravitated toward lobbying and advocacy, directly addressing the British Mandate's officers, appealing to their presumed ethics and morality. And as the Arab Women's Congress had a secretary, and issued many letters, we have a solid record of these urban women's activism.

Proto-Feminism?

Even as we rightly speak of "feminisms" in the plural and appreciate the critical necessity of examining the multiple facets and varieties of this ideology, there are many gray areas of women's organizing, and women's empowerment, that do not easily fit under any of the definitions of feminism, as they neither hinge on a critique of gender roles nor view women's and queer oppression as larger structural, political phenomena, as opposed to localized social ills. Much of the early twentieth-century Palestinian women's activism fits into those gray areas. In villages as well as the cities, Palestinian women were rising up against the British Mandate's colonial designs for their country, and they were negotiating their culture's gender norms as they did so, even though their goal was the overthrow of external oppression—colonialism—rather than Palestinian patriarchy. Indeed, Mogannam had commented on the fact that gender norms within Palestinian society were changing in an effort to confront Britain's intervention, rather than because these norms were found to be oppressive. As secretary of the Arab Women's Congress, and because of her fluency in English, she is presumed to have drafted many of the communications issued by this body. One of these notes:

> We, the Arab women of Palestine, having been faced with great economic and political difficulties and seeing that our cause has not so far received the sympathy and assistance of which it is worthy, have finally decided to support our men in this cause, leaving aside all other duties and tasks in which we have hitherto engaged ourselves. This deputation of all the Arab women in Palestine has now come to lay before Your Excellency their protests and resolutions passed in their first Congress and to ask, as of right, that our demands be granted.[10]

The "cause" and "demands" made by the Women's Congress were nationalist in nature: protesting the Balfour Declaration, Zionist immigration, collective punishment, and the maltreatment of Palestinian prisoners. These initial anticolonial demands should refute the accusation sometimes lobbed at Palestinian feminists that our ideology is a Western, colonial import, irreconcilable with decolonial impulses.

Yet Palestinian women's activism for national liberation certainly challenged the restrictive gender norms of the time, catapulting these women into social and political roles that nurtured their burgeoning enfranchisement, as women. These "random acts of feminism," as I have called them, and in some cases random acts of *proto-feminism*—that is, feminist actions without prior feminist analysis—paved the way for the complex manifestations of today's Palestinian feminisms, which challenge both the ongoing colonial designs on our homeland and our own society's entrenched patriarchy. It is delightful indeed to read that when some men tried to intervene in a Palestinian women's group in Nablus in 1929—specifically, seeking to take control of the group's funds—the women categorically refused and resolved to "never allow men to join."[11] Yet when some of these same women requested a meeting with the British commissioner, and were turned down, they relied on their male kin to drive them around Jerusalem in a protest caravan. The Palestinian men complied, and the 125-car caravan roamed the city, stopping at every foreign consulate, where the women handed out leaflets listing the resolutions of the Women's Congress.

The absence of Palestinian national sovereignty, Mogannam had noted in her book, confined women's organizations to a social and charitable role, which lacked the official capacity to influence the British designs on their nation. Yet Mogannam was instrumental in organizing many women's delegations, marches, and protests against these colonial plans, always pointing out the need to change traditional gender roles while fighting colonialism. For example, Mogannam had requested a meeting with Lady Mary Elizabeth Chancellor, wife of the British high commissioner, John Chancellor, out of deference to her Muslim allies who could not meet with a male nonrelative due to Muslim social norms. Upon being told that Lady Chancellor was not entitled to hold meetings of a political nature, the Palestinian women's delegation decided that their only option to air their grievances and articulate their demands necessitated transgressing their own social norms, and having Muslim women meet with European men. Mogannam writes:

> It should be remembered that even until now Moslem women in the East, and in Palestine in particular, have no free social association with men ... It is true that there are now many highly educated Arab women, yet no Arab Moslem woman could until now speak publicly before a mixed gathering ... But in the history of every nation there are deciding moments which leave their permanent mark in the formation of its future. By force of circumstances a nation is forced to follow without any previous determination a course in which it had no choice.[12]

Mogannam's writing sheds light on many aspects of the Palestinian consciousness. Again, it should be noted that the use of "Arab" as a designation in the literature of the time is a cultural identification, due to pride in being part of the Arab Renaissance (*al-nahda al-arabiyya*) of the late nineteenth century, even as the geographic focus of all the initiatives discussed here was on Palestine, with a clear understanding of the cohesiveness of that diverse nation. "The Arab women of Palestine" of whom she writes are clearly distinct from "the Arab women of Lebanon," or of Egypt. Mogannam also expresses a keen respect for social norms, as she writes:

> The Moslem section [of the Palestinian people] forms the overwhelming majority of the population, and the traditional social order of such a majority must always be given due consideration. The Christian Arab woman, though not under the same handicap, has kept herself within the limits beyond which her Moslem sisters could not well go.[13]

Nevertheless, observing the devastation wreaked by Britain's mandate, she notes that resistance becomes "the highest degree of duty":

> The defence by any person of the cause of his country, though perhaps it may be unintentionally accompanied by acts of violence, is considered under many as a criminal act, although it may appear to the perpetrator as the highest degree of duty as a citizen. It was not strange, therefore, that such distressing circumstances as those in which Palestine was found in 1929 should have resulted in the greatest change in the life of the Arab women in Palestine and in the concentration of their forces.[14]

Mogannam had been raised and educated in the US, yet despite her Western upbringing and education, she clearly displays an Indigenous understanding of the need to resist imperialism, even by armed means ("acts of violence") and even if such resistance is deemed criminal. Moreover, the message she conveyed to the high commissioner articulates a strong sense of self-worth that belies the Orientalist ideas of Arab women as passive, submissive, oppressed beyond all others. Mogannam's entire book reveals self-confidence, astute political incisiveness, even prescience.

Mogannam's book is highly critical both of the West's Orientalist perception of Arab women and of Britain's imperial meddling with Palestine. She writes in the preface:

> If I should be fortunate enough to dispel the illusion, partly if not wholly, which unfortunately has found its way into the minds of many people that the Arab woman, or, to use a more common expression, the Eastern woman, is an ornament of the imaginary harem of old, and to explain to the British people, primarily, the defects of the present administration in Palestine and the evils of the Zionist policy, which has proved to be an unsuccessful experiment, detrimental to a race with a memorable history, I shall feel more than compensated for my labour.[15]

The only fault I find in her writing is the belief that, should the British become better informed about the plight of the Palestinian population, they would reverse their plans out of sheer decency. The British officers were at the service of empire, not indigeneity.

Mogannam was far from the only figure in this period of Palestinian women's organizing driving Palestinian feminism forward. Another participant in the Arab Women's Congress of 1929, Sadhij Baha Nassar, was the coeditor of *El Carmel* newspaper. Born in Haifa in 1900, she was the granddaughter of Baha'u'llah (born Mirza Husayn Ali Nuri), the Tehran-born founder of the Bahai faith who had been banished from Iran and ended up settling in Akka, Palestine. Sadhij attended the Sisters of Nazareth school in Haifa and married Najib Nassar in 1927. Najib was the founder of *El Carmel*, published out of Haifa, and Sadhij had started publishing there in 1923, penning columns that tackled women's issues, including discussions of equality between the sexes and Palestinian women's role in the revolutionary struggle against colonialism. By 1926, she was in charge of two sections of the newspaper: the Women's Section, which addressed gender issues, and another devoted to more general social topics. Historian Ellen Fleischmann writes that between 1926 and 1933, Nassar was publishing prolifically, and that she

> chastised, praised, criticized, encouraged, blamed, and sometimes hectored women to become involved in politics, to raise their female and male children in equality, to unify themselves and avoid factionalism, and to liberate themselves by becoming economically independent through work, among other things.[16]

Within a year of the founding of the Arab Women's Congress, Nassar, along with Mariam al-Khalili, cofounded the Arab Women's Union of Haifa, a militant anticolonial union dedicated to the liberation of Palestine. Realizing the importance of rural resistance, she lived for a while among women farmers in the Baysan district south of Nazareth. As we saw above, many Palestinian women regularly hid guns and explosives in their homes, and in December 1938, Nassar herself became the first Palestinian woman to be arrested and imprisoned by the British Mandate authorities as a result of her nationalist activities. The British charged her with supplying arms to the Palestinian rebels, describing her as a "very dangerous woman" and a "prominent agitator." She was held at the Bethlehem detention camp for eleven months. Earlier that year, in October 1938, Nassar had attended the Eastern Women's Congress for the Defense of Palestine in Cairo, Egypt, where she was elected secretary of the conference bureau. The conference called for an end to the British Mandate and the formation of a sovereign state in Palestine. Upon her release, Nassar resumed her polemic, prompting the British Mandate authorities to temporarily shutter *El Carmel* newspaper several times until, in 1944, they shut it down permanently under "emergency regulations."[17] Also upon her release, Nassar participated in the Egyptian Feminist Union conference in Egypt, organized by Huda al-Shaarawi, widely recognized as a peerless pioneering Arab feminist.

Like the many Palestinian women organizers who looked to her as a role model, al-Shaarawi was born into an upper-class family and devoted much of her early activism toward national liberation, while also tending to the needs of underprivileged women and children. As early as 1908, she had helped found a medical dispensary run and staffed by women, catering to women and children. Her focus gradually shifted from nationalist to feminist causes, and she founded the Egyptian Feminist Union in 1923. These are just a few of the early organizers—there were many more—seeking collective liberation in Palestine during the British Mandate.

Always Already Intersectional

From South Africa to Algeria, the "two-stage liberation theory," which posits that national liberation must come before women's liberation—as if women were not full-fledged members of their nation—has proven bankrupt in every case. Palestine's "proto-feminists," while focused on protesting the Balfour Declaration and what they correctly understood would be its catastrophic consequences, were adamant that social liberation must be part and parcel of national liberation, not a sequel to it. As is clear from Mogannam's and Nassar's writings, education for girls, and women's empowerment, were always high on the agenda of the early Palestinian feminist groups, even as they organized for national sovereignty. But there were also the numerous acts of feminist care, which many of us know from family stories, and which have never been recorded. It is important, then, for readers to engage in what interdisciplinary feminist scholar Charlotte Karem Albrecht, in *Possible Histories*, has called "historical-grounded imagining"—that is, the diligent attempt to imagine various unwritten aspects of the past, based on family lore and the faint traces we have of recorded events around them. Thus, while most of the literature about Palestine in the 1920s and 1930s is focused on the cities and the educated elite, we have sufficient "traces" about the countryside, where the majority of the Palestinian people lived, to construct an educated and realistic idea of their circumstances. Similarly, we can form an idea of the lives of the economically disadvantaged city dwellers from the few stories we have of them, which have been threaded into those of their wealthier neighbors or employers.

One specific example of Arab women organizing, and sometimes subversively scheming, to improve their own circumstances is in the practice of child marriage, which the Arab Women's Congress referred to as an "evil custom" and, though long denounced, is sadly practiced to this day in communities around the world.[18] In 1935, the Palestinian delegation brought the issue to the International Women's Congress in Turkey, yet the Palestinian delegates could not legislate against it, because they did not have a sovereign state. And Mandatory Britain was utterly uninterested in taking up the issue. Palestinian women, however, schemed to protect the children. My own maternal grandmother, Jamila, was married at the prepubescent age of ten years because her parents had found a suitable boy for her—"suitable" meaning, of course, from an appropriate family within the same small religious denomination, rather than someone my grandmother fancied, as if one could ever be mature enough to choose one's spouse at ten years of age. The agreement between the two families was that the marriage would not be consummated before my grandmother reached menarche. When she did, within a couple of years, her mother-in-law hid that from her own son, until Jamila reached the age of fourteen, which was considered mature in the 1920s. My grandmother told me this story when I myself was a teenager, and she emphasized her endless gratitude to her mother-in-law, the woman who saw her as a child needing protection, not a procreator vessel first and foremost. And while I delight in this personal story, I earnestly believe that it was not exceptional—that women did support other women and protect children, because the state did not protect them then, and does not to this day.

The belief that the freedom of Palestinian women, queers, and children is an integral, not subsidiary, part of a nation's freedom is clearly articulated by Palestinian feminists today, in both the homeland and the *shatat*, the motherland and the "otherland." Yet it is obvious that this concept is not a new idea; rather, it is an understanding that started percolating a full century ago, when Mogannam, Abdulhadi, Nassar, and hundreds of other Palestinian proto-feminists, while operating within a nationalist framework, grasped that their activism necessitated a transgression of their society's social and gender norms and viewed this transgression as a positive development, rather than an unfortunate condition of the national struggle for liberation. As is immediately clear from perusing the literature about the Mandate period, both the illiterate rural women and the Western-educated urban socialites knew that their circumstances as Palestinian women could only be improved if they overcame, at once, their society's traditional restrictions on their own potential and the colonial designs on their nation. As we will see throughout this book, all variations of Palestinian feminisms are fully Indigenous, emanating from within Palestinian society, while directed against foreign intervention. This is a useful reminder for those of us who still need to argue against the accusation that feminism is a "Western concept" imposed upon Palestinian society by its European colonizers. As such, ridding our nation of the outside occupier should not suggest an aspiration to rid ourselves of feminism and return to our oppressive, patriarchal ways. Those patriarchal ways, our own society's restrictions on women's opportunities to fully thrive and realize their inherent potential, were being challenged and changed from within by Palestinian women, long before white-savior Western feminists claimed any interest in "liberating" us. The educated members of the Arab Women's Congress advocated against child marriage while bemoaning the absence of national sovereignty that may help end it. Meanwhile, the illiterate rural women successfully schemed against it.

The Political and the Macro-Political

If in Europe and the US, first-wave feminism—understood as the period of women's activism for legal rights dating from the late nineteenth into the opening decades of the twentieth century—focused on women's right to vote, in Palestine, voting per se was not the primary concern of Palestinian women at the time, since no Palestinian, male or female, could vote for their own leader under the Ottoman Empire or the British Mandate. It is true that toward the end of Ottoman rule, Palestinian men, but not women, could vote in strictly local municipal elections. However, this was not of national import, in the context of major political turmoil broiling across the homeland, and Palestinian women did not feel particularly disenfranchised on the national level because of their gender. Instead, they felt disenfranchised because they had no nation capable of legislating their causes and concerns. Palestinian "first-wave" feminism, then, as represented by the members of the Arab Women's Union, founded in Nablus in 1921, then the Arab Women's Congress, launched in 1929, was obviously concerned with national liberation but simultaneously sought to improve disenfranchised women and girls' circumstances across the yet-to-be-liberated country. This early Palestinian feminism was about uplifting the less privileged, rather than acquiring greater individual rights and rising up in society. In her important book documenting much of Palestinian women's organizing during the British Mandate, Ellen Fleischmann also explains that the Arab Women's Executive "clearly situated gender at the forefront of its political consciousness," and that one of the main goals of the Arab Women's Congress was "to act as a catalyst for women all over Palestine to organize their own movement."[19] Indeed, the very insistence of the numerous organizations on placing women's and girls' education and empowerment at the core of the nationalist struggle is indicative of the movement's feminist inclinations, even though the term itself was alien to most of these women.

In the 1960s and 1970s, "second-wave feminism" in the Global North shattered the tranquility that the middle class had supposedly achieved after the challenging, tumultuous years of the Great Depression (1929–39) and World War II (1939–45) and the immediate aftermath. Beginning in the early 1960s, second-wave feminists started openly articulating their frustrations with domesticity and the expectations that they should feel fulfilled as suburban housewives and mothers. Global North second-wave feminism was also predominantly white, with women rallying around the slogan "The personal is political." The slogan correctly underscores that many concerns traditionally understood as "personal" matters, such as a new mother's need to stay home due to lack of affordable childcare, the domestic division of labor, and of course abortion, could not be solved through personal intervention, as they are in reality larger social issues, necessitating collective, "political" action to bring about change. Kate Millett's *Sexual Politics*, published in 1970, broadened the definition of "politics" to encompass sexual hierarchy and all power-structured relationships.[20] The expression "the personal is political" was popularized in the US by Carol Hanisch, a member of the New York Radical Women, whose 1969 essay by that title was widely read in women's consciousness-raising groups across the nation. In it, Hanisch writes that her participation in these groups, which were sometimes derided as "therapy sessions" because the participants talked about intimate matters,

> is not to solve any personal problem. One of the first things we discover in these groups is that personal problems are political problems. There are no personal solutions at this time. There is only collective action for a collective solution. I went, and I continue to go to these meetings because I have gotten a political understanding which all my reading, all my "political discussions," all my "political action," all my four-odd years in the movement never gave me. I've been forced to take off the rose colored glasses and face the awful truth about how grim my life really is as a woman.[21]

Some of the more obvious manifestations of the personal as political in the US today include the persistent gender wage gap in pay for comparable work, sixty years after the passing of the Equal Pay Act, and the fact that a woman's most intimate decision—to continue or abort a pregnancy—is not her own but is granted or denied her by the laws of the state she lives in.

Like the more influential white feminists, however, Hanisch had to wrestle with her society's patriarchy, but not with racism—which she benefited from systematically, simply because she was white, and regardless of her personal or political views, or her own working-class background. That is, she was paid a salary for her antiracism work, whereas Black people whose entire lives were devoted to that cause generally needed a different source of income to support their activism. Hanisch's gripe, "how grim [her] life really is as a woman," did not have to take into account the multiple levels of additional disenfranchisement that Indigenous, Black, or other women of color contended with. Further on in her essay, Hanisch adds that "women are smart not to struggle alone (as are blacks and workers)," and that "women, like blacks, workers, must stop blaming ourselves for our 'failures.'"[22] Apparently Hanisch, a "radical" woman, was utterly oblivious to the existence of Black women workers. Second-wave feminism, then, as has been sufficiently pointed out in recent decades, was a rebellion by discontented educated women, almost all white and middle-class, most of them married, against what society told them should be their ultimate goal: a domestic life caring for their husbands and children. Yet these discontented "housewives" had domestic help: cooks, nannies, and cleaning women, most of whom were Black and Brown. Obviously, these Black and Brown women were not bound to and frustrated by the expectation of "domesticity" that white women complained about. Meanwhile, Indigenous women were focused on reviving and preserving their criminalized traditional ways, while surviving the all-encompassing gendered and racialized violence against them. Asian women were exoticized, sexualized, exploited in sweatshops, and presumed uber-submissive, even as white Americans feared the "yellow peril." Latina women's feminisms hinged on a discussion of imperialism, working-class conditions, citizenship, and belonging. Arab American women were invisible, not yet recognized as women of color, and certainly not members of the "discontented white women's club."

Mainstream Western feminism, then, was essentially different from the feminism of Palestinian women organizing in the homeland. There, Palestinian feminism was very much concerned with collective liberation, not individual rights. This had already begun with the "first-wave" Palestinian feminists, who had a clear grasp of the need to use their privilege to serve those less advantaged than themselves. The urban elite women who formed the various women's organizations in the 1920s and 1930s all discussed ways of assisting rural women, who were disproportionately impacted by the budding Zionist settler colonialism endorsed by the British Mandate. They expressed their deep concern about the implications of the Balfour Declaration, which they viewed as "detrimental to us in every way."[23] Most, just like Matiel Mogannam, had determined that British imperialism is the "principal enemy of the Palestinian Arabs."[24] But their demands always included ways to improve poor and rural women's circumstances. This tending to the collective needs of the community's less privileged members was lacking in white feminism. The multiple jeopardy of intersecting vectors of oppression, then, is the basis of the affinities between Palestinian women and women of color on Turtle Island, who also organized to improve the circumstances of their communities, not their own individual opportunities.

If "the personal" is strictly limited to interactions between two individuals free of the impact of social norms (identical twins, maybe?), and "the political" accounts for the hierarchy of these norms within a society, then the "macro-political" refers to the power dynamics between societies, with their larger vectors of oppression. Like women of color on Turtle Island, Palestinian women have long negotiated the personal, the political, and the macro-political as they have bristled under Palestinian society's patriarchal norms, as well as the added oppressive structure of colonialism. That overarching "macro-political" structure became significantly more onerous under the British Mandate (1923–48) than it had been under the centuries of the Ottoman Empire.[25] This is because Britain, while officially responsible for protecting the civil and religious rights of the Palestinian people, was actually facilitating their dispossession, since it was also charged with creating a Jewish homeland on parts of Palestine, a contradiction inherent throughout the text of the Mandate.[26] Article 6 of the Mandate for Palestine, for example, reads:

> The Administration of Palestine, while ensuring that the rights and position of other sections of the population are not prejudiced, shall facilitate Jewish immigration under suitable conditions and shall encourage, in co-operation with the Jewish agency referred to in Article 4, close settlement by Jews on the land, including State lands and waste lands not required for public purposes.

Article 9 reads:

> The Mandatory shall be responsible for seeing that the judicial system established in Palestine shall assure to foreigners, as well as to natives, a complete guarantee of their rights.

But what rights did foreigners have *to* Palestine, rather than as foreigners *in* Palestine? As they became aware of the colonialist designs on their country, Palestinian women across the nation, from the remote rural villages to the urban centers in Jerusalem, Yaffa, Haifa, and Nablus, actively organized to oppose these designs, forming associations, issuing declarations with political demands, and calling for meetings with Mandate officers—activism that was considered feminist at the time and is still viewed as such to this day.

By Force of Circumstances

The radical transformation of Palestine, from an Arab nation in tune with its natural and regional environment into a new country settled by Europeans, had never been part of the Ottoman vision, which certainly exploited Palestine's resources but did not seek to transmute the country, or the larger part of it, into an essentially different one. The British Mandate, then, catapulted Palestinian women into feminist political activism, guided primarily by an anti-colonial vision, to safeguard the identity of their homeland rather than focus on the personal ills of Palestine's conservative patriarchy. Yet in order to take to the streets, form committees, organize delegations, or write nationalist essays, Palestinian women also had to go against social norms, as women had gone against social norms in numerous other countries that had experienced or were experiencing political turmoil and upheaval. The "political" is also personal: Social disruptions caused by wars invariably translate into social commotion and change.

The common belief that the significant social changes in Palestinian society over the past century began around 1948, following the onset of al-Nakba, is therefore misguided, even as that momentous event, the foundation of the Israeli state, certainly disrupted all aspects of Palestinian life. Yet, as evidenced from the formation of various Palestinian women's groups beginning in the 1920s, Palestinian women's organizing began as soon as they got wind of the Western plans for their nation, when the Ottoman Empire was collapsing during World War I and Lord Balfour issued his declaration of support for a "national home for the Jewish people" in Palestine to the Zionist Federation of Great Britain and Ireland. Palestinian resistance to colonialism, then, is over a century old, and women have been active participants in it from its earliest days, in isolated incidents such as localized village unrest, in collective advocacy by women's associations, and through protests and organized militancy during the Great Revolt of 1936–39. And while nationalist goals guided their activism, the "personal" inevitably percolated for these women, as major social and political changes were afoot in the opening decades of the twentieth century.

The harm inflicted on Palestine by the British Mandate was evident in the British commitment to implementing the Balfour Declaration, and in the facilitation of European Jewish immigration to Palestine. Meanwhile, the British had banned the Palestinians from arming themselves, with very strict penalties for anyone caught with a rifle, no matter how old and rusty, even as it was an open secret that Zionist militias were receiving large quantities of smuggled weapons. As rifles and ammunition were extremely hard to come by, rural women frequently transported these, knowing that the British officers did not (initially) think them capable of political agency. Most of Palestine's population was rural at the time, and rural women also regularly joined the protests against, and confrontations with, the British troops and Zionist militias. Male Palestinian nationalist leaders, and men who engaged in military resistance—and there were many spontaneous outbreaks and confrontations with both the British troops and the newly arrived Zionist settlers and militias—were imprisoned, killed, or exiled. The prominent Palestinian historian Rashid Khalidi estimates that during the 1936–39 uprising alone, 10 percent of Palestinian men between the ages of twenty and sixty were wounded, imprisoned, exiled, or killed, many by hanging.[27] This figure came atop the families that had earlier lost husbands and fathers to emigration, or to being drafted into the Ottoman army. Thus women now found themselves heading their households in larger numbers than they had in the previous century.

The Rebel Fellahat

Poring over publications and records from that period, it is obvious that Mandatory Palestine was characterized by vibrant debates around women's circumstances, including discussions about what constitutes "ideal womanhood" (chiefly education and, for the elite, membership in social organizations catering to the less privileged) and the necessity to overcome traditional social restrictions on women's engagement in nondomestic matters. Importantly, even though most articles were written by the educated urban elite, there was an awareness of the different circumstances of the fellahat (the feminine form of *fellaheen*, Arabic for "peasants") and an acknowledgment by urban women that these fellahat were not passive but as engaged in the political struggle as their male kin, the rural men who constituted the bulk of Palestine's resistance efforts.

Countryside activism was of utmost importance, as over two-thirds of the Palestinian population was still rural by the end of the mandate and was disproportionately impacted by the influx of Jewish immigrants in the 1930s, Britain's privileged treatment of these new arrivals, and the ripple effects of the Great Depression. Palestine's urban women were aware of their privileged status, which they consistently put to use to improve the circumstances of poor and rural women, without dismissing or minimizing the latter's agency. On the other hand, the assumption that rural women had no agency, and no national consciousness, was pervasive in British circles, hence they did not initially suspect that these fellahat would consider rising up against their dispossession. This resulted in interesting consequences, such as, for example, when the British thought they would subdue the restive countryside during the Great Revolt by imposing strict martial law on the restive towns and villages. One village, Baqa al-Gharbiyya, kept up the resistance and mounted attacks on the British, inflicting losses on the soldiers. The British forces then rounded up all the men and took them prisoner in collective punishment of the village.[28] The women and children were left behind—a fortunate consequence of the assumption that they would be helpless without the adult men. Storming the unguarded barracks under the cover of night, these unarmed women and children pounded the doors with their bare hands until they broke them down, liberating their adult male kin.

The story of the women and children of Baqa al-Gharbiyya liberating their menfolk from the colonizer's jails is familiar to many Palestinian feminists and occasionally mentioned as undocumented lore in history books, even as it remains rarely discussed in historical overviews of Palestinian resistance to colonial dispossession. Yet it constitutes one of those glimpses into the past that allow us to engage in historically grounded imagining, as there is nothing to indicate that the population of the village was in any way unique. The women's attack on the British barracks, then, is extremely important as an exemplar marker of both Palestinian national consciousness and Palestinian women's agency in the defense of their families, and of their nation. It is an agency, an awareness of one's role to play in securing sovereignty for one's people, that has been uninterrupted since the first imperial designs on our nation—Great Britain's cavalier decision to create a homeland for Europe's Jews in parts of Palestine. The women of that village were not the educated urban elite but rural women who had long shouldered heavy responsibilities essential for both the family unit and the larger community. They were foragers, farmers, market women; they pressed olives for oil and soap and spun yard for weaving and *tatreez,* Palestine's traditional cross-stitch embroidery.

Without necessarily bearing arms—a rare commodity for all Palestinians at the time—the fellahat were full participants in the turmoil of the Great Revolt. Thousands joined in issuing the alarm calls for villagers warning them of approaching British troops; they hid weapons as well as fighters in their rooms, smuggled food to the revolutionaries who had been rounded up and detained in barracks, and beat the British troops with their bare hands, especially when the latter were sexually assaulting one of them—an unfortunately common crime in military conflicts. Eventually, the British troops had to reconsider their misconception of Palestinian women as devoid of agency. As is so frequently the case, there is little written documentation of their engagement, yet one can glean from the eye-opening fact, recorded in a journal of military history, that British troops at one point had arrested 2,000 rural women, that

> women played their part in revolt and pacification, both as [British] subjects of attritional imperial control and as [Palestinian] active agents of rebellion. Rebels' use of women to avoid security force searches helped the national struggle; women supporting their menfolk or as warriors themselves added to rebel fighting power.[29]

The rural communities were also the underclass that produced the dayat, the traditional midwives who literally brought Palestinian life into being. And unlike most rural women in the early twentieth century, who thought poorly of themselves because they were illiterate and had internalized urban classism (which equated education with social status), the dayat firmly believed their ways were superior to those that the British were trying to impose on them. Here, Fleischmann's work is once again extremely valuable, in that she recorded the defiance of these women. She writes:

> Conflicts with midwives played themselves out in numerous, sometimes overlapping power struggles ... One struggle represented a confrontation between two competing, gendered hierarchies of medicine, representing (male) "science" and "modernity" on the one side, and indigenous (female) authority, folk wisdom, and experience on the other.[30]

When the government required that women be licensed to practice midwifery, beginning in 1918, the women "displayed remarkable defiance of the law."[31] Some midwives practiced gynecology, going beyond assisting a woman during labor; others continued practicing beyond the age of forty, when the British government deemed they should retire; and most if not all knew the critical importance of their work in delivering and maintaining Palestinian lives and ways of living. These dayat proudly earned the reputation of being Palestine's early "uppity women," as the British viewed them: confident, rebellious, defiant. The colonial attempt to control Indigenous lifegiving, and the consequent politicization of motherhood—a concept central to today's Palestinian feminisms—is thus over a century old in Palestine and began with Britain's attempt at regulating midwives, and the latter's rejection of these attempts.

The anticolonial impulse may have been the primary propeller behind the transgression of social norms around gender in Palestine in the early twentieth century. Yet Palestinian women in the 1920s had independently developed a political consciousness of their circumstances that understood the constraints of traditional social norms as limitations to their full potential as women, and as Palestinians, and many appreciated the silver lining provided by the political turmoil, which drew them out into the streets and the meeting halls. Additionally, throughout Palestine's past century, we see that at times of increased political conflict and war, it is primarily men who are arrested, incarcerated, exiled, or killed, leaving women as heads of household—a responsibility they may not have wished for, which nevertheless provided them with a greater degree of freedom and responsibility. Palestinian women overall felt it was their duty to protect their nation against the colonial design of the European outsiders, acting upon this commitment through organizing and taking to the streets. Those born into elite and middle-class advocated for girls' education and gender equality. They took pride in their Indigenous ways, refusing to uncritically accept presumed Western superiority. As such, they were enacting a defiant Indigenous feminist consciousness that emerged out of the cauldron of patriarchy and colonialism, the personal and the political.

The blurring of the boundaries between their anticolonial engagement and their organizing to transform women's traditional roles in Palestinian society is indicative of Palestinian women's activism from the early days of Western colonialism to the present. Palestinian women understood in the 1920s that they could not achieve national liberation without transgressing gender norms and fully embraced the latter "transgression," not only as an improvement in their own circumstances but as an essential aspect of a liberated nation. Sadhij Nassar's urging of Palestinian women to raise their male and female children with equality, the rural dayat's confidence in their skills and their defiance of the colonizer's laws, and the urban elite women's insistence on engaging in the national struggle (even if it meant violating social norms) are all examples of the organic understanding that women's empowerment is an essential part of national liberation. Within decades, as the British Mandate gave way to the foundation of Israel and the onset of al-Nakba, and the dispersal of hundreds of thousands of Palestinians across the globe, Palestinian women in the shatat found themselves continuing in the footsteps of their aunts, mothers, and grandmothers in the homeland—a legacy, not a parting of ways.

2

Surviving: "You Will Be Safe"

And all of us, the daughters of Mama Hind, the women who were fortunate enough to go to Dar al-Tifl, are proud of our upbringing, and remain forever grateful for the opportunity to have been raised by this exceptional woman.

—K, online interview, September 21, 2023

While cities and villages were being depopulated across Palestine, one young woman, a "spinster" by the norms of the time, was criss-crossing the tormented homeland, taking bereaved children in, and soon afterward traveling the world to secure donations to give the destitute a life of dignity and the best education Palestine could offer. She did so with the long-term strategizing of an astute visionary, who organically grasped that safety, independence, and empowerment are only ensured through community, not through government supervision or handouts premised on acceptability. Her legacy—hundreds of confident, powerful women and girls who recall their years under her care at her children's school, Dar al-Tifl, as "the best time of [their] lives"—continues to this day.

Hind al-Husseini, better known by the honorific "Sitt Hind," is the founder of Dar al-Tifl al-Arabi, the Arab Children's Home, more commonly referred to simply as Dar al-Tifl. And she is without a doubt one of Palestine's greatest examples of generosity, resource sharing, nurturing, and selfless toil for those less privileged. Born in 1916 Jerusalem to the prominent Jerusalemite al-Husseini family, Sitt Hind was an educator and social worker with a lifelong interest in women's issues.[1] She first became active in a number of women's social organizations in the 1930s, and rose to become coordinator of the Arab Women's Union in the 1940s. A teacher by training, she worked from 1938 to 1946 at the Islamic Girls' School, which she herself had attended as a child. In 1948, while still motivated primarily by a desire to improve children and women's circumstances, al-Husseini shifted her focus toward social work and helped establish the Women's Cooperation Society (Jam'iyyat al-Takkaful al-Nisa'i) in Jerusalem. Within years, the society grew to twenty-two branches throughout Palestine, which conducted studies to better determine the needs of Palestinian women and children. In order to meet these needs, the society established kindergartens, led campaigns to minimize illiteracy (especially among girls and women), and set up shops to teach women dressmaking.[2]

On the evening of April 9, 1948, al-Husseini and her friend Hanneh al-Karsheh were heading to an organizing meeting in the Old City of Jerusalem when they came upon a number of visibly exhausted, distraught children cowering by the Holy Sepulcher church, near Bab al-Amoud. Some of these children were sobbing unconsolably; others stared into the dark in silent, terrified shock. Al-Husseini asked them who they were and how they had ended up where they were huddled, realizing in horror that these fifty-five children, most of them under nine years of age, were the survivors of the Deir Yassin massacre perpetrated earlier that day by the Irgun and Stern Gang Zionist militias.[3] To quote al-Husseini:

> They had been carried from their homes, snatched from the protecting arms of their parents, and thrown into the streets of the Old City. They stood huddled together against the lofty walls of the Holy City, casting terrified looks toward Heaven as if supplicating and praying for an end to that horrible nightmare. Those innocent puzzled eyes glittering with tears made everyone wonder how such outrages could be committed against humanity in an age of enlightenment and knowledge.[4]

As we seek to reinscribe into history the various individuals who were erased from it, because they were deemed "lesser," I feel it is important to note here that, in all my reading about al-Husseini and

Dar al-Tifl—and there is sufficient literature on both al-Husseini and the institution she founded—I have not come across a single reference to al-Karsheh, who was with al-Husseini on that fateful night. Even Hind al-Husseini's narration of that fateful evening says "I was walking along," a singular, not the plural which would suggest a companion.[5] Nevertheless, al-Karsheh is mentioned by name by al-Husseini's own daughter, Hidaya, in an interview with Al-Qastal news agency.[6] As Hidaya did not herself witness the encounter with the orphaned children on April 9, 1948, I assume that she heard the story from her own mother, who included al-Karsheh in her narration. The erasure, then, in various records of that evening, of the less famous person who was there, is a reminder of the selectivity of historical narratives, and how we must generally assume that "others," especially women of lesser social status, queers, and other socially marginalized individuals, tend to be disappeared in these narratives. The mention of al-Karsheh certainly does not take away from al-Husseini's phenomenal life and accomplishments, yet while a few reports speak of "a colleague" of al-Husseini being there with her, only her own daughter has ever publicly named Hanneh al-Karsheh as her mother's friend. (Hind al-Husseini never married, and adopted Hidaya, whom she raised at Dar al-Tifl, alongside the many other children she cared for.)

By all accounts, the atrocities committed during the Deir Yassin massacre had been unheard of until that day. Testimonies by survivors of the massacre describe how the inhabitants of the village had been indiscriminately slaughtered, with many men, women, children, and the elderly tied up to trees and burned alive, or lined up against a wall and executed by submachine guns. Some of the victims were mutilated, and many of the women and girls were raped before being murdered. Other testimonies speak of cutting a pregnant woman open to murder her infant.

These testimonies are corroborated by a United Nations report dated April 20, 1948, which states:

> The deaths of some 250 Arabs, men, women and children, which occurred during this attack, took place in circumstances of great

> savagery. Woman [*sic*] and children were stripped, lined up, photographed, and then slaughtered by automatic firing and survivors have told of even more incredible bestialities. Those who were taken prisoner were treated with degrading brutality.[7]

Deir Yassin was a prosperous if small village, with a population of 750 inhabitants whose wealth came from the stone they quarried, a hard yellow limestone prized by Jerusalemites. The Zionist fighters looted the houses, too, and stole the gold the women and girls were wearing, roughly snatching their jewelry from their ears and wrists.

The ruthlessness of the killing of civilians during the Deir Yassin massacre marks it as a pivotal event for Palestinians, as it sparked terror among other villages, who feared the Irgun and Stern Gang Zionist militias would attack them next. Indeed, the parading of the Palestinian prisoners in the Old City was intended to accomplish exactly that. Dozens of men from Deir Yassin were driven through Jerusalem in open-bed trucks before being executed at the end of the day. The number of deaths listed in the early United Nations report has since been revised, lowered to around 150, but the overall impact of the massacre was accomplished regardless of the number of casualties. Zionist gangs had been engaging in a concentrated "shock and awe" campaign since February 1948, attacking defenseless villages such as Qaisariya, which was ethnically cleansed in its entirety on February 15, 1948; Barrat Qaisariya, also completely wiped out in February 1948; and Sa'sa', where two massacres were committed in 1948, one in February, and the other in October. Militia leader David Ben-Gurion was pleased with the first massacre in Sa'sa', where "the sky prised open," and where the Zionist militias "left behind 35 demolished houses and 60–80 dead bodies (quite a few of them were children)."[8] Preeminent Palestinian historian Walid Khalidi, cofounder of the Institute for Palestine Studies, writes that Moshe Kelman, the commander of the battalion who attacked Sa'sa', was similarly satisfied in that "it planted a great fear in the hearts of the population of the villages."[9]

In what set the tone for the new state that would be born out of these ruthless executions, the Deir Yassin massacre was committed by the Irgun and Stern Gang militias, respectively led by Menachem Begin and Yitzhak Shamir, each of whom would eventually hold the office of prime minister of Israel. The Haganah militia, precursor to the Israeli army, provided support for the attack with mortar fire and by disposing of the bodies. Its leader, David Ben-Gurion, became Israel's first prime minister only weeks after the massacre.

The fifty-five children Sitt Hind came upon on the outskirts of the Old City had been dropped off there by the Zionist fighters who had earlier killed their parents. They had been transported there in the same trucks used only hours before to parade the Palestinian prisoners in Jerusalem, where they were jeered, spat at, assailed with trash, and stoned before they were returned to Deir Yassin and executed. This was far from an isolated event known only to those around Jerusalem: classified documents reveal that dozens of massacres were committed by Zionist terrorists across the country during the catastrophic months that culminated in the ethnic cleansing of Palestine, with the forced displacement of over 75 percent of its entire population.

The use of informants, or collaborators, during the massacres was similarly meant to sow complete disarray among the Palestinians by adding to the psychological terror: Who could be trusted in such dangerous times? We see this, for example, in Darin Sallam's 2021 historical drama *Farha*. The film, based on a true story about the coming of age of a young Palestinian girl in 1948, depicts how these men would be paraded, hooded, among the villagers and made to point to where fighters may be hiding, or weapons stashed.[10] Again, the terror such scenes spread among the villagers was intentional: The informants—many of whom were captured trying to check on family members—would have been just as effective from inside the Zionist fighters' vehicles but were displayed in the streets to sow further confusion and distrust among the terrified Palestinians.

The concerted campaign of shock and awe achieved its goal. The stories of ruthless executions, rapes, and mutilations circulated widely, and families that could flee did so, sometimes leaving behind one or two members to fend off the enemy. My own maternal grandmother, Jamila Salman Mourey, fled from Jerusalem to

Yaffa with seven of her nine children, leaving behind my two older uncles, who fought in the battle for Jerusalem. Jamila was already a widow by then, one of thousands of Palestinian women protecting large families, hoping to find their way to safety in a world turned treacherous, murderous, as the Zionist European Jews continued with their indiscriminate assaults on Palestine's Indigenous people. Neither she, nor her daughter, my mother, were ever able to return to our homeland.

An Early Form of Mutual Aid

"Stay right where you are. Do not go anywhere. I'll be right back," Hind al-Husseini told the fifty-five bereaved orphans, as she assured them, "You will be safe."[11] She promptly moved the children into two rooms rented by the Social Work Endeavour Society, which she headed. Al-Husseini then visited the children daily, delivering food and clothing she had been collecting from families around the city. She called on her entire community, asking everyone to contribute what they could: blankets, food, clothes, hygiene and first aid supplies. In fact, just as feminism, and feminists, existed before these terms had been coined, so al-Husseini had activated a mutual aid network before this system of resource sharing was named and recognized as an alternative to government handouts.

Mutual aid, as explained by queer organizer Dean Spade, is "collective coordination to meet each other's needs." Spade acknowledges that "there is nothing new about mutual aid" as communities "have worked together to survive for all of human history."[12] Mutual aid is grounded in the awareness that the government is not going to meet the people's needs, hence the grassroots organizing of resources and support. Palestinian women were aware early on of the fact that "the government," as they were growing up in Mandatory Palestine, was utterly uninterested in providing for what they viewed as basic human needs, such as girls' education. Matiel Mogannam had been quite outspoken about the British government's neglect of the needs of the Palestinian people, especially women and girls. Her colleague

Sadhij Nassar had similarly exposed Britain's duplicity, as a "mandatory" power that had no interest in improving the circumstances of the people it was tasked with protecting. This denunciation, beginning in the 1920s, continued in the decades to follow, including with the Arab Ladies' Society of Yaffa decrying, in 1946, the British government's neglect of education, writing that "governments all over the world consider education a duty. This government had a budget of 20 million pounds and spends only 1/2 million pounds on education."[13]

The focus of the various Palestinian women's associations on remedying illiteracy, especially among rural girls, was thus a form of stepping in and sharing resources to transform society and constitutes an early form of mutual aid: providing for basic rights and social needs by offering what one has, where the government fails. Al-Husseini herself viewed education not as a privilege but as a human right, which she devoted her life to securing for as many needy girls as possible. But first, in order to provide the most basic necessities to the orphans she had rescued, she put together a system of communal resource sharing. Availing herself of her high-placed connections in the city, she asked Anwar al-Khatib, the governor of Jerusalem, for help in securing donations, which he offered by requesting, at the start of an official meeting, that everyone present pledge to give something to the Deir Yassin orphans before he would tend to the agenda. Stepping in where the government would not, al-Husseini gathered donations from the community, always making sure the many children she sheltered were well fed and clothed.

The situation of the fifty-five orphans in two rooms was untenable, and al-Husseini's own daily visits there from her nearby home put her at risk, so she arranged with the director of the nearby al-Sahyoun convent for the children to move there. This was literally a lifesaving move, as the two rooms the orphans had been staying in were bombed that same night. And, on April 25, 1948, within a mere two weeks of her getting them off the streets, al-Husseini moved the Deir Yassin orphans into her grandfather's mansion and established the Dar al-Tifl al-Arabi Foundation to raise funds for their support. Al-Husseini was quite adept at raising money and soon started receiving funds from across the world, as the orphanage and its elementary school grew, sheltering bereaved children from different villages and cities and adding one grade a year to its school curriculum. Shortly after it was established as an orphanage, Dar al-Tifl expanded into a boarding school. From its early years until 1967, it hosted about forty students sent there by wealthy Palestinian parents in the Gulf countries, who wanted their children to grow up in Palestine and receive a rigorous and politicized education. The tuition paid by these families was sufficient to cover the needs of the destitute and orphaned, while the attendance of these well-off Diaspora children fulfilled al-Husseini's belief in the importance of socioeconomic mix to children's growth and self- awareness.

The orphanage also had a bus, which drove across the country, where Sitt Hind would pick up needy children, offering them a better life under Dar al-Tifl's roof. Some Palestinians to this day recall "the Dar al-Tifl school bus" and how they would gather in the town square when they saw it arrive, ready to send their children off to the school that would offer them a chance at a better life.

Yamila Channan, a friend I interviewed about her years at Dar al-Tifl, tells me she remembers a local butcher who would drop off meat every week, whose shop she later made a point of patronizing as an adult, in recognition of his generosity to the school. Channan also recalls that on occasion, a car would drive onto the school grounds to drop off hundreds of pairs of shoes, gathered from community members in and around Jerusalem. The orphanage also had a craft studio with sewing machines, so that the children could have new clothes, or to alter donated dresses to fit the young girls, always with the goal of making them feel good about their appearance. Sitt Hind's own daughter, Hidaya, recalls many of the stories she had heard about her formidable mother, and experiences she herself had growing up in the orphanage. "She made each and every one of us feel that we were worthy, and that we had something to be proud of," Hidaya recalls, adding, "She made us walk tall, feel tall."[14]

Hidaya's words about her mother are echoed by many of the women who spent years at Dar al-Tifl when they were younger.

Nihaya Qawasmi, another friend of mine who also spent her formative years at Dar al-Tifl, sent me the following recollection:

> I spent nine years at Dar A-Tifel Al-Arabi (2nd–9th grades), 1977–1983. Like most kids, I hated school and having to do homework and taking exams, but when I look back on these nine years, they were the best years of my life. As a kid, I didn't see the value of Miss Hind because I wasn't as politically aware as I became due to those wonderful years at my school. At the time, I knew that she was the head of the school, but I had no idea what a wonderful woman she was. I saw her a few times during those nine years. She was always abroad securing funds for the school. She was also a member of the Palestinian National Council (PNC).

Qawasmi recalls that al-Husseini was careful to instill political awareness and knowledge of Palestinian history among the schoolchildren, effectively countering the Zionist erasure of Palestinian culture and Indigeneity. "I can't remember which year, but it was the anniversary of Land Day [March 30] when the Secondary level girls ordered us not to attend classes after we were finished with the morning line up," Qawasmi wrote.

> We gathered at the other end of the yard and sat down on the cold and wet ground and refused to move because the older girls wanted to participate in the demonstrations on that day. I didn't know anything about Land Day, and for me, as a kid, it was a day to escape school and classes. When the teachers failed to make us budge, Miss Hind showed up. She stood there in her thin body and gray hair and told us that she understood our need to join the fight against the occupation, but we needed to know what Land Day was and why it's an important day in the history of our people. She asked the PE teacher, who was a member of the PFLP [Popular Front for the Liberation of Palestine], to educate us about Land Day. She told us that she wouldn't force us to attend classes, but we needed to learn about this day.

"The school had two sections, "Dakhili [internal] and Khariji [external]," Qawasmi explained to me.

> The first was for the girls who lived in the dorms and all their needs were provided by the school and the other one was for the girls who lived with their families and only attended day school. I was one of the latter, but I received free education because my family couldn't afford to pay tuition. The school was a private one and had high tuition like the Saint George and Schmidt schools in Jerusalem, but Miss Hind made educating girls more important than funds and that is why she traveled far and wide to secure such funds from charitable organizations and governments.[15]

Channan, mentioned above, an educator herself today, also told me that the education she and the other children received at Dar al-Tifl was fully comparable to that of the private schools that catered to the country's elite families. Ms. al-Husseini also went out of her way to hire teachers who could not find employment elsewhere because of their political activism. Channan recalls the physical education teacher that Qawasmi mentioned—Abdellatif Ghaith, a member of the Palestinian Front for the Liberation of Palestine—and tells me the students were aware that many of their teachers were not only politically active but, in some cases, had actively engaged in acts of resistance against the Israeli occupation. The school was thus an institution that instilled pride in the children, employed highly politicized faculty and staff, and remained independent of government intervention, as al-Husseini had registered it as an Islamic *waqf*—an inalienable charitable endowment—to ensure its self-governance and overall independence.

"Miss Hind was more than the president of my school; she was my mother," Qawasmi wrote, again echoing many of the women I interviewed for this research. She recalled:

> I learned my ethics and political principles from her. She made me who I am now. She could have ignored those 55 Deir Yassin kids and gone on with her life, but she decided to drop everything and

> dedicated her life to improving the lives of girls she never bore. She was/is my inspiration and role model. I learned tenacity and being religiously ethical from her. She was the first Palestinian woman who moved out of her family home and rented her own apartment in the old city of Jerusalem. She single-handedly built this great educational institution in Jerusalem where girls entered in their diapers and graduated with a BA degree.

Qawasmi added, "Miss Hind was the mother I never had. I will always be in debt to her and I will always honor her and tell the world about her. I'm proud to call myself the daughter of Miss Hind al-Husseini."

Another woman I talked to, who asked to be identified only by the initial "K," also told me that Sitt Hind was a mother figure to her, and that the al-Husseini family overall was the only family she knew.

"I am a proud daughter of Mama Hind—neither a foundling, nor an orphan, but a proud daughter of Dar al-Tifl," K told me. (A "foundling" is generally an out-of-wedlock infant who would have been left at the Dar al-Tifl doorstep). K explained that she is one of six siblings, three girls and three boys. She was only three years old when she entered Dar al-Tifl in 1985. Her Palestinian father, wanted by Israel, went into exile, and her Egyptian mother returned to Egypt after leaving the six young children at Dar al-Tifl, trusting the school would offer them what she, effectively a single mother, could not. Indeed, many of the children who were taken to this orphanage by their own parents were taken there because the parents trusted they would receive the shelter, food, clothing, and education that the parents lacked, all within a loving environment.

K's younger brother was only seven months old at the time, and even though Dar al-Tifl was a girls' school by then, Sitt Hind did not want to separate the siblings and let the boys spend their first few years there, before transferring them to the nearby Dar al-Awlad, "the Boys' School," in the same Sheikh Jarrah neighborhood. "We were in the internal section, with the children (orphans) who did not go home for the holidays, but Dar al-Tifl was our home. It felt like home. During the holidays, when other children went back to their families, those from the internal section were made to feel they were members of the al-Husseini family, visiting al-Husseini uncles and aunts, while the rest of their schoolmates were also visiting family, on the outside," K recalls, feeling particularly privileged to have this greater proximity to the extended al-Husseini family than the day school children. "We always had a feast on the first day of Eid. And presents. We never felt lesser. Sitt Hind would bring my brothers over from the Boys' School for these occasions, so that we six siblings celebrated together as a family. We remain close to this day because of how she brought us up."

K repeated what other "daughters of Dar al-Tifl" shared with me, namely that Sitt Hind always told them: "Keep your shoulders up. Hold your head high. Be proud to be a woman. Never let anyone boss you around. You are strong." "And all of us, the daughters of Mama Hind, the women who were fortunate enough to go to Dar al-Tifl, are proud of our upbringing and remain forever grateful for the opportunity to have been raised by this exceptional woman," K told me.[16]

Sitt Hind al-Husseini directed Dar al-Tifl until her death in 1994. In 2018, novelist susan abulhawa, who had lived there from age ten to thirteen, wrote a statement that was read at Dar al-Tifl following her own deportation from Palestine: "She saved a lot of us girls. She gathered us from all the broken bits of Palestine. She gave us food and shelter, educated and believed in us, and in turn made us believe we were worthy." abulhawa adds:

> I lived the best years of my childhood there, despite my separation from family and the sometimes difficult conditions we faced living under Israeli occupation. Dar el Tifl is the legacy of one of the most admirable women I have ever known: Sitt Hind el Husseini. She saved me in more ways than I suppose she knew, or that I understood at the time.[17]

Into the Diaspora

One of the many Zionist canards about the dispossession and forced displacement of the Palestinian people is that the 750,000 fleeing Palestinians left "of their own volition," seeking temporary shelter in the neighboring countries (Lebanon, Jordan, Egypt, Syria, and Iraq) because they believed these would wage a victorious war on Israel, enabling them to return to their homes within weeks. In reality, even if the fleeing Palestinians had fostered such naive hopes, reliance on the promises of Arab countries was not what drove them into the Diaspora. The Palestinians had been effectively terrorized, and they were fleeing in fully justified fear for their lives. Their anticipation of return was grounded in their conviction that their dispossession and displacement were wrong, along with the erroneous belief that the powerful countries that played with their fates would realize the gravity of their error and consequently redress it. But again, their flight was a result of well-orchestrated Zionist terrorism campaigns, and they did not have the luxury of some thought-out plan for the future.

My own maternal grandmother, Jamila, already widowed by then, had left Jerusalem in April 1948, in the aftermath of the Deir Yassin massacre, gathering seven of her nine children and heading for Yaffa. But Yaffa itself would soon come under attack too, as Irgun fighters launched a full-scale assault on the city on April 25, 1948, in an offensive that included a continuous three-day bombardment of the town center. Here, too, the intent was to cause a mass exodus of the Palestinians, with Yaffa, known as "the bride of Palestine," holding a special significance because, up till 1948, it was Palestine's second city and the country's cultural and literary center. Surrounded by expansive citrus orchards, including its namesake orange fruit, it was also a hub for Palestinian journalism, where two newspapers, *Filastin* and *Al-Difa'* (The defense), were established. In Yaffa, the Irgun and Haganah bombardment achieved its goal of ethnic cleansing: The prosperous, thriving city, which boasted 100,000 residents in the mid-1940s, lost most of its population, with only an estimated 15,000 to 25,000 left by mid-May 1948.[18] Tens of thousands of

Palestinians fled by boat toward Gaza and Egypt in the south, or northward toward Lebanon. Scores drowned in the sea, an early precursor of today's refugee crisis in the Mediterranean. Following the expulsion of Yaffa's Palestinian population, the newly established nearby Israeli city of Tel Aviv expanded its municipal boundaries to annex Yaffa and several other Palestinian villages in 1950.

My mother was only days short of her sixteenth birthday as her family fled in 1948, and years later, she told me about her trip from Yaffa to Beirut, aboard a pontoon that had previously been used to transport sheep. The pontoon reeked of the stench of farm animals, my mother recalls. Later, she gave me more details of the dangerous journey that could have ended her life, and that of the many families aboard the pontoon. The flatbed, loaded with refugees, had been hastily tied to a tugboat. At one point, the rope attaching it to the tugboat began to loosen, and was about to come completely undone, leaving the refugees to drift away, and potentially sink, within sight of the coastline. Nobody knew how to swim, my mother tells me, but two young boys lowered themselves in the water and tightened the rope again, in a courageous act that saved the pontoon's human cargo, which eventually made it to Lebanon.

It adds insult to injury that Palestinians, who were terrorized into fleeing their historic homeland, are the ones who are accused of wanting to "push the Jews into the sea."

Defying Gender Expectations

In 1948, my two uncles, the elder sons of the family, stayed behind to fight the Zionist militias. The family was eventually reunited, in Lebanon, when my uncles fled Palestine shortly after the battle of Jerusalem, which they could not effectively participate in, because they had not been able to find any guns to fight with. The heavy-handed British suppression of Palestinian resistance since the 1936–39 Great Revolt meant that Palestinians caught with a rifle, if not summarily executed, would be jailed or possibly exiled. Indeed, the ethnic cleansing of the Palestinian people in 1948 would have been impossible were it not for the harm inflicted on that population during the 1936–39 revolt, when the British violently quelled the widespread uprising against their imperial plans by killing thousands of Palestinians, injuring and imprisoning thousands more, applying collective punishment on entire towns, and jailing and deporting leaders—all measures of repression which Israel later adopted.[19]

Considering the social norms and expectations at the time, it was typical for some male members of the family to stay behind to fight. But as Matiel Mogannam had noted in 1937, these gender norms were also regularly being transgressed, "by force of circumstances," with many women active in armed resistance. In "Nariman Khurshid and the Chrysanthemum Flower Organization," Janan Abdu writes about her challenge researching Palestinian women's participation in armed resistance up till 1948. She explains that she could gather the everyday experiences of rural women relatively easily, as she was able to arrange to meet with them, or their daughters, to conduct interviews. As for the stories of women who were active in armed resistance, "this was more like a legend," she notes. One name, Fatima Ghazal, kept popping up—the first woman to carry a rifle, and to be killed, in the battle of Jal Azoun. Most remained nameless, listed only as casualties: So many women were imprisoned, so many injured, and so many killed in battle. Yet the folklore suggested Palestinian women were agents, not just casualties. Yes, hundreds of thousands had fled. But many stayed behind to fight.

Abdu persevered in her research, unearthing three militant women's groups that were active from the 1930s to 1948: al-Kaff al-Aswad (the Black Hand), active in Jerusalem, whose members were arrested, tried in military court, and imprisoned; Rafiqat al-Qassam (the Companions of al-Qassam), who were trained to bear arms by the anti-British, anti-Zionist guerilla leader Izzadine al-Qassam himself, and were active mostly around Haifa; and Zahrat al-Uqhuwan (the Chrysanthemum Flower), active around Yaffa.[20] Only Zahrat al-Uqhuwan, named after the flower that grows wild in fields throughout Palestine, was founded by women, sisters Mahiba and Nariman Khurshid of Yaffa. Mahiba was a teacher, Nariman a secretary. Mahiba's date of birth is given in different sources as

1920 or 1925, with Nariman a few years younger, making them both in their twenties in 1948. The sisters were active in a number of women's organizations and began their political activism by providing medical care to the wounded. Growing up in the 1920s and 1930s, Mahiba and Nariman witnessed many atrocities, but one particular incident, the shooting by a British sniper of a ten-year old boy, who died in his mother's arms, convinced them that liberation could only be achieved through armed revolt, and that all Palestinians, men and women, should join the military resistance.[21]

In 1947, upon being told by male fighters that they could not join them because they were women, Mahiba and Nariman, along with twelve other women, formed the first Palestinian women's armed resistance group. Zahrat al-Uqhuwan soon became known as one of the best-trained Palestinian armed groups, securing many military victories. The Arab press lauded the group's successes, comparing Mahiba to Khawla Bint al-Azwar, a legendary woman from the early history of Islam who fought many battles disguised as a man.[22] The newspaper *Filastin* wrote that Zahrat al-Uqhuwan had restored Palestinian women's dignity.

And all along, even as they engaged in military battles, the fighters in Zahrat al-Uqhuwan continued to tend to their communities' many needs by providing medical care, meals to the needy, and relief to displaced families.

Rape as a Weapon of War

The principle of "purity of arms," written into the "The Spirit of the IDF," or code of ethics of the Israeli military, states:

> The IDF serviceman will use force of arms only for the purpose of subduing the enemy to the necessary extent and will limit his use of force so as to prevent unnecessary harm to human life and limb, dignity and property. The IDF servicemen's purity of arms is their self-control in use of armed force. They will use their arms only for the purpose of achieving their mission, without inflicting

> unnecessary injury to human life or limb; dignity or property, of both soldiers and civilians, with special consideration for the defenseless, whether in wartime, or during routine security operations, or in the absence of combat, or times of peace.

Yet throughout the history of the Zionist dispossession of the Palestinian people, we have a plethora of cases illustrating the deliberate, state-sanctioned violation of this haughty principle.

The principle had already been formulated in 1946, when David Ben-Gurion, addressing the Haganah, the precursor to the Israeli army, stressed the supposed moral superiority of the Jewish fighters over the Palestinians, who are described as barbarians, deceitful, cowards, and lowlifes.[23] Indeed, just as the European settlers on Turtle Island described the Indigenous of this land as "merciless savages" whose "known rule of warfare, is an undistinguished destruction of all ages, sexes and conditions," and just as these colonizers thought they were being "attacked" on what they perceived as their own frontiers, so the Zionist fighters must have seen all Palestinians as aggressors. For only by perceiving them as such could the Zionists kill, and rape, while believing they retained their "purity of arms."[24] Like most fleeing Palestinians, my grandmother was terrorized by the possibility that she, and her daughters, could be raped. Recently declassified documents reveal that this horrific crime was a standard accompaniment to the depopulation of the villages and served two functions. One was psychological, inflicting collective social trauma on the Palestinian people; the other was more self-serving for the militiamen, providing them with sanctioned instant gratification.

Indeed, one can conceive of the magnitude of Israeli sexual violence against Palestinians at the onset of al-Nakba from the many recently declassified documents dating back to 1947–48, as well as interviews, testimony from survivors, and oral history collected among the fighters who engaged in the concerted terror assaults that lead to the creation of Israel. Israeli historian Ilan Pappe's *The Ethnic Cleansing of Palestine* lists some of these instances, including the horrific rape of a twelve-year-old who became the sex slave of an Israeli platoon, with a total of twenty-two soldiers gang-raping her over a few days before finally murdering her.[25] Pappe, who left Israel out of fear for his own safety, also writes about instances recorded in the Israeli archives, but these only list cases where the Israeli soldiers were brought to trial. "David Ben-Gurion seems to have been informed about each case and entered them in his diary. Every few days he had a sub-section: Rape Cases."[26]

Other instances of rape were only recorded later. Thus Pappe explains:

> Oral recollection also exposed cases of rape throughout the occupation of Palestine's villages ... Many of the cases were corroborated by UN officials who interviewed a number of women from the villages who were willing to come forward and talk about their experiences. When, many years later, some of these people were interviewed, it was obvious how difficult it still proved for the men and women from the village to talk about names and details, and the interviewers came away with the impression that they all knew more than they wished or were able to tell.[27]

Rape is a crime whose impact lasts a lifetime, often across generations, and the trauma of this gendered violence at the onset of al-Nakba is still being unearthed today. And as the horrors of these early days continue to be revealed, we are becoming more aware of the specifically gendered nature of Israel's violence against the Palestinian people, from the very foundation of that state. What we still need to foreground is the resilience of the women and children who were subjected to sexual atrocities and persevered in their determination to help one another survive and to live in dignity. Beginning with the British Mandate, Palestine's proto-feminists not only denounced the imperial designs on their country; they confronted them with every means at their disposal. Some opened schools when the government wouldn't; others rejected the imposed Western ways; and yet others took up arms to fight the colonizers. All showed the Indigenous defiance and steadfastness that come from being grounded in one's soil and proud of one's culture.

I do not think it is an exaggeration to say all Palestinians are indebted to Sitt Hind al-Husseini, the young woman who assured fifty-five orphans in 1948 that they would be safe and has since delivered on her promise to them, and thousands more. Like Indigenous feminists everywhere, Sitt Hind and the many women who ceaselessly toil to improve the circumstances of their dispossessed communities show us how individuals frequently step up and fill in the gaps when the state fails to do so.

Hind al-Husseini was the scion of one of Jerusalem's most privileged families, an educated, wealthy woman who not only gave generously but also made sure others in similarly privileged positions gave what they could, or would, to the most vulnerable members of society. My own grandmother, Jamila Salman, was of the same generation and also hailed from Jerusalem, but she came from a poor family and was barely literate. Despite their widely different socioeconomic circumstances, Hind and Jamila are proof that Palestinian women are survivors and do not need to be saved from the men in their lives—fathers, husbands, or brothers—but from structural violence by a state that does not care, and will not provide, for the people whose land it occupies. Nor do they need to be saved *by* their fathers, husbands, or brothers. They are the women who, as our nation was violently stolen from us, ensured the survival of the new generation, so that today we persevere in the struggle to liberate ourselves from colonialism and patriarchy.

3

Sustaining Communities: The Preservation of Culture

> *My only identity is my national dress. It is my own work which I inherited from my ancestors through my mother and my grandmother ... My history is recorded on my dress. I believe in my dress more than I believe in scholars and historians, because their books and accounts are easily distorted and biased. But, not my dress. Embroidery was created by common people who do not know distortion at all.*
>
> —Feryal Abbasi-Ghnaim, in Wafa Ghnaim, *Tatreez and Tea*, 2018

Wealthy Palestinian women's social work was unlike Western-style, self-serving philanthropy, where one donates 10 percent of one's wealth for tax-relief purposes without being in the least inconvenienced. The prioritization of collective empowerment over individual advancement is one of the defining characteristics of Third World feminism, and from the early 1900s, as we saw in the previous chapters, privileged Palestinian women were walking away from their leisurely lifestyle to crisscross their country, setting up schools in underserved rural towns. They did so out of their conviction that offering poor rural girls a formal education was a pathway to empowerment. Many of these women were also highly politicized and believed women had an important role to play in liberating the nation from the colonial plans European countries had for it. A formal education, to them, was necessary for such national advocacy, and everyone was needed. Most of these "society ladies" had gone to private schools as young girls and took pride in being cultured;

many had hosted literary salons at their own homes. They came from, and lived in, comfortable homes which had well-furnished libraries, with shelves lined with books in Arabic, Turkish, French, and English. They traveled abroad on lecture tours or to visit schools in other Arab countries, primarily Egypt, Syria, and Iraq, but also Jordan and Lebanon. In Egypt, they had gathered with Egyptian feminist Huda al-Shaarawi, a remarkable woman whose dedication to women's issues earned her the title of "Egypt's First Feminist," as well as Nabawiya Musa and Saiza Nabarawi, both of whom had participated in the 1923 Conference of the International Women's Suffrage Alliance in Rome, Italy—which remains to this day the world's biggest conference on women's suffrage. Al-Shaarawi, Musa, Nabarawi, and their peers and followers advocated for equal rights for all citizens, and for women's full participation in political matters. And whether they spoke of "the women's agenda," women's "rights," or women's "responsibilities," their social and political work made it clear they believed education should not remain a privilege afforded only to wealthy urbanites.

As they realized that their traditional ways were threatened as a result of their dispossession, Palestinian women were also committed to preserving and passing down their cultural heritage in the form of oral history, cooking techniques, making coin headdresses (which brides wore on their wedding day), weaving both textiles and baskets, and *tatreez*, the traditional Palestinian embroidery deeply rooted in Palestinian culture and heritage, with distinctive patterns for each region of the country.

A Cultural Nakba

As a people, Palestinians are known to have high education rates and to rank among the nations with the highest proportion of college graduates in the world. In her 2023 book *Refuge and Resistance: Palestinians and the International Refugee System*, British historian Anne Irfan discusses how Palestinians are known as "the world's best educated refugees," a people determined to pursue education no matter how harsh their living circumstances. This, however, was not always the case among a primarily rural nation and can be attributed to two factors: the urban elite women's commitment to "social work," which for them consisted primarily of educating rural girls and women, and the catastrophic dispossession that began in 1948. As they fled their villages and started living in tents, Palestinian refugees developed a growing appreciation for education, a wealth they could carry with them. Indeed, one early indication of how important schooling had become to Palestinians is the fact that, following the 1949 establishment of the United Nations Relief and Works Agency for Palestine Refugees in the Near East (UNRWA) to tend to the needs of refugees, they successfully petitioned the agency to prioritize education among the services it offered them.[1] Moreover, when it began operations in May 1950, UNRWA did not have to start the refugee schools from scratch as much as take over those schools started in 1947 and 1948 by the Palestinians themselves, as they were being displaced first by Zionist terrorist militias, then by Israeli soldiers. Indeed, the mid- to late 1940s, and the 1950s, saw a burgeoning of Palestinian education, even as Palestinians were struggling to establish new lives in what they hoped would be temporary conditions. Having lost their land, Palestinians now looked to education as an alternate form of social capital.[2]

The European Jews who were colonizing Palestine had also learned the hard way the importance of education as social capital. Jewish land ownership had been proscribed in Eastern Europe, and Jews had been barred from many guilds and professions throughout the continent. This pushed them into financial transactions such as tax and rent collections and money lending, considered "inferior" trades by Europe's Christians. Another venue open to European Jews centered cultural and intellectual pursuits. They excelled at both, earning scorn and resentment for their financial successes but social acceptance, even admiration and respect, for their cultural accomplishments. These were the colonizers of Palestine in 1948, and they were determined to own land, even if they had to steal it, just as they were determined to erase the cultural heritage of the Palestinians, so as to absolve themselves of the guilt of displacing a civilized people. As Edward Said would write later in *Culture and Imperialism*, widely viewed as the successor to *Orientalism*, all colonial enterprises frame the colonized as culturally inferior and project themselves as spreading civilization where it is nonexistent.[3] Looking specifically at the connection between literature and empire, he noted that literature has "the power to narrate, or to block other narratives from forming and emerging" that might otherwise challenge the idea of colonization as spreading civilization.[4] The Zionist colonizers were no exception in their desire to eradicate the Indigenous culture, as evidenced from the discourse they created, which presented Palestine as a barren land awaiting their touch to "make the desert bloom."

Part of the Zionist attempt at the cultural erasure of Palestine consisted of renaming of the cities and villages. As they lay claim to the land between 1925 and 1948, the early settlers had limited themselves to giving Hebrew names only to the newly established Jewish communities purchased by the Jewish National Fund. Beginning in 1948, however, they immediately started changing the name of the towns and villages they were taking over, in an effort both to erase their Arab identity and to claim legitimacy for the settler colonial theft. Thus David Ben-Gurion wrote in his diary, "We must give Hebrew names to these places—ancient names, if there are, and if not, new ones," later explaining to the chair of the "Committee for the Designation of Name Places in the Negev Region" ("Negev" being itself a Hebrew renaming of "Naqab"), "We are obliged to remove the Arabic names for reasons of state. Just as we do not recognize the Arabs' political proprietorship of the land, so also do we not recognize their spiritual proprietorship and their names."[5]

In this, too, Zionism was simply following the general colonial model. Just as all colonial enterprises claim to be bringing civilization to a savage, barbaric land, so all settler colonial countries—as distinct from extractive colonial countries—have changed the names of the land they occupy to reflect their own cultural heritage. A prime example is the US, where towns and cities are named after European conquerors. Thus there is a city or town named "Columbus" in Ohio, Mississippi, Montana, New Mexico, and New York, among other states, and an even greater number of cities named "Columbia," including the nation's capital, the "District of Columbia." Similarly, "Virginias" abound, named after the "Virgin" Queen Elizabeth the First. And so do "Washingtons," all the way from the East Coast to the West. It is only when the colonial entity feels completely unthreatened by the Indigenous people that it is willing to engage in performative "land acknowledgments," which nevertheless remain unaccompanied by any measures to return the stolen land.

Our colonizers have always been threatened by the Indigeneity of the Palestinian people, our belonging to the land, hence the Zionist need to "Hebraize" the names of the conquered cities. In *The One-State Solution: A Breakthrough for Peace in the Israeli-Palestinian Deadlock*, Professor Virginia Tilley writes that a

> body of scientific, linguistic, literary, historical, and biblical authorities *was invented* to foster impressions of Jewish belonging and natural rights in a Jewish homeland reproduced from a special Jewish right to this land, which clearly has been occupied, through the millennia, by many peoples.[6]

The Great Book Robbery

Along with changing the names of the towns they now occupied, the early Israelis were also looting libraries, stealing books, and destroying Palestinian artifacts, so as to better convince themselves that the people they were dispossessing were culturally inferior. In what has become known as the Great Book Robbery of 1948–49, an estimated 60,000 to 70,000 books were stolen from private homes in the affluent neighborhoods of Jerusalem, Yaffa, Nazareth, Akka, Haifa, Ramallah, and other conquered cities. Approximately 75 percent of the dispossessed urban families were quite rich in both money and assets, which were stolen from them and never returned. Intellectuals such as Khalil Sakakini had an impressive private library; other elite families such as the Nashashibi and the Dajjani also had substantial private libraries. Novelist Ghada Karmi's father, Hassan Karmi, a linguist, had been working on an English-Arabic dictionary and had gathered hundreds of books in both Arabic and English, so as to capture all the nuances of a word he was entering in the dictionary. These collections are all gone.

The looting was first done by individual thieves—soldiers who stole what they found in the houses the Palestinians had been forced to leave, rummaging through shelves, armoires, cabinets, drawers, grabbing armfuls of what they fancied and tossing the rest to the side. Then came the official looters—an Israeli-government-sponsored joint operation between the Hebrew University and the Israeli army, which lasted from April 1948 to February 1949. Israeli soldiers participated in it, as well as some Palestinian prisoners of war who were ordered to go into the houses from which other Palestinians had been expelled and loot fine china, Persian rugs, silverware, furniture, and books, which were then loaded into separate trucks and taken away. In an interview with Israeli Dutch documentary maker Benny Brunner, Mohammed Batrawi, who recalls he was "POW number 6704," says he and a number of young men from his town of Isdud were made to loot Palestinian houses in Ramleh, Safad, and other towns he was unfamiliar with at the time.[7]

An unknown number of the looted books had their pages ripped out and used as wrapping paper at markets. Others were recycled into paper after they were deemed by the Israeli government to "incite against" Israel, probably because they expressed nationalist ambitions. And yet others were taken to Israel's National Library, where some 6,000 remain housed to this day, with the letters *AP* ("Abandoned Property") stamped on their spines.[8] The library, which claims it is "preserving the books," refuses to release them to their owners despite having a record of some of the books' origins and who they were stolen from. As Adam Horowitz, managing editor of the anti-Zionist news website *Mondoweiss*, writes in a short essay about the looting, "A particularly chilling document, [at the Israeli National Library] from March 1948, lists tens of Jerusalemites whose libraries were looted—it reads like a Who's Who of the Palestinian cultural elite of the time."[9] Since individual thieves had gotten to the books prior to the Israeli-sponsored looting, there is no telling where some of the more valuable ones ended up, which are not at the Israeli National Library; they may be lining the shelves of Israeli citizens' private libraries, or they could have been thrown away.

Khalil Sakakini, a towering Palestinian intellectual and visionary educator of the early twentieth century whose private library was looted, penned this lament:

> Goodbye, my books! Farewell to the house of wisdom, the temple of philosophy, the scientific institute, the literary academy. How much midnight oil did I burn with you, reading and writing in the silence of the night, while the people slept ... farewell, my books. I do not know what became of you after we left. Were you looted? Burned? Were you transferred, with due respect, to a public or private library? Did you find your way to a grocer, your pages wrapping onions?[10]

One of the effects of this book robbery was that many Palestinians growing up in *al-dakhil* (the interior), also known as "1948 Israel," did not know Palestinian literature had even existed before the 1960s and 1970s. They were bereft of a sense of civilization—the exact intention of settler colonialism. As the books were "disappeared" and Palestinians were prevented from studying their own culture in Israeli schools, they were dispossessed of the cultural heritage that would have sustained them as a collective, cultural entity. Ala Hlehel, a Palestinian writer born in 1979 in Jish, in present-day northern Israel, speaks of having a "thirst for knowledge" of Palestinian culture as he went through the Israeli education system, calling himself a "cultural orphan" for having been deprived of his heritage.[11]

Empowering Families, Preserving Culture

Realizing the gravity of the cultural erasure Israel planned for them, many Palestinians grasped the urgency of preserving their ancestral heritage, and teachers and parents alike felt the need to educate the youth about their villages, their towns, their crafts and folklore.

Passing down their threatened culture was an act of Indigenous resistance, instrumental in preserving the newly displaced people's language, their history, and the knowledge accumulated over millennia. With the *shatat*, the dispersal, came *lamlama*, the gathering, an intentional nurturing of communal knowledge of the traditional ways. One young woman in particular, Samiha Khalil, made this endeavor her life's mission, a corollary to her commitment to improving Palestinian families' overall circumstances.

Like her contemporary Sitt Hind al-Husseini, founder of Dar al-Tifl, Samiha Khalil had devoted her life from a young age to humanitarian relief for destitute Palestinians, before focusing on the needs of the children of martyrs post-1967. Born in 1923, Khalil was in her teens when she witnessed the violence of the British Mandate in her own home. Her father was mayor of her hometown, Anabta, and during the 1936–39 revolt, he stored food that had been donated by wealthy neighbors, to be distributed to the poor. But British soldiers broke into her family home, pushed her father to the floor, and slit open the bags of rice and flour with their bayonets. During that Great Revolt, the British also killed five of her cousins. Khalil carried those memories with her till her last days. Indeed, she was one of hundreds of thousands of Palestinian women who became politicized during the Great Revolt, joining protests against the British in cities and smuggling guns and food to the fighters in the countryside.

As she turned seventeen, and before she had a chance to complete her secondary education, Samiha's parents determined she should marry and found her a suitable husband—who indeed proved to be a wonderful partner to this phenomenal woman. Motherhood came next, as she bore and raised five children: Khalil, Saji, Sa'ida, Samir, and Samih. But early marriage and motherhood were no hindrance to her ambitions, and her husband, a teacher who soon became school principal, supported her desire to pursue higher education. Almost twenty years after leaving high school without graduating, "Umm Khalil," as she came to be known, finally sat for the *tawjihi* (high school graduation) exam, at the same time as her son Saji. Shortly afterward, at the age of forty, she enrolled at the Beirut Arab

University, majoring in Arabic literature. She was about to graduate when the 1967 war put an end to that plan.

Samiha Khalil's life trajectory is in many ways representative of that of her people at large—women, men, and children whose dreams, ambitions, and aspirations were irrevocably impacted by Zionism, and who nevertheless persisted, adapted, and never stopped caring for each other as they continued to dream of liberation. My own mother was sixteen in 1948. Her parents had pulled her out of school one year earlier, as tensions were escalating in Jerusalem, and I remember her enrolling in secretarial school and practicing her typing and stenography next to us as my sisters and I did our own homework in Beirut, Lebanon, in the early 1970s, our dining room table doubling up as a homework desk for five. My father had died in 1967; she was a widow who overcame the disruption of her middle school education to become a secretary almost twenty-five years later, as she determined to offer us a better life than what she'd had. My maternal aunt, only a few years older than my mother, became an UNRWA teacher. She never married, devoting herself instead to the many Palestinian children she taught for decades.

Similarly, the indomitable Samiha Khalil was not one to let her personal disappointments hinder her activism. In 1948, she was only twenty-five, and without her coveted tawjihi, when she began what would become a lifelong commitment to relief work with displaced refugees, beginning with collecting donations for the survivors of ethnically cleansed villages. Most politically involved women at the time had joined the Arab Women's Association (AWA), and in 1952, Khalil started a chapter in her new hometown of al-Bireh, where the family had moved after Khalil's husband became school principal there. There, she also founded the Arab Union Society in 1955 and, along with other politically active women, in 1965 cofounded the al-Bireh chapter of the Palestinian Women's Union, which shortly afterward became a chapter of the General Union of Palestinian Women. The GUPW itself had been established shortly after the first Palestinian National Congress convened in Jerusalem in 1965, under the slogan "Towards unifying the efforts of Palestinian women's committees to liberate the usurped homeland." The Preparatory

Committee consisted of Zulaikha al-Shihabi, who became GUPW president, Samira Abu Ghazaleh, Souad al-Kilani, Fayza Abd al-Majeed, Salma al-Khadra al-Jayyousi, Wadi'a Khartabil, Rashida al-Masri, and Hajja Andalib al-Amad. Samiha Khalil was elected secretary of its executive committee, consequently becoming a member of the Palestine National Council in 1966.

The many chapters of the AWA, the Arab Women's Union (AWU), and, as of 1965, the GUPW across the nation were a barometer of the very active participation of women in political affairs. The AWA, which morphed into the AWU in some cities, had spawned out of the Arab Women's Executive that formed at the 1929 Congress. Its goals were to organize around issues that were directly political, such as advocating for the release of Palestinian men imprisoned by the British authorities, or petitioning the British authorities against their colonial plans, as well as tending to the social needs of women and children. In an interview with Ellen Fleischmann, Matiel Mogannam explained: "There are times when you can't do anything except go out and do something. We had to do something to help the men." Fleischmann then comments: "It is interesting that the women felt that they *could* help the men. This unobjectionable motive, modestly phrased and continually reiterated in the press and interviews, cleverly articulates a rather disguised, collective self-confidence and assertiveness."[12]

The numerous chapters had their distinct characteristics, leadership, and priorities, and many established clinics, infant centers, educational centers, and playgrounds for children. The Jerusalem chapter played the most diplomatic role, as its members were in closest contact with Mandatory diplomats and politicians and were viewed as representing the Palestinian people nationally. But other chapters were often more political: The Haifa chapter, for example, under the leadership of Sadhij Nassar, was one of the more radical chapters, and the AWUs, which viewed themselves as chapters of the AWA, tended to prioritize political concerns over strictly social ones.

By 1944, the AWU had changed its name to the Palestinian Women's Union, a move to reinforce the distinctive cultural identity that Palestinians felt was under attack. Eventually, the GUPW, an umbrella organization grouping the various AWA and PWU chapters, was officially formed at a February 1965 meeting, called by Zulaykha al-Shihabi, another prominent Palestinian feminist with a long record of political organizing stretching back to the convening of the first Palestine Arab Women's Congress in 1929. Al-Shihabi was a member of the women's delegation that had met with the British high commissioner, Lord Chancellor, to present their petition against the arrests of Palestinian men, and against the harsh repression Palestinians were enduring under the Mandate, in addition to opposing British-facilitated Zionist migration to Palestine. The delegation threatened to launch massive demonstrations should he not accept their demands.[13] Al-Shihabi also played a pivotal role during the 1929 Buraq Revolt, as she organized a large audience to attend the trials of Palestinian rebels, to show solidarity for them in court and raise their morale. She also visited prisons and detention facilities regularly to provide support to political detainees.[14]

The GUPW did not have its own offices when it was first launched, relying instead on the General Union of Palestinian Students for space and resources, yet the energy behind it was such that within three months of its formation in June 1965, it was recognized as the sole official organization for women under the Palestine Liberation Organization (PLO). Shortly afterward, it acquired its own offices and moved away from prioritizing social work, focusing instead on national and gender liberation. And since it viewed itself as a Third World women's organization, it encouraged Palestinian women to establish relations with women's groups in communist and socialist countries such as Cuba, East Germany, and the Soviet Union.

Samiha Khalil remained politically involved in women's organizations and national politics until her death in 1999, when she was still serving on the Palestinian National Council, the "parliament" of the PLO. Meanwhile, she was also directing Jami'iyyat In'ash al-Usra (Inash Alusra Association, better known simply as In'ash al-Usra), the association she founded to fulfill three goals: to empower women by offering them vocational training to help them become financially independent, to educate children, and to preserve Palestine's cultural heritage.

In'ash al-Usra

Like other Palestinian feminists, Khalil deftly juggled political and social work, actively opposing Western colonial interventions and Zionist occupation while caring for the widows and children of martyred fighters. She was often seen at the forefront of demonstrations, including the massive 1956 women's demonstration against the Baghdad Pact, a Cold War–era agreement between England, Turkey, and the US and some of its protégés: Iraq under King Faisal the Second, and Iran under the shah, Mohammad Reza Pahlavi. Egyptian President Gamal Abdel Nasser, generally perceived as King Faisal the Second's chief rival in the region, viewed the Baghdad Pact as Western intervention and convinced Lebanon, Jordan, and Syria not to join it. Khalil, who organized with the more left-leaning political groups, was determined to see the agreement annulled and led a protest with women from twenty-seven West Bank towns and villages. She was reported to have stated at that time: "We killed the Baghdad Pact. We kept demonstrating until it expired."[15]

In 1967, following Israel's occupation of the rest of historic Palestine, Khalil started organizing and leading protests against Israel and was arrested and imprisoned a total of six times, in addition to being placed on house arrest for two and a half years and prevented from traveling for twelve years. None of this slowed her down, as she continued to organize, representing Palestinian women at multiple international gatherings and radicalizing those around her. Two of her children were deported, and the other three denied reentry into the homeland after having traveled abroad. In 1996, at the age of seventy-three, she became the first Arab woman to run for president, challenging the patriarchal status quo as she ran against PLO Chairman Yasser Arafat. Even as she knew her chances of winning were slim, she did it to prove that women had a place at the highest echelons of politics, not just in the margins or in strictly women's organizations. She garnered 11.8 percent of the vote, a significant achievement for women, and for democracy: She was Arafat's only challenger. Khalil was also the first and only female member of the National Front Committee and served on the Palestinian National Council until her death in 1999.

Her political activism notwithstanding, what Umm Khalil is best known for today is In'ash al-Usra, which she had founded in 1965, as she was still matriculated at the Beirut Arab University. The association had a very humble beginning, in one room in Khalil's home, where women came to learn sewing skills to support themselves and their families on the one sewing machine Khalil had purchased for that purpose. Within months, however, as the popularity of this program increased, with women seeing they could earn an income out of their labor, Khalil decided to rent a separate location and set up a total of eighteen sewing machine stations. Next came the steam iron, adding a touch of professionalism and pride to the women's production. The first item commercially produced was men's pajamas, then boys' pajamas, and gradually the center expanded to produce all the clothing that Palestinian schools and hospitals would need: lab coats, doctors' robes, bedsheets, and school uniforms.

Matters changed immediately after the June 1967 war. The association's three goals, "women, children, cultural heritage," were unchanged, but economic self-sufficiency became paramount as poverty increased, with many men jailed or killed. Like Sitt Hind before her, Umm Khalil understood the importance of a woman's financial independence for her mental independence, as she also understood how important it was that In'ash al-Usra be financially independent in order to not compromise its mission and political agenda. While only accepting "no strings attached" donations from individuals, In'ash al-Usra has long been mostly self-sustaining, generating approximately 80 percent of its monthly budget by selling products made by women on the premises, ranging from clothes to food. More so, Khalil was so intent on being financially independent of the occupier that she refused to use Israel's currency, first the lira, then the shekel, and promoted noncooperation through the economic boycott of Israeli products shortly after 1967, laying out a detailed plan for Palestinian self-sufficiency that dispensed with Israeli products. (Boycotts became a widescale campaign twenty years later, during the First Intifada.) She never paid herself a salary as director, living ascetically, with financial help from her children. And also like Hind al-Husseini, Umm Khalil called upon the generosity of privileged fellow Palestinians to support her association, in a form of mutual aid: She would ask women to donate the jewelry and antiques they could spare, which she then sold to other Palestinians, always careful to keep cultural treasures within the community. She used the proceeds from these sales to grow the facilities of her association.

And grow it did. Today, In'ash al-Usra is one of the largest and most effective Palestinian welfare organizations, training thousands of women and offering a wide range of educational and welfare activities for the children of jailed Palestinians and the orphans of those killed while fighting to liberate the land. With Israel's relentless crackdown on and incarceration of Palestinians, the association also added prisoners' clothing to their products. Cooking followed, as In'ash al-Usra provided commercial-grade kitchen facilities, and women could cook traditional foods that they would sell at the market or deliver to catered receptions. Palestinian women who would have otherwise been dependent on charity were working; they were earning money, and their self-esteem was high. In 1972, Khalil also founded the Palestinian Museum in Ramallah, a small space which nevertheless proudly displays numerous books, replicas of villages, and the all-important traditional *thobes*. Indeed, In'ash al-Usra is perhaps best known today for the many tatreez items its members produce, with these embroidered pieces preserving the distinctive patterns and designs of the different Palestinian regions and cultures, telling stories of a deep connection to the land, with the added touch of political defiance. It is where, in 2005, I bought my mother an embroidered jacket, which she henceforth proudly wore to all important occasions including, most recently, my niece's wedding.

The Palestinian Thobe

Palestine's cultural heritage, its arts and crafts, go back thousands of years, with many regional distinctions. Gaza's traditional cuisine, with its unique blend of spices, garlic, chili, pomegranate molasses, and a whole lot of dill, flavoring a primarily fish-based diet, boasts many dishes considered delicacies outside of that region. Gaza has also long been known as a center for cloth production, including fine silken cloth, as well as the loose-weave fabric known today as "gauze," a reference to its place of origin. Bethlehem's mother-of-pearl inlaid olive wood jewelry boxes, photo frames, crosses, and other religious artifacts can be traced back to the fourth century CE. Nabulsi soap, made with virgin olive oil following a simple and ancient recipe, confidently tells the modern world there is no need to mess with modest perfection. Jerusalem is known for its ceramics, hand-painted in vibrant colors, often depicting Jesus's miraculous multiplying of the loaves and fishes as narrated in the Bible. And al-Khalil boasts a glassblowing cottage industry that goes back millennia.

Among the many sources of national pride, however, the Palestinian thobe enjoys a unique status as a repository of culture, history, personal identity, and a deep connection to local roots. The thobe, or embroidered dress, prominently features tatreez, the age-old intricate art of cross-stitching that is passed down from mother to daughter. Simply, no two hand-embroidered thobes are alike, and each one tells a story grounded in deep knowledge of the lore, the flora, the fauna, and the history of Palestine.

This is because tatreez requires not only patient attention to detail but also a knowledge of the local plants, the trees, and their symbolism. It is known as a *fellahi* craft, *fellah* meaning a farmer, a tiller of the soil, a land-based person. Those deeply familiar with the art can tell where it was produced, and by whom, as the dyes, dominant hues, and motifs are specific to every region. Ramallah tends to favor bright reds, Khalil the darker, browner tones. Orange trees are used as a symbol for Yaffa, world-famous for its citrus. A camel represents Jenin, and flowers Beer as-Sab'a. The cypress tree also stands for Khalil, and for rural Palestine generally. Bethlehem is frequently represented by the Balat Beit Lahem or "tiles of Bethlehem" motif. The Bethlehem chest panel, generally the most intricate part of a thobe, frequently features four branches emerging out of a water jug, depicting the tree of life. Yet a single motif, such as the *saru*, or tree of life, would vary from one maker to another.

Indeed, as Wafa Ghnaim, author of the book *Tatreez and Tea*, writes: "The governing style of each *thobe* signified a woman's village, tribe, or town; her marital status; and whether her life was materially impacted by missionaries, colonialism, or war."[16] For example, it is only after Queen Victoria's 1840 wedding to Prince Albert, in a white dress, that white became the preferred color for a bridal thobe in Ramallah. Other Palestinian cities, however, did not follow suit, and by the early 1900s, Ramallah women and young girls were wearing white embroidered thobes for various occasions, not just their weddings. Also in Ramallah, women had, up till the early twentieth century, traditionally used a home-dyed deep burgundy but switched to an imported, bright-red dye by the middle of the century. Al-Khalil has a rich history of glassmaking, and its headdresses are prized for the beads that decorate them, which sometimes also find their way into a thobe—a practice unique to that city. Gaza's style features rows of the cypress tree motif, usually both upright and upside down. Seemingly random spots of color delivered messages: single women would include a touch of blue, widows willing to remarry a purple streak. Crafting a thobe, then, is an inscription not only of the personal history of its maker but also of the collective history of her town or village, passed on through the cross-stitching. Again, as Ghnaim writes: "Palestinian *tatreez* patterns, thread colors, and adornments often express the maker's relationship with her village and society, and the materials and techniques she used attest to her regional identity, individual personality, interests, and at times her sense of humor." Tatreez is a repository of history, a transmitter of culture, a living art, and ever evolving. Soraida Hussein, a Palestinian women's rights activist based in Ramallah, says the thobe has an undeniably Palestinian identity. As she puts on an inherited dress, she ponders:

> This dress is us. How long did she spend embroidering it? It's made of art, of *tatreez*, of the threads of an unfinished story. Each color, the orange, red, lilac, green, yellow, says something about us. A crystal clear identity. There's no doubt, it's Palestinian. When I wear it, I feel relaxed, beautiful.[17]

Today, tatreez is also an act of Indigenous defiance. Most Palestinians are familiar with some version of the story of how the watermelon became a symbol of Palestinian rebelliousness and resistance. Popular lore says that in the 1980s, the artist Sliman Mansour was planning an exhibition of his art, along with that of fellow Palestinian artists Issam Badr and Nabil Anani, when an Israeli soldier informed them that not only were they not allowed to exhibit paintings with the Palestinian flag; they were also barred from exhibiting ones that included its *colors*. Indeed, Israel's repression of any symbol of Palestine was such that any painting that depicted olive trees, or women in thobes, would be confiscated. Mansour responded with his famous *Watermelon Boy* painting, a watermelon being, of course, red, green, black, and white—the four colors of the Palestinian flag. The watermelon thus became a symbol of insubordination and cultural resistance. And Palestinian women started introducing new patterns and colors in the tatreez they were cross-stitching in centers like In'ash al-Usra. The silhouette of historic Palestine became prominent on chest panels; poppies, which are native to Palestine, growing wild all over the countryside as well as in cracks in the cement of the cities—and which also happen to feature the colors of the Palestinian flag—sprouted on the sleeves and skirt bands of the thobes.

Samiha Khalil, determined to preserve the nation's cultural heritage, made sure that Palestinian women could continue the tradition, art, and newly acquired political meanings of tatreez, offering them the raw materials, the training, and the space to work in groups, sharing stories about their patterns and setting up a store where they could exhibit and sell their products. To date, In'ash al-Usra has supported thousands of women in achieving dignity through financial independence, while steadfastly resisting the cultural erasure violently enforced by the occupier.

Samiha Khalil, founder of In'ash al-Usra, died in 1999. Her legacy lives on in the institution she founded in 1965, which continues to inspire and empower thousands of women to overcome circumstantial limitations by providing them with the space and resources needed for them to sew, cook, proudly display their crafts, and preserve Palestinian heritage. A truly extraordinary woman, she is one of many phenomenal Palestinian feminists who understood that the nation cannot survive without empowered women, and who devoted their lives to lamlama, the gathering of the dispersed, and the preservation of our cultural heritage. Yes, our books have been looted, burned, and used to wrap vegetables at Israeli farmers' markets. But we have not stopped writing, and our children are the world's best-educated refugees. And our cultural heritage remains, worn with pride in our thobes, where, as vlogger Leanne Mohamad put it, "Every stitch is a statement, every pattern tells a story, every garment feels like home."[18]

4

Speaking Out: Normalizing the Anticolonial Discourse

It was a critical time. The war in Vietnam and the antiwar movement spurred many young people to get involved. Many of us got involved in the social movements for social justice beyond the Arab world and against colonialism in Africa and Asia, apartheid in South Africa, Central and Latin America, as well as the struggles of Native Americans, Indigenous people, and Chicanos here in the United States.

—Camille Odeh, Chicago-based community organizer

Born in Jerusalem in 1940, Jean Makdisi (née Said) was a young undergraduate student at Vassar College in the late 1950s when she was invited to participate on a panel about women in the Arab world. In her presentation, she spoke about her upbringing as a young girl in a relatively conservative setting, sheltered "from men and sexuality."[1] She certainly was not expecting the barrage of hostile questions she had to field when she concluded her brief presentation—questions she says had little to do with the presentation she had just given. The audience, she writes, was "impatient with the topic" and "launched an attack which almost literally took my breath away. 'Why do you hate Jews?' 'Why do you want to throw all the Jews into the sea?' 'Why can't one hundred million Arabs leave two million Jews in peace?'"[2] She was taken aback but, very soon, resolved to set the record straight.

Clearly, the young Makdisi had been sheltered from more than "men and sexuality." Makdisi's father, Wadie Said, had fought in the American Expeditionary Forces during World War I and had been granted US citizenship for his service. In 1919, he established a stationery business in Cairo, Egypt, and the family led a comfortable life between al-Zamalek, one of Cairo's more affluent neighborhoods, and Jerusalem, where they had a family home in Talbiyah, in what would become "West Jerusalem." Makdisi recalls spending every summer there as a child, until the family moved to Cairo year-round in 1948. She was eight; her brother, Edward Said, born in 1935, was just shy of thirteen. Growing up between Jerusalem and Cairo, the young Makdisi had thus also been sheltered from the Zionist discourse, which portrays all Palestinians, indeed all Arabs, as Jew haters.[3] But her new environment as a college student in the US was completely different, as she found out almost immediately upon arrival.

A continent away, another Palestinian woman, Fadwa Tuqan, was experiencing the same dissonance between her lived experience and the Western perception of her people, a misrepresentation rooted in the lazy and racist ideology Makdisi's brother would later expound on at length in his groundbreaking book *Orientalism*.[4] Tuqan was attending Oxford University at the time, and she recalls spending Christmas 1962, and the advent of 1963, with an English family who asked her if Arabs had chairs, slept on beds, or drank water out of crystal glasses.[5] These questions, she writes, reminded her of similar ones she had earlier fielded from French children. Then she comments, "It is indeed strange that the image of the tent and desert sticks in the British mind in this fashion, as if they had not colonised our countries for several decades."[6]

Since the catastrophic expulsion of over 75 percent of the Palestinian population from our hometowns in 1948, more and more Palestinians are growing up and living their entire lives in the Diaspora. The Palestinians organizing in "the West," and primarily in the US, continue to face the anti-Palestinian, anti-Arab, and anti-Muslim racism that Makdisi experienced as a young undergraduate. In the 1960s, such organizing took place in the streets, frequently at rallies against the Vietnam War or during civil rights marches, where Palestinians broached the links between various anticolonial struggles. Thus the 1960s saw the rise of Black-Palestinian solidarity, as well as an understanding among US antiwar activists, particularly anti–Vietnam War activists, that the Palestinian struggle is an anti-colonial struggle. Perhaps above all, what characterized Palestinian resistance in the 1960s was its shift to a new Diaspora battlefront, the US academy. Makdisi writes:

> I went to America for college and almost immediately was wearied by the effort of trying to bridge a gulf between two worlds, the Arab and the Western ... I gradually came to feel like a kind of modern Atlas, holding up a mountain of hostility threatening to crush everything underneath it; or a female Janus, with one face looking this way and the other looking that.

Makdisi adds that, following her painful experience on that panel, she set out to educate herself about the history of Palestine so that she could better respond to and refute the accusations.[7] But her newly gained knowledge was of no avail: The accusations were not so much grounded in ignorance or unfamiliarity, Tuqan had insightfully observed, as they were steeped in the racism of the colonizing mind.

The feeling of not having adequate knowledge of one's history was shared among many Arab Americans. Linda Simon, another college student in the US in the late 1960s, recalls a similar experience with one of her classmates: "One day I walked into a college sandwich shop and Miranda was sitting there with people discussing something. It must have been after an Israeli invasion somewhere. She said to me, "Linda, come here, you're an Arab, you tell me what ..."

Linda then realized she knew very little about the situation in the Arab world, as immediately obvious by her extremely vague "an Israeli invasion somewhere." She recalls that her interlocutors knew more about the topic than she did, which prompted her to educate herself.

> Here she was asking me questions [about the Arab world] and she knew a lot more about it than I did, and so did all the other people sitting there hammering out the world situation. I forgot how I got

> out of that spot, but afterwards I thought "Gee, I'd better learn about this."

As Linda set out to educate herself, she came to a jarring realization.

> I began reading about the Middle East and realizing how much of a Zionist I was. I think a lot of America, without realizing it, is Zionist. They think of Israel, or the land of Palestine, as a place that the Bible gave to the Jews, that after World War II the Jews actually went home, as if they were the same Biblical Jews. I was really ignorant about a lot of things.[8]

Tuqan's, Makdisi's, and Simon's experiences were all too common. Racism has been foundational to US hegemony over parts of Turtle Island, just as it was an integral impulse behind the global reach of the British Empire. But since the 1948 creation of the new Israeli state, Palestinians and Palestinian Americans were dealing with a growing hostility that viewed them as particularly inimical to democratic values because of their opposition to Zionism, which most Americans viewed as a positive ideology, a redemptive movement. This is because to most Westerners, as Linda Simon observed, Israel was a safe haven for European Jews in the aftermath of the Holocaust. Few were concerned by the fact that it had been established upon another people's historic homeland. The importance of Israel as a "strategic ally" and important military satellite would not become the determining factor in US-Israel relations until post-1967, but coming out of World War II, Israel, for most Americans and Europeans, was perceived as a much-needed antidote to Jew hatred. It was certainly not recognized as a settler colonial project that had been conceived of decades before the horrors of the Holocaust. Opposition to the establishment of this new country, especially as it promoted itself as the antidote to fascism, was thus deemed a continuation of Jew hatred rather than a basic anticolonial response to dispossession. That the question posed is "Why do you hate Jews?" instead of "How could any people not resent ethnic cleansing, the violation of their human rights, and the loss of their sovereignty?"

reflects this basic flaw in Western discourse. Nor is there a questioning of why the Palestinian people should be dispossessed to remedy the evils of Europe's antisemitism. Simply put, the Palestinian experience was utterly erased, dismissed.

Many American and European politicians who were involved in Middle Eastern affairs were aware that the creation of Israel would be catastrophic for the Palestinian people: a Nakba.[9] But the dispossession, even genocide, of an Indigenous people deemed inferior had never stopped such politicians. On the other hand, tens of millions of American and European nonpoliticians were utterly ignorant of the injustice done to Palestinians, and if they had any ideas about the Arab world, those came primarily from the essentially flawed literature Edward Said would dissect and denounce thirty years later. Meanwhile, Leon Uris's novel *Exodus*, a portrayal of the creation of the modern state of Israel laden with historical inaccuracies and pervaded with anti-Palestinian racism, fed into the popular Western discourse about Israel as a righteous victim finally achieving liberation in an otherwise-neglected land awaiting caring stewards.[10] The denial of the existence of the Indigenous people, even as most mythopoetic narratives include them, if only to tell of the mighty dangers the righteous colonizers overcame, is a common phenomenon. Equally common is the designation, by colonizers everywhere, of Indigenous resistance as terrorism.

Exodus was published in 1958, ten years after the onset of al-Nakba, and became a record-setting bestseller in the US. The movie based on that novel came out in 1960, and again, millions of Americans watched it uncritically, absorbing a narrative of Jewish resourcefulness and perseverance (in the face of British recalcitrance), a willingness on the part of Zionists to "share the land" (with no mention that it does not belong to the colonizers, who therefore are in no position to "share" it), and of course, a generous serving of "Arab hatred of Jews," rather than Indigenous resistance to dispossession. Indeed, the racism that permeates the writing is such that almost every mention of Arabs appears as "dirty Arab" or "stinking Arab." For years, the book and movie were the only source of any information about Israel for the majority of Americans. On the other hand, there were no popular books available in the US in the 1950s that told the Palestinian story of dispossession. Ghassan Kanafani's *Men in the Sun*, about the misery of Palestinians in refugee camps, was first published in Arabic in 1963, and another novella, *All That's Left to You*, set in a refugee camp in the Gaza Strip, was published in Arabic in 1966, but neither was translated into English until the late 1990s.

Fadwa Tuqan's nationalist poetry, penned in Arabic, had been published and widely acclaimed in the Arabic-speaking world since the 1940s but would not be translated into English for decades. Echoing Matiel Mogannam, who had earlier written that England was the worst enemy of the Arabs and that the British Mandate over Palestine was the greatest threat to that country, Tuqan also fully grasped that England was an imperial force rather than a facilitator of Palestinian sovereignty. Of the year of her birth, she writes:

> I arrived at a time when one world was in its death throes, and another one was about to be born; the Ottoman Empire was breathing its last; and Allied armies were continuing to open the way for a new Western colonization—1917.

This passage reveals a clear understanding that England was pursuing Western colonization in Palestine. Indeed, Tuqan was just an infant when she was personally impacted by the British Mandate over, or occupation of Palestine, as she correctly names it: "The British occupation of Palestine was completed in September of that year [1917]. In Nablus the British authorities arrested Father, banishing him to Egypt along with others aware of the dangers of western imperialism."[11]

This organic, lived experience understanding of Zionism as occupation, disenfranchisement, dispossession, and family separation is the discourse that Palestinians had to introduce in the Diaspora. Similarly, there was a need to redress the misinformation Westerners had been fed, beginning with the unwarranted accusation that "Arabs" had always hated "Jews"—as if the two categories, one a cultural affinity group, the other a religious one, were mutually exclusive rather than occasionally overlapping. Thus Jean Makdisi recalls:

> As for the whole question of Palestine and the Jews, I knew that while Jews had been victims in Europe, they certainly were not in Palestine: The broken lives of all my relatives there attested to that. I knew that it had never occurred to me to hate Jews—the memory of all the Jewish boys and girls who had shared my childhood in Cairo flooded over me—and the distinction between Zionism and Judaism was very clear in my mind.[12]

Educating Westerners, then, became an integral and critical aspect of resistance in the Diaspora. Frequently, it started with self-education, because while Palestinians knew their own lived experience of displacement and disenfranchisement, their Nakba, most were not familiar with the political reasons behind it, the global agreements between imperial powers that led to their dispossession and dispersal. As Makdisi writes: "Later, reeling from the bitterness of the experience [the hostile reception to her presentation], I went to the library and studied modern history from an altogether new viewpoint."[13] In the library, she recalls:

> I read about McMahon's dealings with Hussein, promising independence to the Arabs if they helped in the fight against the Ottomans; I read about how, while these promises were being made, Sikes and Picot, complicit in imperial treachery, were already dividing up the map of the Arab world; I studied the Balfour Declaration and its background and development; I read about the beginnings of the Zionist movement, read Herzl and others; I followed the strain between the two World Wars and the final accomplishment of Israel. I read diaries and journals, books, and newspapers; I was determined never again to be caught unawares.[14]

Of course, most Americans are not as committed to learning history from primary sources as Makdisi was. Yet anti-Palestinian racism would not be redressed without knowledge of what had truly taken place, rather than what the dominant mythopoetic Zionist narrative presented. Hence the critical need Makdisi and her peers felt to arm themselves with irrefutable historical facts that would inform their interlocutors: agreements between Western leaders, negotiations between politicians, United Nations resolutions. Maybe ignorance, rather than anti-Arab racism, was at the root of Western support for Israel? The battle had moved to a new front: the academy, and the production of knowledge.

Prelude to 1967

Two continents away, the Arab world was restless. In 1953, Israel had unilaterally started a water-diversion project within the Jordan River to irrigate the coastal plain and the Naqab Desert. "Making the desert bloom," Israel's claim to tend the land better than its Indigenous stewards, required water theft. Syria immediately protested to the United Nations, setting into motion a number of deals between the neighboring countries, including a 1955 US-brokered deal between Israel and Jordan, which both countries failed to ratify. As Israel continued with its unauthorized water diversion, a number of Arab countries held a summit in Cairo in 1964, where they decided to form a unified military command that would give Jordan control of the headwaters of the Jordan River, thus preventing Israel's theft. The Arab leaders also agreed on the need to establish a Palestinian political entity. Accordingly, the Palestine Liberation Organization was formed later that year, on May 28, with Ahmad al-Shuqayri as its first chairman. Meanwhile, Palestinian guerilla groups had formed in Lebanon, Syria, and Jordan, determined to liberate the parts of the homeland Israel had pushed them out of, and occasionally launching cross-border attacks against their occupier.

Then, on November 13, 1966, Israel launched a large-scale attack on the West Bank village of al-Samu', killing eighteen and injuring fifty-four Palestinians. Israel's excuse for the attack was that it had lost three soldiers in a land mine explosion there the previous day. Ever expansionist, Israel did not care that the Israeli soldiers had crossed the "Green Line" into the West Bank and were not supposed to be in Palestinian territory. The "Green Lines," or "pre-1967 lines," are generally viewed as the 1948 internationally recognized borders of Israel with its neighbors Lebanon, Jordan, Syria, and Egypt, even though Israel has never officially declared its borders. Additionally, there was no evidence the Palestinian guerilla fighters who had planted the land mines came from the village of al-Samu'. And even if that had indeed been the case, Israel's air strike on the village was an act of collective punishment, a violation of international law. None of these critical facts about the illegality of Israel's actions made it to mainstream America—only that Palestinian fighters were "launching attacks" against Israel, which Israel was "responding to." The skirmishes between Palestinian fighters and Israeli soldiers continued until, in April 1967, Israel shot down six Syrian fighter jets after Palestinian guerilla forces staged attacks across the Syrian border. This was a major escalation, which the Arab countries that had met at the 1964 Cairo summit determined should be met with a proportionate response.

By late 1956, Egyptian President Gamal Abdel Nasser had become the towering political figure in the Arab world after his successful nationalization of the Suez Canal, wrestling control of this strategic maritime route from British and French interests and expelling the ten Israeli brigades that had invaded the Sinai in October of that year. This victory against old and new colonizers catapulted him to the status of hero in the Arab world, as well as among colonized and anticolonial peoples across the globe. But by 1967, Nasser was coming under harsh criticism for not rallying to the defense of Syria and Jordan, and in May 1967, he determined to take decisive action to support these two countries against an emboldened Israel. On May 14, 1967, Nasser mobilized Egyptian forces in the Sinai Peninsula, days before formally requesting the removal of the United Nations peacekeeping forces that had been stationed there since 1957. And on May 22, he closed off the Gulf of Aqaba to Israeli shipping. One week later, on May 30, Nasser signed a mutual defense pact with King Hussein of Jordan, placing Jordanian forces under Egyptian control. Shortly after, Iraq joined the coalition.

Concerned by the mobilization of its neighbors, on June 5, 1967, Israel, with support from the United States, launched preemptive air assaults against both Egypt and Syria, destroying 90 percent of Egypt's air force while the latter was still on the tarmac, and similarly incapacitating Syria's air force. Israel then followed with a ground invasion, capturing the Gaza Strip, which had been under Egyptian control, and Egypt's Sinai Peninsula. On June 7, Israel also pushed the Jordanian forces out of East Jerusalem and the West Bank. And on June 9, it captured Syria's Golan Heights.

Israel's surprise assault, combined with its military might, dealt the Arab countries a stunning defeat. By the end of the Six-Day War, it occupied all of historic Palestine, as well as Egypt's Sinai Peninsula and Syria's Golan Heights. Over 300,000 Palestinians were displaced during the invasion, including over 100,000 who had been refugees since 1948. Around 100,000 Syrians were displaced from the Golan Heights. Egypt's fatalities topped 11,000, Jordan lost 6,000, and Syria 1,000, compared to Israel's 700.

Israel's victory gained it a new status in the US. Between 1948 and 1967, the new country had been viewed, albeit misguidedly, as a form of Euro-American restitution for the horrors of the Holocaust. But its newly demonstrated status as the overwhelming military power in a geographically important region made it the "strategic ally" that the US needed in the region. In the eyes of the imperial, colonial power itself occupying a large part of Turtle Island, Israel the illegal occupier could do no wrong.[15]

The Association of Arab American University Graduates

Many Palestinians in the US point to 1967 as the year that catalyzed their activism. Suffocating amid increased US adulation of Israel, they felt compelled to educate those around them about Israel's violation of international law and the human rights of the Palestinian people, as well as its illegal occupation of East Jerusalem, the West Bank, Gaza Strip, Sinai Peninsula, and Golan Heights. The work had to be done in the streets, and the civil rights marches and community rallies against the war in Vietnam provided many opportunities to discuss Palestine as a human rights, anticolonial issue. But, importantly, it also had to be done in the academy, which was churning out Orientalist textbooks that buoyed the Zionist narrative. Thus the battle for Palestine had to be fought at the site of the production of knowledge.

Jean Makdisi's brother, Edward Said, closed his groundbreaking study *Orientalism* with an insightful observation: Empire was transitioning from Europe to the US, and the new Orientalists were the scholars in American universities. Specifically, Said noted in the concluding chapter, "Orientalism Now":

> Since World War II, and more noticeably after each of the Arab-Israeli wars, the Arab Muslim has become a figure in American popular culture, even as in the academic world, in the policy planner's world, and in the world of business very serious attention is being paid the Arab. This symbolizes a major change in the international configuration of forces. France and Britain no longer occupy center stage in world politics; the American imperium has displaced them.[16]

He then explains that the new US-based Orientalism is ensconced in the university, as he states:

> A vast web of interests now links all parts of the former colonial world to the United States, just as a proliferation of academic subspecialties divides (and yet connects) all the former philological and European-based disciplines like Orientalism. The area specialist, as he is now called, lays claims to regional expertise, which is put at the service of government or business or both.[17]

Palestinian scholars and their Arab allies in the US felt the critical importance of introducing the anticolonial discourse into mainstream Western culture, as millions of Americans looked at Israel with admiration following its defeat of three Arab armies within days. Shortly after the June 1967 war, they formed the Association of Arab American University Graduates (AAUG), with the mission of educating "educated" Americans about the reality of Israel as a settler colonial state, thus countering the dominant discourse about Palestine in the US. Palestinian American founding member Michael Suleiman observed:

> Israel has been greatly successful in its efforts to persuade Westerners to view the Middle East and its peoples through Israeli eyes. Consequently the American public and its political leaders have accepted the Israeli version of Middle East developments as at once more "objective" or "realistic," and more helpful in advancing U.S. interests in the area, than the assessment of the situation advanced by the Arabs.[18]

While the association never claimed to be feminist, it was cofounded by a total of thirty-seven women and men, many of whom identified as feminists, and it always numbered many powerful women who wove their activism for Palestine with their broader embrace of other progressive causes. AAUG board member Janice Terry recalls:

> Unlike most other Arab-American organizations, the AAUG was not a patriarchy. The AAUG welcomed full participation from women, several of whom including Elaine Hagopian, Faith Ziadeh, and later Ghada Talhami and Hala Maksoud became president. Women were also nominated and elected to the board; indeed, an office manager later informed me that whenever women ran for the board, they were elected by the membership.[19]

Indeed, the AAUG championed gender equality throughout the Arab world, as it did in the United States, just as it located the Palestinian liberation struggle within the context of global anti-imperialism and anticolonialism, like Palestinian feminists had always done.

The association's first annual conference, held in 1968, focused on "The Arab American Community: Its Contribution and Role," in a clear indication of the need to organize in the Diaspora. The theme of the second annual conference was "The Palestinian Revolution:

Its International, Social, and Technical Dimensions," again revealing a holistic approach to liberation.[20] The AAUG remained active for decades, producing groundbreaking work that normalized anticolonial discourse from its formation in 1967 to its dissolution in 2007. And it allowed its feminist members to hone their scholarly and academic skills by providing venues for intellectual exchanges, writing, and public speaking, thus challenging the Western views of Arab women as devoid of agency.

Among the feminist founding members were Elaine Hagopian, who served as AAUG president in 1970. Hagopian also served as secretary of the AAUG and was on its board of directors for five terms. She was prompted to form the AAUG at the end of her first year of teaching at Simmons College, as she watched with dismay the jubilation over Israel's victory and the accompanying misrepresentation of Palestine and the Palestinian people. Hagopian was of Syrian descent. Another founding member of the AAUG, who also served as its president twice, was Faith Zeady, who served as president twice and helped every administration as secretary, officer, or board member. Zeady was of Lebanese descent but understood that the question of Palestine was one of justice that went beyond the borders of the historic nation, just as the Palestinian people had been dispersed beyond the land of Palestine. Another prominent cofounder, also of Lebanese descent, was Hala Maksoud, who later served as president of the American-Arab Anti-Discrimination Committee.

Ghada Talhami, a Palestinian born in Jordan, also served as president of the AAUG. Talhami later wrote critically of the AAUG, saying it reproduced the broader social dynamics of elitism and sexism within the institution:

> Despite its dazzling success in its earliest years, it [the AAUG] clearly suffered from a host of issues that led to its inevitable decline. Among these was the insidious system of star-based prominence that both defined the organization and attracted many promising young scholars to its ranks while at the same time perpetuating its elitist nature and structure.

Indeed, the fact that the first names most people offer when asked about the AAUG leadership are Edward Said and Ibrahim Abu-Loghd, whom Said described as "Palestine's foremost academic and intellectual," rather than Hagopian and Zeady, is proof of the truthfulness of Talhami's observation.[21] She continues, "Younger members, especially women, were made beneficiaries of a system of tokenism and were expected to remain content with the star system permeating the entire structure."[22]

The AAUG may have been flawed, but it allowed Palestinian feminists to flourish. Talhami herself went on to write prolifically about Palestinian feminism, noting that it could not be separated from nationalism. "Few would question the fact that the identity of Palestinian women was forged in the crucible of war and revolution," Talhami wrote, adding that "the case of Palestinian women remains an inseparable part of the Palestinian national narrative."[23]

The AAUG's advocacy for Palestine integrated support for other anticolonial, Third World struggles from its very inception. Reflecting on the AAUG's attention to the causes of non-Palestinians, Hagopian wrote:

> It was important to us to not become a one-issue organization. If you don't support other people's causes, why should they support yours? But it was more than just that; it was the commonality of the dehumanization. You have solidarity out of the commonality.[24]

Another cofounder, Fauzi Najjar, expressed a similar feeling as he wrote:

> From its inception the AAUG refused to limit its concerns to issues only affecting Arab-Americans, although Palestine was its first and dearest cause. On the contrary, AAUG members constructed a transnational collective identity by standing in solidarity with Black Americans, Africans, South Asians, and Latin Americans. Thus, Palestine was an issue that brought Arab-Americans into conversation with other groups that grappled with racism, settler colonialism, and decolonization.[25]

While the AAUG was unique in many respects, not least in that it was an activist organization restricted to college graduates, its mission resonated fully with the political culture of the New Left that was flourishing across universities across the country. In *Intellectuals in Action: The Origins of the New Left and Radical Liberalism, 1945–1970*, Kevin Mattson notes that scholar-activists who identified as progressive during that period intended their lectures and publications to be "forums for alternative politics" that would empower their audience to confront the imperial, militaristic power structures.[26] The 1960s and 1970s were the era of the teach-ins, of students demanding a new kind of education, and the scholars of the AAUG were prolific in both giving lectures and publishing, thus normalizing anticolonial discourse from an Arab American perspective.

The scholar-activists who founded or later joined the AAUG were educating themselves about the sociohistorical context that had led to their dispossession: the Sykes-Picot Agreement, the Balfour Declaration, the duplicity of Britain's mandate over Palestine. They were also educating fellow Palestinians, who did not necessarily spend hours in libraries. And they were learning about other struggles, as well as educating other activists about Palestine. Living in the Diaspora meant they navigated two worlds, and many felt the deep connections between their own circumstances as disenfranchised communities and those of other such communities in the United States.

In the Streets

A new battlefront may have opened up within the academy, the site of the production of knowledge used by politicians, but this in no way lessened grassroots organizing and popular education. In the streets and in homes, churches, and cultural centers, Palestinian community members were actively preserving their culture by gathering around food and music. Multiple times a year, they held fundraisers for needy Palestinians by selling tatreez, olive oil, and Nabulsi soap from the homeland, in a loop that had never been severed, despite the forced exile.

Two acronyms are well-known to many Palestine-rights activists: PEP, or Progressive Except for Palestine; and POOP, or Progressive Only on Palestine. In reality, both are misnomers. One cannot be truly "progressive" yet exclude Palestine, because Palestine is an anticolonial, antiracist, anticarceral, gender justice, and disability rights justice issue, among many other progressive issues. Similarly, one cannot be "progressive" only on Palestine, because whether one approaches the Palestinian struggle for liberation from an anticolonial, Indigenous, or antiracist perspective, one must realize Palestine is not the only nation enduring racist settler colonialism. The Palestinian activists organizing in the 1960s in the US understood how their cause was related to the many social and political issues around them. If the AAUG was never a "one-issue organization," as Elaine Hagopian noted, the interconnectedness of the Palestinian struggle for liberation with other struggles against dehumanization in the US was also deeply understood by Palestinian grassroots activists.

Camille Odeh (also known as Camilia Odeh), a Chicago-based organizer, recalls the rallies she participated in, which addressed multiple related issues. Odeh, a Diaspora Palestinian who grew up in Lebanon before moving to the US, also points to 1967 as the year of her political awakening. "The 1967 war was a turning point for me and many other Arab Americans," she writes, expressing what was clearly a common experience with Palestinian Americans of her generation. "At the time, we did not understand what was happening. Arab Americans did not know who we were, we were invisible, we did not fit in either the dominant culture or the marginal spaces," she elaborates, again articulating the need for Palestinian Americans to learn their own history. "So the issue of identity is fundamental to one's development of self-confidence, role in society, self-love, love of family and community, and even more so, central to organizing and political development." Indeed, the Palestinian desire to better understand one's position in society reflects the impulse toward identity politics that describes the 1960s and 1970s, with students calling for the creation of ethnic studies departments in their universities, even as grassroots organizations opened up cultural centers across the nation. The AAUG, Odeh felt, was for "academics and intellectuals," whereas the Organization of Arab Students was "the political home of Arab American students. There, students learned about their own history, but also participated in public education, actions for social change, and actions against colonialism." Since an approximate 49 percent of all Arab Americans have at least a bachelor's degree, almost twice the national average for all Americans, with an estimated 35 percent of all college-aged Arab Americans enrolled in college, student organizing was not elitist, but represented a large segment of Arab American youth.

This is obvious in the recollections of Odeh, who writes about her student days:

> We had a vibrant sense of community, cultural events, and political rallies on campuses across the United States. We connected to and brought to the forefront of people's minds the pain of people's struggle against oppression around the world. It was a critical time. The war in Vietnam and the anti-war movement spurred many young people to get involved. Many of us got involved in the social movements for social justice beyond the Arab world and against colonialism in Africa and Asia, Apartheid in South Africa, Central and Latin America, as well as the struggles of Native Americans, Indigenous people, and Chicanos here in the United States. It was an uplifting time and as Arab Americans, we felt transformed, affirmed, and uplifted from within.[27]

Odeh, who had an organic understanding that community and culture are essential to nurturing well-being, was part of a handful of women who poured their energy into providing such spaces. "The community developed organizations to support and serve our community," she recalls. "The Arab community organizations served students and others who needed housing, employment, and other basic needs. How could they organize if they lacked their basic necessities? We also provided places for the newcomers to learn English. We provided cultural classes and summer camps for children to learn Arabic, music, dance, and the arts."[28]

The 1960s in the US also saw the maturation of alliances between Arab Americans and other marginalized communities of color, and Odeh herself played an important role in forging these. In 1983, Odeh went on to serve on the electoral campaign of Harold Williams as he ran for first Black mayor of Chicago, carving out a space for Arab Americans to engage in progressive legislative politics. And she continued her grassroots activism as she founded the Southwest Youth Collaborative, catering primarily to Black, Latinx, Arab, and Arab American youth in one of Chicago's most diverse neighborhoods. Recalling her many years as an activist building bridges with other communities, Odeh wrote of the importance of movement building, asserting: "Solidarity is the oxygen that keeps our communities alive—let us build networks, coalitions, and work together for Justice."[29]

While Odeh's activism—a form of Third World feminism, catering to the social and identity needs of a community—focused on Chicago's marginalized communities, other Palestinian women were equally engaged across the United States, from Detroit to San Francisco to New York to Houston—basically wherever there was a significant Palestinian community.[30] The community activism of Palestinian Americans was influenced by the Black civil rights movement, which knew it could not depend on the government and elected officials to cater to marginalized communities. Thus ACCESS, the Arab Community Center for Economic and Social Services in Dearborn, Michigan, modeled its own work upon that of the Black Panthers, who were setting up cultural and food-distribution centers around the country. Black leaders such as Malcolm X, Jesse Jackson, and Martin Luther King Jr. had all traveled to the Arab world and viewed the question of Palestine as an antiracist, anticolonial liberation struggle. And it was a young Black student, Ethel Minor, who penned the 1967 letter by the Student Non-Violent Committee on Palestine. Written that July, in the aftermath of the June 1967 war, Minor's article, "The Palestine Problem: Test Your Knowledge," a four-page exposé in the form of questions followed by hard-hitting facts, was highly critical of Zionism and Western intervention in the Third World.

Feminist Tensions

As anticolonial, Third World coalitions were forming among Blacks and Arab Americans in street protests, within the labor unions, and on college campuses, one US activist community that lagged behind was the women's movement. So-called second-wave feminism has been rightly criticized for its centering of middle-class white women's issues, the "problem that had no name" of being an educated housewife whose accomplishments were restricted to and within the elegance of her home. Betty Friedan's important book *The Feminine Mystique*, published in 1963, had catalyzed a national discussion around the social and intellectual limitations imposed upon women by conventional expectations. Yet as Friedan denounced the ennui of her peers (*The Feminine Mystique* was based on interviews with her fellow Smith College alumnae), Black women and women of color generally were confronting a different set of challenges, fighting for the very recognition of their experience and different circumstances. The poet and essayist June Jordan, for example, recalls that while an undergraduate student at Barnard College,

> No one ever presented me with a single Black author, poet, historian, personage, or idea for that matter. Nor was I ever assigned a single woman to study as a thinker, or writer, or poet, or life force. Nothing that I learned, here, lessened my feeling of pain or confusion and bitterness as related to my origins: my street, my family, my friends. Nothing showed me how I might try to alter the political and economic realities underlying our Black condition in white America.[31]

Jordan was one of the early Black feminists pushing her sisters toward a recognition of the plight of the Palestinian people, frequently sparring with the otherwise-radical Audre Lorde, for example, over this issue, and also frequently ostracized and censored for her views.[32] Meanwhile, the mainstream, predominantly white women's movement of the 1960s and 1970s also reflected the mainstream, predominantly white political views about Israel and was thus openly Zionist, dominated by such influential writers as Gloria Steinem and Adrienne Rich, alongside Friedan. Rich has since renounced Zionism but was a firm supporter of Israel up till the mid-1980s. In July 1982, for example, following the Israeli invasion of Lebanon, she was one of seven Jewish Ashkenazi lesbian writers who penned an open letter, "What Does Zionism Mean?," published in the feminist journal *Off Our Backs*, in which they emphasize, "*Zionism is one strategy against anti-Semitism and for Jewish survival. Anti-Zionism is anti-Semitism*" (underlined in original).[33] With such strong conflations of anti-Zionism with antisemitism being the norm in US feminist communities, Palestinian feminists and their allies were alienated from the majority of American feminists, where their opposition to Zionism was viewed as racist rather than political. It is indeed ironic that while Palestinian activists were making major forays in the academy, in labor circles, and in Third World communities across the US, one supposedly progressive enclave glaringly lagged behind. Within most feminist circles, the battle for Palestinian rights had yet to be won.

5

Rising Up: The "Women's Intifada"

All the girls my age fought in the First Intifada; we were in the streets throwing rocks and blocking roads and screaming at the protests just like the men.

—Raja Mustapha, active during the First Intifada (in Sherene Khalel, "The Women of the Intifadas," *Al Jazeera*, October 23, 2015)

"My parents were concerned that the man I planned on marrying had been imprisoned," Naila Ayesh told Julia Bacha, a Brazilian film director of Palestinian descent who was in Palestine to make a documentary about the First Intifada. "But I told them this was the main reason I was in love with him. We were both determined to resist the occupation."[1] Ayesh did indeed marry her "jailbird" partner, but the couple were together for less than two years, during which she herself was imprisoned for six months before her husband, Jamal Zakout, was deported to Jordan. From there, Zakout relocated to Egypt, which felt closer to Gaza, where Ayesh was raising their child alone. And helping organize women's collectives, nurseries, schools, and all the structures that sustained Palestinian society as it rose up against twenty years of brutal Israeli occupation.

Soraida Hussein, who ran a clandestine school during what has become known as "the First Intifada," says she felt "reborn" during that uprising, as it channeled the myriad frustrations she had experienced while navigating the hardships of life under occupation into alternatives that gave her a longed-for taste of self-determination and self-sufficiency.[2] Hussein was one of thousands of women all over the West Bank who were setting up underground schools, medical clinics, food-distribution networks, and the occasional sewing centers where precut sections of red, green, black, and white cloth, the colors of the forbidden Palestinian flag, were pieced together minutes before being flown with unmitigated pride during protests. Individual women would have bought each color separately, so as not to come under suspicion by the ever-watchful Israeli occupation soldiers, and they would have measured and cut them in the privacy of their own homes, before meeting just once to assemble the flag.

Raja Mustapha, one the hundreds of thousands of women who took to the streets during the uprising, grins as she looks at a photograph of herself in a nightgown, one arm clutching a broomstick, the other raised high in the air, about to swoop down. The photo was published in the last year of the Intifada, in a 1993 issue of *Palestinian Revolution* magazine. She recalls proudly:

> The soldiers were known for stealing things when they did home raids. One of them stole my gold on my nightstand and wouldn't give them back. I'd had enough and just started hitting them to get my gold back and to get them out of my house.

She adds that she had already knocked down one Israeli soldier, who was outside the frame.[3]

As the subjugated people rose up in protest of Israel's brutal and illegal military rule, Palestinians were experiencing an exhilaration they had not felt in decades, after their initial dispossession in 1948, followed by the occupation of the rest of historic Palestine in 1967. In the West Bank and Gaza Strip, youth under the age of twenty in 1987 had never known a day of freedom in their lives. Refugees displaced since 1948 were naming "return" as their first demand, followed by an end to the occupation, and could once again entertain the hope of going back to the villages they had been expelled from, in *al-dakhil* (inside the 1948 borders). The draconian measures Israel was employing to subdue the resistance did not dampen the hopeful enthusiasm and deep commitment to liberation that permeated all sectors of society: students, laborers, teachers, shopkeepers. This uprising was different. It was not the domain of armed fighters and politicians. Everyone was involved, had a role to play, and felt empowered to play it. This uprising was radical, transformational. Not only were women and children visible everywhere; they were the leaders and decision-makers.

A Long Time Coming

Most historical analyses mark the beginning of the First Intifada as December 8, 1987, when riots erupted after an Israeli settler rammed his truck into parked civilian cars at the Eretz crossing in Gaza, killing four and seriously injuring seven residents of the Jabalia refugee camp. The Palestinians suspected that the "accident" was intentional, as retaliation for the stabbing of a settler in Gaza the day before. But Israel maintained that was not the case. Another frequently given date for the beginning of the Intifada is December 9, when another young man was killed in confrontations with the Israeli military following the funeral of the four refugees. Either way, the Palestinians had reached a boiling point, where any provocation was likely to lead to an uprising. The first protests erupted in Jabalia camp, followed almost immediately by riots in Balata refugee camp in Nablus. Soon, the Intifada, or "uprising," spread throughout the West Bank and Gaza Strip.

The full-scale grassroots revolt was a long time coming. Unrest had been simmering for years, occasionally boiling over into limited protests or riots. Larger protests, not restricted to a single town or refugee camp, had erupted just over one year earlier, in 1986, after Israeli soldiers shot two students from Gaza at the Birzeit University campus in the West Bank. Israel had responded to the demonstrations with harsh punitive measures that included arrests, beatings of handcuffed youths and activists, and extended "administrative detention," the imprisonment of civilians without charge for up to six months at a time, often renewed multiple times. Over 250 Palestinians had been taken from the West Bank to just four cells in a converted army camp, Ansar 11, also known as "the Beach camp," outside of Gaza City. "Ansar 11" was named after the original Ansar prison set up by Israel in South Lebanon, which it had invaded and occupied since 1982. Ansar prison in Lebanon was notorious for its vicious torture of prisoners held there, and Ansar II proved to be no different.

To further quash the 1986 protests, and in blatant violation of international law, Israel introduced a policy of deportation of activists in January 1987. Naila Ayesh herself had only recently returned from Bulgaria when she was first arrested in February 1987. She was tortured for two weeks, leading to a miscarriage, before confessing to being a member of the Democratic Front for the Liberation of Palestine. As Israel had banned membership in any political protest group, Naila was imprisoned for forty-five days. This period would bring the first taste of prison not just for her but for hundreds of women Israel arrested during the Intifada for their organizing and activism.

Meanwhile, political organizers, mostly adult men, would be rounded up and taken across the border into Jordan. It wasn't long before Naila's husband, Jamal, was arrested and deported to Egypt, in early 1988. Naila, pregnant for the second time, gave birth alone before being arrested and imprisoned again. Since her child, Majd, was only a couple of months old, he was allowed to stay with her in prison.

Naila Ayesh's story is one of many similar ones. Between the beginning of the Intifada and the end of 1992, Israel deported 489 Palestinians from the West Bank and Gaza Strip and arrested up to 120,000, mostly men. But after decades of Israeli rule, coming on the heels of the British Mandate, Palestinian women were used to being "heads of household" and the decision-makers for their communities. They also knew the importance of social support networks as they navigated employment outside the house, political organizing, and family responsibilities. They understood that "the struggle" had multiple fronts, from the kitchen to the streets.

The Israelis, both soldiers and settlers, were engaging in daily acts of violence against Palestinians: Soldiers would pursue and shoot at young boys from their jeeps, and settlers would uproot Palestinian olive trees or terrorize families harvesting their produce. Palestinian home demolitions were routinely conducted, either as collective punishment for a suspected attack on Israelis or to clear the land for an illegal, Jewish-only settlement, or a bypass road leading to it. No one was spared: Snipers targeted women hanging laundry to dry on the rooftops of their own homes; a settler shot dead a teenage girl in the schoolyard, claiming she had been throwing stones. The settler was arrested, only to be released a few days later in response to settler protests. In the summer of 1987, after the Israeli soldier in charge of the Ansar 11 prison was shot dead while stuck in a Gaza traffic jam, Israel responded by imposing a three-day curfew on Gaza, during Eid al-Adha.

The curfews were a frequent occurrence for Palestinians, forcing them to remain indoors for extended periods, as collective punishment. Anyone who risked stepping outside their home could fall to an Israeli sniper's bullet. Life under Israel's draconian occupation was subject to the individual whims of thousands of Israeli occupation soldiers whose duties consisted of making the lives of Palestinians a Kafkaesque nightmare. As early as 1948, Israel had devised a system of permits to restrict the movement of Palestinians between their towns and cities, as it issued different identification cards to Palestinians depending on which part of the country they came from, and where they resided. Within al-dakhil, Palestinians were subjected to military law, while Israelis enjoyed civilian law. (A 2017 report by Adalah: The Legal Center for Arab Minority Rights in Israel lists over sixty-five laws that discriminate against Palestinian citizens in Israel, even as the country claims to be the region's only democracy. The number is closer to 100 laws now.) With its 1967 occupation of the rest of historic Palestine, Israel put in place various schemes aimed at further controlling and restricting the movement of both people and transportation, as it initiated a system of color-coded permits to distinguish between different groups of Palestinians, this time based on their place of residence and their political or "security" status. The residents of East Jerusalem were issued blue ID cards, residents of the West Bank and Gaza Strip had an orange card, and anyone with a security file, generally from having been arrested by Israeli forces, was given a green ID.

Palestinians over the age of sixteen residing in these newly occupied territories had to register with the Israeli authorities to be issued their IDs, but anyone from the West Bank and Gaza Strip who was out of the country in 1967 was denied the Israeli-issued ID and thus could not return to the homeland. Many families were separated this way, never to be reunited unless those in the homeland left it. East Jerusalem residents with a blue ID who left the city for three years—to study abroad, for example, or be with family members denied residency in Jerusalem—would lose their ID, and thus their right to reside in their city. Palestinians with orange cards were allowed to travel between the West Bank and Gaza, but since these occupied territories were not contiguous, they had to go through Israeli border control for movement in between their own towns and cities. More often than not, showing a green card at a checkpoint was sufficient to be denied passage.

Additionally, over 40 percent of the Palestinian workforce in the West Bank and Gaza Strip crossed into Israel daily for work, almost exclusively in construction and agriculture. This made for a grueling workday for the men, as they had to line up as early as three in the morning at the checkpoints to be allowed to go to their workplace. Many had lost their land in the West Bank and Gaza through expropriation—illegal, of course, as Israel's entire presence in the occupied territories was illegal. They were routinely denied permits to build homes for their own families, even as they built homes for Israelis. They were losing their beloved trees to Israeli land appropriation and uprootings, even as they worked on Israeli farms. Protests led to more arrests, beatings, and home demolitions. Underemployment—college graduates unable to find degree-related work—was pervasive, the norm rather than the exception.

In the meantime, the Palestinians had learned to set up the social infrastructure that would sustain them in the absence of a government of their own, and under the brutal rule of an occupying military power. The illusion that somehow Arab armies would help liberate Palestine had been dashed with the resounding defeat of 1967. And the departure of the PLO fighters from Beirut in September 1982 drove home to most the reality that they alone, as teachers, students, cooks, nurses, social workers, mothers, and daughters had to be the agents of Palestinian liberation. And the women, hundreds of thousands of whom had long been in charge of their household and extended communities while the men were imprisoned, or even just working long days in Israel, were quite familiar with taking matters into their own hands.

Taking the Helm

Soraida

For Soraida Hussein, participation in the Intifada to the full extent of her capacity was a rite of passage, an entry point into being Palestinian. Having been born and raised abroad, and having fought for a decade for the right to live in her own homeland, she said she and her siblings felt "a need to prove we belong here," and the Intifada offered them that opportunity.

Soraida's parents, both Palestinian, had moved to Colombia after getting married to pursue better economic prospects, and Soraida and her nine siblings were born there. Hussein's father, Abed, had always planned to return and never applied for Colombian citizenship. He had told his wife that should he die abroad, he wanted to be buried in Palestine. Upon Abed's death, in 1977, Soraida's mother, Hajar, packed up the house in Colombia and took her husband's body and her ten children back to Kobar, their village. The trip was long, expensive, and obviously difficult for the bereaved widow and mother of ten, but she was determined to fulfill her husband's wish and eager to be back home, surrounded by family for much-needed support. But as she and Abed had been away from the country when Israel took the population census in 1967, they were not registered, and Hajar set on what would turn out to be a protracted, ten-year battle in Israeli courts to be allowed to reside legally in her hometown. A persistent woman, she was not going to be defeated by Israel's deliberately complex administrative maze. Three times during her ten-year battle to regain the right to live in her village, Hajar would be deported to Jordan. But she never gave up. Since she was her children's sole guardian, and was deported without them, she was able to repeatedly win the legal case to return to Palestine on a temporary basis. Then she would immediately file another case in another court, buying herself and her family some time in the homeland. Finally, in 1987, after three different law cases, the family received their Palestinian identity cards—just as the Intifada was starting. Soraida was twenty-five; two of her brothers had been arrested and imprisoned by the occupation forces, one more than once, and she herself had been briefly detained a couple of times.[4]

"I experienced the First Intifada as a rebirth," Soraida recalls, as she describes the suffocation she felt living under Israeli rule.

> The occupation was everywhere. They control every second of our lives. They know we go to sleep thinking of them, and wake up thinking of them. They control when we can go out, and when we have to stay home. We are like puppets on a string that they hold.[5]

So when the Intifada erupted, she was more than ready to do her part to sever the marionette string. Soraida immediately joined one of the popular committees that were springing up across the occupied territories. As Israel forced the schools shut in an attempt to control the uprising, Soraida and one of her brothers started a clandestine school that digressed from the official curriculum to focus on pragmatic decolonial education. She had read Frantz Fanon and Paolo Freire, and she was teaching accordingly. The students were reading history books that spoke to their lived experience under occupation; they were learning biology and nutrition by growing their own vegetables; they were practicing math by trying to share resources equitably, calculating how many loaves of bread a family would need, based on how many children there were. Soraida's courtyard school was so popular it served as the model for many of the clandestine schools set up by parents and teachers during the Intifada. Eventually, representatives from the major Palestinian political parties came to observe this alternative school so as to incorporate its critical components into their own schools.

Just as Britain had done during the Great Revolt, Israel's response to the Intifada, and the setting up of an alternative social structure, was ruthless. Israeli soldiers shot at protestors, arrested activists, and imprisoned the young men who were slinging stones at armored tanks. Every family was impacted; everyone had a loved one arrested, injured, deported. So Soraida started another initiative in her village, which was also soon copied elsewhere: a women's collective that helped families who had a loved one in prison. Women from the village would know which family needed help when, and they showed up. "We would help them with the harvest if the young men were gone, or with whatever they needed in the absence of their imprisoned loved ones," she explains.[6] The Intifada was truly an "all hands on deck" moment, and women were stepping up everywhere.

Zahira

Born and raised in Jerusalem, Zahira Kamal had been active at the grassroots level for years before the Intifada. She was first placed on "town arrest" for six months in 1979 for protesting the Camp David Accords between Egypt and Israel, and for founding and chairing the Palestinian Federation of Women's Action Committees (PFWAC), which mobilized women all across the West Bank to join trade unions and improve their social standing. This initiative was a direct challenge to Israel's exploitation of Palestinian labor, as poor rural Palestinian women made up the overwhelming majority of the workforce in West Bank garment workshops, which sold cheap clothing items to Israeli companies. Kamal believed that improving the circumstances of the more disenfranchised members of a society was essential to improving a people's overall well-being. Rather than focus on women's circumstances in Jerusalem and nearby towns such as Ramallah and Nablus, Kamal sent out employees of the PFWAC to remote villages to listen to the concerns of illiterate rural young girls. When she found out that some would work ten- to twelve-hour days in sweatshop conditions without even knowing how much or when they would be paid, she mentored them into joining trade unions. Like many Third World feminists of that era,

Kamal incorporated class into her analysis of women's systemic oppression and frequently argued that Palestinian women's struggle is threefold: against the occupation, against Palestinian social norms, and to surmount class, as they are at the bottom economically. While chairing the PFWAC, she also served on the board of In'ash al-Usra, the association founded by her colleague Samiha Khalil, from 1978 to 1988.

Kamal was placed under town arrest again between 1980 and 1986, becoming the Palestinian woman with the longest town arrest to date. She was finally free to leave her hometown in 1987, when the Intifada broke out. A seasoned feminist, Kamal soon got involved in leadership positions in the Intifada, and when that uprising's years of collective civil resistance forced Israel to agree to negotiations in 1991, Zahira Kamal was one of three women who traveled to Madrid as part of the Palestinian delegation.

Naila

Like Zahira Kamal, Naila Ayesh had experienced Israel's ruthlessness from a young age and was primed to immediately jump into action when the protests erupted in Gaza in 1987. Naila was only eight years old in 1969 when, shortly after hearing an explosion while she was at school with her four sisters, she overheard an employee tell her school principal that the Israelis had "demolished Ibrahim Ayesh's house." Ibrahim was Naila's father; this was her home. Naila says that as she and her sisters saw the sadness in her father's eyes later that day, as the family looked at the ruins of their home in Lifta, on the outskirts of Jerusalem, she grew to hate the occupation and determined to put an end to it.

After graduating from high school in the West Bank, Naila enrolled at the Academy of Science in Bulgaria in 1982. There she met Jamal Zakout, another Palestinian student equally determined to free his homeland. They spent many evenings deep in political conversation with fellow Palestinians, discussing nationalism, socialism, and the importance of women's contributions to the struggle for political liberation. Many Palestinians were studying abroad at the time, some in Western Europe and the US, where they were challenged by, and challenging, the disconnect between leftists and Palestine; others studied in Eastern Europe, where countries generally had a more supportive political stance. Bulgaria had established diplomatic relations with Palestine as early as 1973, and in 1988, it recognized the Palestinian Declaration of Independence, issued by the PLO.

The young couple got married upon returning to Palestine in 1986, during the very tense period in the lead up to the Intifada, and shortly afterward moved from the West Bank, where Naila had grown up, to Zakout's hometown in Gaza. There, they immediately got involved in political organizing, putting into action the ideas they had first discussed as college students in Bulgaria. Ayesh started working for Save the Children, while becoming increasingly involved in grassroots organizations focused on women's issues. Defying Israel's criminalization of political organizing, she joined the Democratic Front for the Liberation of Palestine, a Marxist-Leninist party that promoted socialism and aspired to create a democratic state for Muslims, Christians, and Jews, free of Zionism and imperialism. She and her husband frequently hosted political meetings at their home, and the newlyweds were closely watched by Israel.

One evening in February 1987, Israeli soldiers stormed their house, kidnapped Naila, and took her away to prison in the dreaded military wagon that was an all-too-familiar sight in the streets of occupied Palestine. As she was being brutalized, she informed them that she was in the early stages of pregnancy. Not surprisingly, the soldiers told her this would make no difference. She was handcuffed, blindfolded, made to sit for extended periods in extremely uncomfortable positions, and eventually taken out in the cold rain, still blindfolded and handcuffed, and left to shiver in a prison courtyard for three days. Fearing a miscarriage, she eventually confessed to being a member of the DFLP. Naila's confession did not spare her this misfortune, however, and she did miscarry. The occupation had once again managed to impact the most intimate parts of a Palestinian woman's life.

The UNLU and the Popular Committees

But there was no suppressing the deep yearning for freedom. Upon her release in the spring of 1987, Naila went back to political work, joining the tens of thousands of Palestinians who defied Israel's iron-fist repression to strategize, agitate, and fight for liberation. Thus, when the Intifada erupted in December of that year, the people were already well organized. Local leaderships emerged within days, and Naila was part of the group that issued the first official communiqué of the Intifada on January 8, 1988, calling for a "total, general strike ... until the fall of the occupation."[7] The communiqué was signed by the newly formed Unified National Leadership of the Uprising (UNLU), which had coalesced at one of the many evenings Naila and her husband had attended.

The UNLU, also known as the United National Leadership of the Intifada (UNLI), was made up representatives of the four principal PLO-affiliated groups: Fatah, the Popular Front for the Liberation of Palestine, the Democratic Front for the Liberation of Palestine, and the Palestinian Communist Party. Women's issues, from education to labor practices, were very much at the core of the concerns the groups focused on, and each of these groups had a women's committee, often with local chapters: Fatah had the Women's Committee for Social Work, the PFLP had the Union of Women's Committees, the DFLP had the Women's Section Committees and the PCP had the Working Women's Committees. Similarly, the four parties were united around the clear goals of the uprising: Right of Return, self-determination, and an independent country. Naila Ayesh believed education was fundamental to women's empowerment, Zahira Kamal was establishing a Women's Studies center at Birzeit University, and Soraida Hussein was gravitating toward work in domestic violence prevention. An overall understanding of the importance of women's contributions permeated the popular committees. Soraida's husband articulated an understanding of the trickling down of oppression, as he noted that when Palestinian men are brutalized, some believe that they can regain their social status by brutalizing women. This was yet one more way the Israeli occupation impacted the most intimate aspects of Palestinian family life. The women's groups also came to an understanding that, as Sama Aweidah, cofounder with Zahira Kamal of the PFWAC, put it, "We can't be free as women unless we're in a free country, and even if we're free of the occupation, we can't know freedom as long as we're subjugated in our own society."[8]

The communiqués became the preferred mode of communication among the leadership and the people, calling for and explaining the parameters of strikes, protests, and boycotts. Strategically, these would be held in one town or city, only to be transferred to another once Israel had reestablished its hold on the place where they had erupted first. Women also frequently distributed these pamphlets, smuggled in food baskets and grocery bags, throughout the West Bank and Gaza. And youth were charged with making sure calls for strikes were being heeded. By the spring of 1988, there were popular committees in the cities, villages, and refugee camps throughout the West Bank and Gaza Strip. Most were an expansion of the well-trusted preexisting committees that had sprung up over the twenty years of occupation, as Israel refused to set up any social work agencies in the West Bank and Gaza Strip. Israel's convenient excuse for neglecting the territories was that it was only temporarily occupying these, and that any official administrative work on its part would be tantamount to annexing and claiming them as part of Israel. The neglect by the occupying force, however, coupled with the absence of a national government, meant that people took matters into their own hands. And as the popular committees had organized at the grassroots level while the PLO leadership was in exile, their members enjoyed a legitimacy that high-ranking PLO officials lacked, if only because they were not "in the streets" like the women and youth.

In the first year of the Intifada alone, Israel had killed more than 300 Palestinians and injured more than 11,500, nearly two-thirds of whom were children under the age of fifteen. Over the six years of the Intifada, an estimated 120,000 Palestinians were arrested, and close to 500 deported. Because of the killing, arrest, and deportation of so many of the politically involved men, women were the majority in most committees and made most of the decisions. Rabeha Diab, who headed Fatah, the largest Palestinian political party, for over a year during the Intifada, said that when people came asking for advice, she would tell them, "Give us a couple of hours, so we can ask the brothers in the organization." This was a nod to traditional roles, "but there were no brothers," she recalls.[9]

Women also started "victory gardens" to grow produce for self-sufficiency, and they set up food-distribution networks, focusing first on the besieged refugee camps that were most frequently subjected to extended curfews. The popular committees also set up agricultural cooperatives to reduce dependence on Israeli produce, as well as health committees to provide medical care when protestors were injured and would have been further endangered by trying to reach a hospital. The impact of the economic boycott on Israel's economy was significant, as Palestinians in the West Bank and Gaza had depended on Israel for 90 percent of their produce prior to the Intifada and were now setting up their own agricultural cooperatives. Women ran these coops, as well as the nurseries and schools, and were deeply involved in grassroots political organizing while doing the dangerous work of sustaining the people. Their political organizing was permeated with Third World feminist praxis: at once caring for and empowering the community, the people, the downtrodden. "Publicly, the women's committees were known for their social work. But in reality, and covertly, it was all political organizing," student activist and Union of Palestinian Women's Committees member Naima al-Sheikh Ali has noted. "Nurseries, sewing workshops, teaching women how to knit, cook, etc., that was all window dressing."[10] The window dressing was necessary, as all of the organizing during the Intifada was clandestine, since Israel also declared the popular committees illegal and threatened with ten-year sentences anyone known to be a member of these committees.

Women were also literally putting their own bodies in between the occupation soldiers and vulnerable youth or adult men. As Raja Mustapha was hitting the Israeli soldiers with a broomstick during a night raid on her home, she explains that she was also acting as a decoy, keeping the soldiers occupied while five of her cousins escaped on the other side of the house. Women also frequently claimed that any child they saw being brutalized by soldiers was their own, demanding that child be let go. If the soldiers insisted on taking the child away, the women would jump in the jeep and go to the interrogation center with them. Sometimes, the argument these women had with the soldiers as they insisted that they let the children go was sufficient to give the arrested youth the opportunity to jump out of the jeep and run away. Again, the occupation soldiers responded with harsh repression, with many women arrested while trying to protect the youth, or killed by bullets or tear gas inhalation.

Land Before Honor

Just as the Intifada was a long time coming, so women's activism during the uprising did not come out of the blue but was, rather, a continuation of the social and political work they had engaged in for decades. As Raja Mustapha put it, "The wonderful thing is it isn't a question as to why a girl should participate now, or if she can. It's a given that they can."[11] Mustapha adds that "Palestine has always raised strong women because of the hard life they are born into. With these two things, I think it may be the girls who are the fiercer force, even, not the boys."[12]

And throughout the country, as women became more involved in overtly political actions, they also paid a gendered price for their activism. The expression *al-ard qabl al'ard*, or "land before honor," which started circulating in the 1970s and 1980s, is a clear illustration of Palestinians' awareness of the pervasiveness of sexual torture and rape in Israeli prisons, to extract information from women prisoners, especially during interrogation. And while one needs to problematize the idea that a woman's honor should in any way be impacted by whether she has been raped or not, the slogan also reflects changing social dynamics, assuring women that they will not be shunned by their society for what they have endured in prison. More importantly, the slogan "Land before honor" was also a way for women to resist Israel's manipulation of Palestinian conservative patriarchal tendencies, which viewed a raped woman as "family dishonor," which could only be cleansed through the killing of the rape survivor. And as large numbers of women were being arrested, while actively protecting young men and sustaining the Intifada, the conservative views were also waning, making space for a greater appreciation of women's contributions and the price they were paying for their leadership in the uprising.

A routine interrogation of Palestinian women by Israeli soldiers entailed being undressed, handcuffed, blindfolded, and strip-searched, most frequently roughly and in the presence of male officers. The soldiers would generally comment on the woman's body shape, her size, or her body hair. Frequently, the naked woman would be paraded in front of Palestinian male prisoners, who were ordered to look at her. But in many instances, the interrogation went beyond humiliation and abuse into torture. Nor was Israeli state-sanctioned sexual violence a new development. Rape had been used as a weapon of war in 1948, and beginning in 1967, Israel used rape to obtain confessions from women suspected of political work. Rasmea Odeh, who was arrested in 1969 on suspicion of planting a bomb in a Jerusalem café, is one of the better-known cases of Israel's use of sexual torture. Rasmea recalls that the worst part of her torture was when they brought her father into the interrogation room. She had been stripped naked, and they tried to force him to have sex with her. "It broke everything in my father," she told documentarian Buthina Canaan Khoury. But Odeh also understood the larger dynamics, adding, "I am not the cause [of her father's collapse]. The occupation is the cause."[13]

Odeh also mentions what she considers the second-hardest moment in her torture, after the episode with her father. She says she was dragged, still naked, into an interrogation room where the previous detainee had died from torture, and was made to believe she would share the same fate. After forty-five days of torture, Rasmea Odeh eventually confessed to having planted a bomb in a Jerusalem café, and was sentenced to life in prison—even though confessions extracted under torture are not valid in a court of law.

While Rasmea Odeh was being tortured, another woman, Aysha Odeh (no relation to Rasmea) was brought into the interrogation room. Aysha recalls that her interrogation first took on the form of psychological torture: If she did not give out information, Rasmea was tortured even harder, in front of her. Aysha could see Rasmea's hands turning deep blue from the tight handcuffs, and at one point, she thought Rasmea was going to become paralyzed from the torture. She confessed, giving out information about where weapons had been hidden.

Like many of the women active in resisting Israeli occupation, Aysha had not limited her involvement to civil disobedience and protests. Instead, she had smuggled weapons and arranged for *feda'yeen* fighters to go to Jordan for training. "The occupier stole our land with weapons, and will only be ousted with weapons. It takes the use of force," Odeh explains. Yet even as she rationalized her participation in armed struggle, Odeh says that she was never comfortable with the idea of having to kill for liberation, that she never rejoiced when she heard Israelis had been killed. But she did believe that armed struggle was necessary to free Palestine. "I did it all," she recalls. "I wrote the pamphlets by hand, then cranked them through the stencil machine by hand, and distributed them door-to-door. In my home, my mother and sister-in-law cooked for the feda'yeen. I smuggled weapons. I hid weapons. I took part in all kinds of resistance. The enemy occupied our land by military force, not through petitions and demonstrations, and I did not believe civil disobedience and pamphlets and demonstrations alone would liberate us."[14] When she was arrested, Aysha was interrogated for forty-five days, which involved sexual torture. In one episode she recounts, three soldiers were torturing her. The first—a woman—was holding her down; one was squeezing her breasts really hard; the other was penetrating her with a wooden stick. They then paraded her naked in front of a row of male prisoners. Still, she only confessed when she became convinced Rasmea Odeh's torture would result in her being paralyzed. Aysha was sentenced to life imprisonment for her militancy, of which she served ten years before being released in a prisoner exchange.

Women were indeed "doing it all" during the Intifada. While it is important to note that they were not just full participants but leaders in the organizing of the protests, the strikes, the cooperatives, the schools, and the food-distribution networks, one should not forget the daily responsibilities they shouldered. When all Palestinians were home during a curfew, men tended to play seemingly endless rounds of backgammon while the women cooked. And when water, which was frequently shut off during the day, came on at night, the men slept as the women got up to do laundry and wash the dishes piled in the sink. And in the morning, they'd write the communiqués and distribute them, giving directives for the day's protests and strikes while inquiring about the people's needs.

The Betrayal

"Negotiations" is a dirty word for Israel—something it will only very reluctantly be dragged into. But the Intifada was showing no signs of abating, while the administration of US President George H. W. Bush was indicating its disinclination to offer more loan guarantees to Israel without a settlement freeze. Through checkbook diplomacy, the American Israel Public Affairs Committee (AIPAC) and the pro-Israel lobby usually obtain what they want from the US president, but three years into the Palestinian uprising that had changed global perception of the Palestinians and their plight under Israel's ruthless military rule, the US Jewish community was divided over the issue of settlements, and President Bush was able to force Israel to the negotiations table. The Madrid Conference of 1991, which took place from October 30 to November 1, was one of the pivotal moments of the Intifada, as it was the first time Israel consented to talks with an official Palestinian delegation aimed at achieving a peace treaty.

Israel placed many conditions before it would agree to participate in the conference. First was its categorical refusal to negotiate directly with the PLO, and only with representatives from the West Bank and Gaza Strip, excluding East Jerusalem. The Palestinian team complied, even though it was no secret to anyone that members of the PLO were present backstage. Another Israeli condition was the revocation of UN Resolution 3379, which "determines that Zionism is a form of racism and racial discrimination." That resolution had been adopted by the UN General Assembly in November 1975 with seventy-two votes in favor and thirty-five opposed. Coming after UN Resolution 1904, the "Declaration on the Elimination of All Forms of Racial Discrimination," which had been adopted in November 1963, Resolution 3379 officially condemned Israel's very ideology. Satisfied with these two important conditions being met, Israel agreed to participate in the talks. The spokesperson for the Palestinian delegation was Hanan Ashrawi, and two other Palestinian women, Zahira Kamal and Suad Amiry, were on the Palestinian negotiating team's advisory board. Ashrawi recalls that when Israel realized the Palestinian team was the only team that included women, they sent an Israeli woman to their negotiations team, too, who had not been part of the organizing prior to the talks.

By successfully bringing Israel to the negotiations table, albeit with weighty conditions, the Palestinians had secured a major public relations victory. And as the delegation members had been part of the grassroots leadership of the Intifada, rather than career politicians, the Palestinians were laying the grounds for democratic power sharing in the future state. There was reason to be cautiously hopeful.

The 1991 Madrid Conference was intended to launch a series of bilateral talks that would address separate issues such as water, the environment, refugees, and arms control. But progress stalled as Israel repeatedly rejected the terms of the negotiations, or individual members of the Palestinian delegation. The greatest betrayal, however, did not come from Israel—if only because Israel was known to be a foe, opposed to Palestinian sovereignty. The betrayal came from the PLO itself.

Unbeknownst to all but a handful of high-ranking politicians, PLO Chairman Yasser Arafat and Israeli Prime Minister Yitzhak Rabin had started meeting in Oslo, Norway, to reach an agreement that would allegedly pave the way to the two-state solution. The talks, conducted between hawkish Israeli negotiators and PLO leaders who had been away from Palestine during the transformational uprising, culminated in the signing of the Oslo Accords, resulting in the recognition of Israel by the PLO and the recognition, by Israel, of the PLO as the representative of the Palestinian people. The accords were crowned with a handshake between Arafat and Rabin on the White House Lawn in September 1993, officially putting an end to the Intifada.

Most Palestinian, however, immediately saw the built-in flaws of the Oslo Accords. Edward Said called the agreement the "Palestinian Versailles," a complete capitulation that did not stipulate the Right of Return for refugees, did not address the status of Jerusalem, and did not call for a dismantlement of the settlements.[15] Instead, a transitional "Palestinian Authority" (PA) would be established, headed by Arafat, who was allowed to return to the 1967 Occupied Territories, from where he would administer the implementation of the accords. Hanan Ashrawi observed correctly that the accords were intended to never allow for Palestinian sovereignty, and the PA was thus seen by Palestinians as a subcontractor of the Israeli occupation.

The Oslo Accords also proved to be a major setback for Palestinian women, as they effectively sidelined them, suggesting their leadership was over, and that they could now go back to domestic chores. As they had been the primary agents of the uprising which created the conditions for Israel to come to the negotiations table, Palestinian women felt betrayed by their exclusion from those very negotiations. "How could the PLO think it could set up negotiating teams without us present?" Naima al-Sheikh Ali asks. "Women were left out of all preparations for the formation of the Palestinian Authority. We represent 50 percent of society, sometimes more. If 50 percent of the population isn't participating in decisions, that means society is half-paralyzed."[16]

And as the PA took over the "management" of the still-occupied territories, women were aghast as they learned they would now need a male guardian to get a passport from the PA. "By the time the men returned, women had achieved a lot in their position, but the expectation was that men would slot straight back into their position," Zahira Kamal adds. "And women would have to step aside."[17]

Despite the betrayal, two aspects of the First Intifada will forever be sources of pride for Palestinians. One is that this popular uprising transformed global opinion about Palestinians, as it exposed Israel's ruthless treatment of a dispossessed people rising up in nonviolent protest against its illegal occupier. The other is the grassroots nature of this uprising, with collectives sprouting up across the Gaza Strip and West Bank, as women and youth took on the tasks to sustain their community's needs.

Even though many were repeatedly arrested, imprisoned, tortured, and raped, women were at the helm of most of the mobilizing: They set up the clandestine schools, nurseries, and cooperatives; they carried the banned Palestinian flag during protests; they made the economic boycott of Israel possible; and, broadly, they created parallel institutions to sustain society in the absence of a Palestinian government. This model of an alternative society ended abruptly with the Oslo Accords, which brought back the old guard of patriarchal leadership to Ramallah. But Palestinian women and youth had shown the world not only the true face of Israel as a brutal occupier but also that the alternative can only come from the grassroots.

The First Intifada is sometimes referred to as "the Intifada of the stones," with the first image associated with it being that of young boys hurling stones at Israeli tanks. But the grassroots uprising would not have lasted five years, from 1987 to 1993, were it not for women's organizing and political work in their homes, the streets, the underground schools, and the political arena. And wherever they fought, Palestinian women were waging a dual struggle: for national liberation, and for gender equality.

6

Persevering: Navigating Social and Political Fault Lines

We can only be free as women in a free country, and even if we're free of the occupation, we cannot be free as women if we are subjugated in our own society.

—Sama Aweida, in *Naila and the Uprising*, dir. Julia Bacha, 2017

Maha Abu-Dayyeh's mother, Wedad Makhlouf, was only fifteen when she married Maha's father, Emile, a man more than twice her age. But the young Wedad, originally from Beit Jala, had placed a condition upon her marrying the thirty-two-year-old suitor: She would only agree to the marriage if the couple could live in Jerusalem, where she would be allowed to work. A respectful and loving man, Emile Abu-Dayyeh agreed, and the newlyweds moved to the Musrara neighborhood in Jerusalem. The 1948 fighting forced them to flee their home and, like so many displaced Palestinians in the early years of al-Nakba, they moved from one temporary living arrangement to another until finally being able to return to Jerusalem, now with four young children. There, from a modest apartment that doubled as their office, they started a hospitality and tourism cottage industry, with Wedad helping organize tours for tourists and pilgrims. Wedad's enthusiasm and diligence were such that, in 1964, the couple were able to launch the Near East Tourism Agency, a business that is run by the Abu-Dayyeh family to this day. All the while, continuing the legacy of other relatively privileged Palestinian women, Wedad was encouraging women and girls around her to get an education and secure an income of their own. Wedad's contributions are recognized today at Bethlehem University, which gives out an annual award for academic excellence in hotel and tourism management named after the young child who had demanded to move to Jerusalem at the age of fifteen, and from there, worked tirelessly to launch and codirect the family business.[1]

While the business was thriving, the political situation in Palestine was deteriorating. Maha Abu-Dayyeh was a teenager in 1967, the year Israel seized the rest of historic Palestine, and she got to experience firsthand the daily impact of life under occupation. After graduating high school in 1969, and encouraged by her parents to pursue higher education, Abu-Dayyeh went abroad for her university education, first receiving a bachelor's degree from the University of Tennessee, then graduating with a master's degree from Columbia University in New York, before returning to Jerusalem, where she taught at Birzeit University. Noticing the worsening circumstances of Palestinian women in the oppressive political climate, Abu-Dayyeh determined to organize to end it. According to one of her biographies, Maha Abu-Dayyeh credited her mother as her source of inspiration whenever she discussed her development as a feminist organizer. This is not surprising, as "Umm Hani," as Maha's mother became known after giving birth to her son, had blossomed into a role model for all of Palestinian society, a feminist encouraging women to get a higher education and enter professional fields of employment.[2]

Nearby, Randa Siniora, also a Jerusalemite and ten years younger than Abu-Dayyeh, was still a child when she began to notice that her three older sisters were regularly denied permission to go to certain places because they were girls. Unwilling to put up with such discrimination, when she herself became a teenager and wanted to go out, Randa would challenge her father to a debate, where the two would share their individual perspectives on an issue. If she won, she would be allowed to go out. More often than not, she was successful. Recognizing her potential, her father encouraged her to pursue a law degree. But Siniora preferred to study sociology and anthropology at Birzeit University, where Abu-Dayyeh was teaching, just outside Ramallah. She then went on to graduate school at the American University in Cairo, where she wrote her master's thesis on Palestinian female textile workers employed in West Bank factories that produced goods for Israeli companies.[3] That research gave her insight into the gendered aspect of disenfranchisement under occupation, setting her on a path to examine and address Palestinian women's challenging circumstances as they navigate traditional social restrictions at the domestic and family level, and the larger systems of oppression brought on by the Israeli occupation.

Soraida Hussein, born in Bogota, Colombia, had returned to Palestine with her family in 1977, at the age of fifteen. She was twenty-five when the Intifada erupted ten years later. She was working at Birzeit University at the time and started a clandestine school during the Israeli-imposed curfew. As she grew more familiar with neighbors and parents of the children she was teaching, Hussein was shocked when she first encountered a survivor of domestic violence. Like Maha, Randa, and thousands of other young Palestinian girls, she had been raised in a loving home, where fathers loved and respected their wives, and by parents who empowered their daughters to reach for anything they aspired to. Seeing that this was not necessarily the case all around her, and horrified at the abuse her trained eye noticed all too frequently, she determined to devote herself to ending this normalized plague.

Hussein, Siniora, Abu-Dayyeh, and thousands of other Palestinian women had been active on numerous fronts during the Intifada, and they had no intention of stopping when that ended with the signing of the Oslo Accords. Indeed, many of them felt that their work was more critically needed than ever, now that the situation on the ground had shifted from one of emergency meetings, most often in response to an immediate crisis, to organizing within the structures of a nascent state—as was supposed to be the outcome of the Oslo Accords.

But statehood proved a mirage. The signing of the Oslo Accords dealt a heavy blow to the grassroots innovation that characterized the Intifada, as it allowed for the old guard leaders to return, in what would soon prove to be a pyrrhic victory, to a still-occupied Palestine. After decades in exile, including, most recently, twelve years in Tunis, Palestine Liberation Organization leader Yasser

Arafat, now the proud president of the Palestinian National Authority, known simply as the Palestinian Authority or PA, returned to much fanfare to the homeland, flanked by fellow high-ranking PLO officers.[4] Shortly after arriving to the Gaza Strip, where he resided until his 1996 move to the Ramallah *muqataa* that would become the headquarters of the Palestinian government,[5] Arafat instituted policies that completely sidelined women's issues, effectively marginalizing the leaders and organizers of the uprising that had made his return possible. The shift, from the PLO's encouragement and support of women's participation in the national struggle to its prioritization of traditional gender roles that would limit women's contributions to the home and family, indicated the regressive path Arafat would henceforth take as he transitioned from guerilla leader and chairman of a liberation organization to titular president of a nationless "national authority." The "Oslo Years," as the period from the signing of the accords in 1993 until the eruption of the Second Intifada in 2000 came to be known, were ones of deep discontent with the multiple missed opportunities for positive change, as the accords were only ever meant to quash the Palestinian uprising so as to bring peace to Israel, with no justice for the Palestinians.

For most Palestinians, Arafat's legacy is complicated at best, irrevocably tainted at worst. Along with other Gulf-based Palestinians, he had cofounded the Fatah movement in 1959, insisting on the Palestinian people's right to armed struggle for liberation. Fatah soon became the dominant group in Palestinian politics, joining the PLO in 1967, with Arafat becoming chairman of the latter in 1969. In 1974, the United Nations recognized the PLO as the sole representative of the Palestinian people. This made Arafat the first representative of a "nonmember body" at the United Nations. For many, the concluding sentence of his November 1974 speech at the United Nations remains one of his proudest moments, as he stated: "Today, I have come bearing an olive branch and a freedom fighter's gun. Do not let the olive branch fall from my hand. I repeat: Do not let the olive branch fall from my hand."

Arafat's signing of the Oslo Accords, however, signified a major turning point in his, and the Palestinian people's, political path, as the accords ended the Palestinian liberation struggle without providing for Palestinian independence. Instead, it set into motion an open-ended process of fragmentation of Palestinian territories and a surrender of sovereignty over most of the West Bank to the occupying power, with no mention of the key issues to Palestinians: the status of Jerusalem, the Right of Return of refugees, or the borders of the future Palestinian state. As Diana Buttu, a Palestinian lawyer and former adviser to the Palestinian Authority, put it in a fifteen-year retrospective: "It is wrong to think of Oslo being derailed, or trying to identify the moment the Oslo process died. Oslo never died. It is still doing today exactly what it was set up to do."[6]

This is because the Oslo Accords were always meant to transform the overarching framing of the Palestinian struggle. What had been, since 1948, an anticolonial struggle seeking liberation, justice, and the right of Palestinians to return to their towns and villages became a prolonged "process" of negotiations, concessions, and stop-and-go state-building within shrinking boundaries, always prioritizing the occupier's need for more land and "security zones." Hailed by the West as a resounding success—as indeed it was for Israel—the Oslo Accords also opened the gates to a major influx of international nongovernmental organizations that significantly impacted Palestinian society while remaining detached from the lived reality of the Palestinian people, focusing instead on a depoliticized facet of international aid. The all-too-real context of a subjugated people denied basic rights and living under brutal military occupation was an additional challenge, rather than the core issue, to the international NGOs. Unlike the popular committees that had formed in response to Israel's neglect of its obligations, and which were affiliated with a political movement seeking liberation, the new, post-Oslo NGOs steered as clear of politics as realistically possible. As they stepped in to fill a void that is Israel's responsibility under international law, the internationally funded NGOs also enabled Israel's ongoing neglect of its obligation to provide for the social and economic welfare of the Palestinian people whose land it illegally occupied. And as most analysts agree, with the generous donor aid that poured into the occupied territories after the signing of the Oslo

Accords, the focus of these organizations shifted from liberation toward "development."

Nongovernmental organizations, of course, were not new in Palestine: Many had begun under the British Mandate as a substitute for nonexisting governmental services. Following the 1967 war, Palestinians formed even more NGOs in the West Bank and Gaza Strip, which were intended to step in where Israel was failing in its obligation to provide necessary services for an occupied people. These NGOs were founded and led by Palestinians, and most were directly affiliated with the major Palestinian political factions of the PLO, especially the Popular Front for the Liberation of Palestine (PFLP, a secular, militant Marxist group founded in 1967, historically the second-largest group within the PLO after the Arafat-founded Fatah), and the Democratic Front for the Liberation of Palestine (DFLP, a more moderate splinter group of the PFLP founded in 1969). They were "nongovernmental" organizations by virtue of the fact that there *was* no Palestinian government, even as some of them functioned like ministries. The Union of Palestinian Medical Relief Committees, for example, substituted for a ministry of health, operating hundreds of medical and dental clinics and rehabilitation programs throughout the West Bank and Gaza Strip. The Palestinian Agricultural Relief Committee was the prominent organization dealing with agriculture, substituting for a ministry of agriculture. The General Union of Palestinian Women (GUPW), established in 1965 as the official representative of Palestinian women within the PLO, acted like a ministry for women's affairs. It had chapters across Palestine, and beginning in the 1970s, it opened chapters in numerous Arab countries, as well as in Europe and the United States.

Most of the popular committees that had sustained the First Intifada were local chapters of these larger Palestinian NGOs. Many, especially the women-led ones, had also facilitated the creation of small women's cooperatives, which gave women dignified employment and income. Overall, the NGOs of the 1970s through 1993 were a vibrant, localized manifestation of civil society taking care of its needs. Most functioned like mutual aid societies, with members supporting each other through appeals for donations, sponsorships, fundraisers, and volunteering. Islamist organizations, which were independent from the PLO, secured funding through *zakat* (almsgiving, one of the five pillars of Islam) from their own members, while the Communist Party, also independent of the PLO, relied primarily on European funding.

The signing of the Oslo Accords, and the consequent establishment, in Ramallah, of a Palestinian Authority—the Fatah-controlled government body exercising partial civil control over Palestinian enclaves in the Israeli-occupied West Bank—drastically changed these dynamics. Indeed, the "Palestinian Versailles," to use Edward Said's apt description of these accords, was a betrayal of all the innovative grassroots organizing that Palestinians had engaged in for years, even prior to the Intifada. The Oslo Accords were also a stab in the back of the Palestinian women who had been at the helm of this organizing and now saw themselves disenfranchised by their own president. One egregious initiative by Arafat was his reviving of the *hamula* system, a deeply patriarchal clan or extended family structure that gives the male elder of that family power to allow or disallow certain behaviors or actions, such as requiring women to obtain a male guardian's approval to get a passport. That had not been the case when Zahira Kamal, Hanan Ashrawi, and Suad Amiry had flown to Spain for the Madrid Conference, shaming the all-male Israeli delegation into hastily appointing female members, so as not to look more conservative than the Palestinian delegation.

But Arafat is not the only political leader who betrayed Palestinian women. The PFLP, the DFLP, and the newly formed Hamas party ("Hamas" being the Arabic acronym for Islamic Resistance Movement), while all three opposing the Oslo Accords, nevertheless failed to address women's concerns. Because of its opposition to the Palestinian Authority's signing of the Oslo Accords, the PFLP, generally viewed as the more progressive of the main Palestinian parties, had withdrawn from the PLO and refused to support Palestinian women's request that their needs be addressed through PA legislation and executive institutions. The DFLP, a splinter group of the PFLP, did not feel it could insist that the women's demands be addressed, as its leadership did not believe there would be popular consensus around this priority. The Hamas charter, issued in 1988, shortly after the group had formed in 1987, supported women's contribution to the armed struggle and encouraged women's education, primarily to allow them to better raise their children and build strong families, thus essentially reinforcing a domestic role for them when they were not engaged in national liberation.[7] Even the GUPW, which holds a strong nationalist agenda, prioritized national independence, which it viewed as a prerequisite for securing women's rights. Thus, despite their significant contributions to the Intifada, Palestinian feminists, and Palestinian women generally, found themselves in the same circumstances as women in other anticolonial struggles globally. Their needs were deemed secondary to those of the "national struggle," even though they had insisted that there can be no national liberation without social liberation.

It is hard to overemphasize how significantly occupation impacts women, taking on very gendered manifestations, slithering its way into every aspect of our lives. It is no mere coincidence that gender violence, and reproductive injustice, are among colonizers' and occupiers' weapons globally. The expression "rape, pillage, loot" is testimony to the mainstream recognition that sexual violence occurs in militarized contexts globally. In the case of settler colonialism, the goal is not just to exploit the resources of the colonized country but to transform that country into another one altogether—one that reflects the colonizer's worldview. Therefore, as the colonizer recognizes that Indigenous women are the preservers and transmitters of Indigenous knowledge and culture, as well as the carriers of future life, the colonizer feels the need to target women in order to "eliminate the native."[8] Thus gender violence is not a potential feature of settler colonialism; rather, settler colonialism *is* gender violence, as it seeks to rid itself of the Indigenous people whose land it covets. The sexual abuse of anywhere from 95 to 100 hundred percent of Indigenous children in Indian boarding schools across Turtle Island is not coincidence; it is a pattern of settler colonialism.

This is a global phenomenon, and Israel is no exception. Following the documented record of rape beginning in 1948, Israel has continued its assault on Palestinian women's bodies and reproductive rights by sanctioning sexual violence in its treatment of the Palestinian people, especially during interrogation and detention. Additionally, Israel restricts Palestinian women's movement at critical life-bearing moments, effectively sanctioning reproductive injustice. After strictly impeding traditional midwifery in the West Bank and Gaza Strip beginning in 1967, forcing women to depend on hospital facilities for pregnancy care and childbirth, Israel increased the number of checkpoints throughout the West Bank and Gaza Strip in 1993, obstructing women's access to health care, education, and social services. A United Nations report estimates that prior to the year 2000, 20 percent of pregnant Palestinian women in the occupied Gaza Strip and West Bank could not receive prenatal care due to the difficulty of traveling through checkpoints. Consequently, many suffered serious health complications that would have been addressed by a medical team. Pregnant women have been forced to deliver, or miscarry, at checkpoints in unsanitary, dangerous circumstances, and newborn infants have died at checkpoints for lack of medical care.[9]

In addition to normalizing gender violence, the occupation has also led to a stagnant economy in Palestinian society, with all the detrimental consequences of poverty—one of the greatest forms of violence—compounded for women. The "feminization of poverty," a phenomenon first studied in the 1970s, which gained currency in the 1990s through a number of United Nations studies revealing increased income inequality between men and women, points to the fact that the majority of the 1.5 billion people around the world living on one dollar or less per day are women. It is important to look at the specific consequences of this phenomenon. In Palestine, as employment opportunities for all Palestinians were diminished as a result of the decades-old occupation, women frequently had no option but to work in exploitative and dangerous conditions in the illegal settlements, with no contract and no job security, where they were extremely vulnerable to harassment and disrespect. Due to the wage gender gap, their income was and remains overall lesser than that of their spouses, leading to increasingly unbalanced dynamics within the household. Most societies disregard the value of uncompensated nurturing and domestic care, and women often feel they cannot even express an opinion on important matters if they are not contributing financially to their household. The overall economic pressure on Palestinian society thus exacerbated existing social tensions, frequently leading to an increase in domestic violence, with women and children on the receiving end.[10]

With the stagnating economy, food was not always affordable, and when food is scarce, many women serve themselves a smaller portion, or skip a meal altogether, in order to feed their husband and children. When a family's home is demolished and the family moves to more cramped quarters, women and girls usually lose what little personal space they had, often leading to increased domestic violence. If a child is arrested, generally for throwing a stone at occupying soldiers, or even for simply being near a protest, and if that child is fortunate enough to have legal representation, the lawyer sometimes successfully negotiates house arrest for the child instead of detention. (Israel does not provide lawyers to Palestinian children, in violation of international law, and imposes systematic restrictions on their access to legal support or family visits. Some organizations, such as Defence for Children International, are occasionally allowed to provide free legal advice to some of the detained children.) But house arrest means one parent, almost always the mother, must stay home to supervise the child and prevent them from going outside. If she is employed, the mother has to quit her job to do so. The family of a child under house arrest who is found at a protest site is subject to a hefty fine, and the mother is generally the one blamed, with the father frequently taking out his frustration on her.

Globally, the assumption that women and children are spared the impact of war because they are not combatants has been repeatedly debunked, as numerous studies show that civilians make up the largest proportion of those killed and injured during armed conflict. The ratio of civilian to combatant casualties grows significantly when there are no "battlefronts," because the fighting takes place in the cities. This is particularly true under Israeli occupation, where not only are there no battlefronts; there are no "two armies." Rather, there is a powerful occupying army hounding unarmed civilians in their streets, their homes, their schools, their hospitals. Thus it is becoming increasingly rare to see reports of casualties that do not mention "women and children." Many peace plans and processes, however, *do* ignore their specific needs as they prioritize "the country" over its people.

Treacherous Terrain

It is in this context of increased violence that the women organizers and leaders of the Intifada decided to focus on women's needs post-Oslo. Globally, feminists everywhere were mobilizing for the 1995 Fourth World Conference on Women, to be held in Beijing. In preparation for this conference, they had produced surveys, research, and analysis to argue for equality and gender justice, with an initial emphasis on legal and policy reform. Birzeit University, which many of the Intifada organizers were affiliated with, had just launched, in 1994, the Institute of Women's Studies, the first such academic program in the Arab world. Palestinian feminists were also in regular communication with members of the global feminist movement, even as they pondered which "government" to hold accountable for legislating Palestinian women's rights. The establishment of the Palestinian Authority seemed to offer this venue.

In the meantime, by transforming the nature of the Palestinian struggle from one of national liberation to a process of state building, the Oslo Accords had set the tone for what Islah Jad, a feminist professor at Birzeit University, has called "the NGO-ization" of Palestinian society. Jad argued that "the NGO as a form of organisation is different in critical ways from another kind of organisation aimed at social change, namely the social movement."[11] Jad explains that whereas the women's charitable associations that proliferated in the early twentieth century "recruited hundreds of women in their administrative bodies and general assemblies, while women's unions had large memberships extending to women in villages, and after 1948 in refugee camps," the reach of the new, post-Oslo international NGOs was significantly smaller. Jad also notes that the leaders of the women's committees that had sustained the

Intifada had been successful because they organized and mobilized the masses and because "they had a cause to defend, a mission to implement."[12] They were known and trusted by the people and frequently engaged in face-to-face interaction, which originated in, and further cemented, trust among these women. Not all the directors of the post-Oslo NGOs, on the other hand, were grassroots organizers; their allegiance was, in most cases, to their funders, and their primary concern was to craft well-written reports for their donors. The post-Oslo NGOs, then, frequently became a place of employment and individual advancement—the Global North feminist aspiration—rather than collective empowerment and liberation—the Indigenous and Third World women's commitment.

Yet many of the women organizers of the First Intifada ended up working for these NGOs, hoping to wield the master's tools—organizing seminars and workshops, drafting legislation, training in "development"—to dismantle the master's house, without abandoning their visions of full liberation. One organization that stood out as optimal for leading such work was the Women's Centre for Legal Aid and Counselling (WCLAC), which had been founded in 1991, during the Intifada, rather than post-Oslo. The founders included Maha Abu-Dayyeh, Soraida Hussein, Zahira Kamal, and other seasoned grassroots organizers. As the post-Oslo years were supposed to usher a new political system in Palestine, they and other members of the WCLAC were intent on addressing gender-based violence within Palestinian community, and on drafting legislation to protect and make equal the rights of women in civil society.

The WCLAC founders and staff understood the precariousness of women's circumstances in the political context of a protracted, brutal military occupation. Randa Siniora, who currently heads the WCLAC but at the time (1987–97) was legal researcher and coordinator of the women's rights program at the human rights organization Al-Haq, explains: "The Israeli occupation and the resulting humanitarian crisis are deeply gendered and exacerbate existing gender inequalities. Women disproportionately endure the violence of occupation borne by all Palestinians, and often with gender-specific consequences."[13]

Indeed, the post-Oslo years witnessed an alarming rise in femicide —the murder of women, often by their own kin, generally a father or brother, supposedly to save the family's honor. The term "femicide" was first used in Palestine by feminist scholar Nadera Shalhoub-Kevorkian, and Palestinian feminists overall refuse to use the expression "honor killing," arguing that a girl's or woman's transgression, whether real or perceived, of entrenched regressive social restrictions does not reflect on her or her family's "honor" and therefore cannot excuse or justify her murder to cleanse the "dishonor." As Hanan Ashrawi put it,

> The woman is not an emblem of honor for the man or her family. The categorization of such crimes under misleading labels constitutes the exploitation of women, and in turn, it safeguards the offenders and promotes more crimes of this nature.[14]

Increased violence within the household—a manifestation of what I have described elsewhere as "intensifying patriarchy"—is a regrettable but predictable consequence of living under settler colonialism and militarized violence.[15] By the 1990s, this phenomenon had noticeably increased in the West Bank and Gaza Strip, aggravated by Israel's decades of occupation and the Palestinian people's overall anger at the fact that their "National Authority" was in such a precarious position that it had to please Israel, rather than tend to the needs of the Palestinian people, in order to retain the little nominal power it had. As with cases of domestic violence and femicide everywhere, exact numbers are hard to ascertain, since such homicides are frequently passed off as suicides or accidental deaths in official documents, or because of underreporting due to societal pressure and stigma.

Palestinian women, however, were duly alarmed at the spiraling number of such murders and at the leniency of the legal system, which frequently pardoned the murderers under a 1960 Penal Code article that allows for "extenuating circumstances," to be determined at the discretion of the judge. According to that code, itself a slight modification of 1936 British legislation, the judge can fully pardon the perpetrator, not even handing out a reduced sentence, should the judge establish that there were "pardoning excuses" for the crime.[16] The Palestinian women organizers, then, felt it necessary to address the legal system that allowed for such crimes to be excused.

The Model Parliament

Maha Abu-Dayyeh had a vision: the WCLAC, which she had cofounded with fellow Palestinian feminists, would organize a Palestinian Model Parliament (PMP), where women's rights would be centered for discussion and legislation. This initiative, she hoped, would address Palestinian women's deteriorating circumstances while upholding their contributions to the struggle for national liberation. It would change the archaic Personal Status Law, a mosaic of relics from the British, Ottoman, Egyptian, and Jordanian legal systems, mixed with religious laws, all of which disenfranchised women. This would come from two sets of actors: "outsiders" to the system, meaning the grassroots feminists who had organized during the Intifada, when civil society and emergency committees were all the people could turn to; and "insiders," including Hanan Ashrawi, the PLO's official spokesperson at the Madrid Peace talks, who later was elected to the Palestinian Legislative Council. Ashrawi, who had started her activism as a student in Lebanon, where she was the spokesperson for the General Union of Palestinian Students, had gradually evolved into a "femocrat," a bureaucratic employee with a feminist background, working within the system.[17] She was, and continues to be, held in high esteem by most Palestinians for her numerous accomplishments in organizing, both as a student and during the First Intifada; academia, including establishing and chairing the Department of English at Birzeit University; and politics.

Feminist analysis of social change locates power in various hubs. For structuralist feminists, oppressive power, while concentrated in the state apparatus, is not located exclusively there. Rather, state-sanctioned oppression relies on various vectors of oppression, such as class, the family, the courts, religious institutions, and more. Effecting change, therefore, must come through attacking the "weaker" structures that support the state apparatus and, from there, spreading the resistance throughout, thus undermining the state's power to oppress. The "femocrats," as bureaucratic employees with a feminist background are sometimes known, were certainly committed to improving women's circumstances and believed they could do it from within the system.

Agency-based feminist analysis, on the other hand, emphasizes the power of the individual to effect broader change. Such agency-based change can happen within the structures of the state—in ministries and other government-funded offices—or completely outside them. The distinction between structural analysis and agency-based analysis, then, is that structural analysis always assumes that change must come from the structures that uphold the state, whereas agency-based analysis sees individual agency as the operative factor, with that individual agent working within or outside state structures.[18] In Palestine, the "outsiders" worked primarily within NGOs—organizations dedicated to social change, yet independent of the Palestinian government. Yet other agency-based feminists believed that a simultaneous push from NGOs and "femocrats" within state institutions was the most effective approach to achieving change in women's rights.

Spearheaded by Abu-Dayyeh and enthusiastically embraced by her colleagues at the WCLAC, the Palestinian Model Parliament was an ambitious, meticulously planned multiyear initiative to change the popular discourse around women's rights, so as to ultimately also change the legal system that denied them equality. Palestinian women had often articulated the belief that because they had no national institutions of their own, it was impossible to legislate change, as they remained under the rule, and laws, of a different country. However, as the Oslo Accords had resulted in the election of a Palestinian Legislative Council, the organizers of the PMP felt there was now a forum where their grievances and concerns could be taken up. The presence of the council, they thought, would finally give them the opportunity to demand women's equality before the law. Beginning in 1994, before the public launch of the initiative, they spent weeks weighing their options, envisioning new opportunities, planning workshops, and cementing partnerships with other Palestinian women's organizations, including the GUPW, the Women's Affairs Technical Committees, and numerous human rights organizations. As the project began to take shape, they reached out to trade unions, political parties, and to the popular committees of the Intifada in an intentional effort to expand their network of allies, so as to be most inclusive and representative.

The initial stage of this initiative, which lasted from 1994 to 1998, called for regional parliaments where specific aspects of the law impacting women would be discussed on a local level. These regional gatherings aimed to increase the legal literacy of the future citizens of the sovereign Palestinian state, with lectures, courses, seminars, and workshops around various issues such as women's contributions to society, the Personal Status Law, and interpretations of *shari'a,* the Islamic canonical law based primarily on the Qur'an and *hadith*, the corpus of sayings by the Prophet Muhammad and his close companions, revered by Muslims as a source of moral guidance and religious law. Then, through increased legal literacy, seminar participants would eventually propose modifications of existing laws and recommend legislation that would promote equality for women.

Each of the regional committees selected one area to focus on, and all were to come together at the culminating event, the actual "model parliament" where proposed legislation would be made.[19] The northern regional committee, including Nablus, Tulkarm, Jenin, and surrounding towns and villages, chose public health and education; the central regional committee, covering Jerusalem, Ramallah, and surrounding towns and villages, chose women in criminal law; the southern regional committee, consisting of Hebron, Bethlehem, and surrounding towns and villages, focused on labor laws; and the Gaza regional committee chose family law. From 1994 to 1998, the regional committees held discussions, debates, and townhalls, deepening the political discourse throughout the West Bank and Gaza Strip, often broaching topics that had previously been taboo. These included the minimum age for marriage, women's right to initiate divorce, feminist interpretations of both the Qur'an and hadith, violence against women, rape (including marital rape), and many other personal issues that had hitherto never been discussed publicly. As these necessary, if frequently heated, debates increased popular knowledge of social and legal issues in Palestine, the WCLAC also organized workshops to train both women and men who were committed to participate in the culminating PMP activities in mobilization, lobbying, and advocacy. The plan was for the regional committees to eventually meet at the Palestinian Model Parliament in Ramallah, to act upon the many discussions held regionally.

But as these important debates spread across the occupied territories, opposition to the PMP came hard and fast, and from multiple directions. The attacks were as fierce as they were unanticipated, as Palestinian society in the West Bank and Gaza Strip had just come out of years of emancipatory activism, and the WCLAC organizers were justified in their assumption that Palestinian society was ready for change. Still, conservative Islamists accused the PMP workshop facilitators of fomenting social strife and of encouraging divorce, which, they suggested, would result in the destruction of the family.[20] Some of the attacks were personal, accusing individual women of adultery or corruption. Nor were Islamists the only foes of the WCLAC: Other women's organizations were also critical of the PMP. While still committed to women's rights, many members of the "femocrat" cadre of the GUPW believed that national liberation was a necessary prerequisite for securing women's rights and organized accordingly, focusing on state building delinked from feminist concerns. Smaller, lesser-known women's organizations intentionally distanced themselves from the PMP, so as to avoid being subjected to the vicious attacks the WCLAC organizers were coming under.

Abu-Dayyeh understood the treacherous terrain women's movements were navigating in the post-Oslo context. In an essay published posthumously, she writes:

> The PMP was conceived and implemented between 1994 and 1998, a time when Palestinians were supposedly moving from a situation of occupation and colonisation to independence and statehood.

> This much-anticipated transition affected our society on many levels including our core value system and the terms of engagement—politically, economically, socially, and culturally. For example, prior to this period, everything had to be conducted in secrecy. Other dramatic changes were from underground community mobilisation to open public political participation, and from an assumed and agreed-upon politics of resistance against occupation and colonisation to a diverse and often contradictory range of politics and political engagements in relation to the Oslo Agreement and the newly established Palestinian National Authority.[21]

Nevertheless, she also believed the changed political landscape made it opportune to launch a national discussion around women's rights. The regional committees certainly did that. Nahda Sh'hada writes:

> One of the main achievements of the project was its success in reaching thousands of men and women in the West Bank and Gaza Strip. Other achievements included raising the awareness of political parties, especially the leftists, about issues specific to women, and lobbying them for better laws for a Palestinian society based on justice and equality. The MP initiative sparked a debate that had been missing from Palestinian society for a long time.[22]

But Abu-Dayyeh and her colleagues were working within the system; here, as in the NGOs discussed above, those who sought change plied the master's tools in hopes of dismantling the master's house. The Palestinian Authority, and by extension the Palestinian Legislative Council, were designed to serve Israel, not the Palestinian people, who still had no sovereign institution to represent them. And the PA president, Yasser Arafat, was growing more authoritarian as he polished his "father of the nation" persona, demanding the respect of the people while groveling at the feet of their occupier. Thus patriarchy was still entrenched in Palestinian society, and even if the PMP had held its projected culminating session, no proposed legislation could have much impact while Palestine was still occupied. Meanwhile, the opposition to the proposed changes proved overwhelming, and the PMP failed to hold its final session and did not issue any resolutions or make any modifications to the Personal Status Law. As scholar Sarah Ihmoud, a member of the Palestinian Feminist Collective, writes: "While some liberal feminist actors were absorbed into the Palestinian Authority structure, the delinking of feminism from anticolonial struggle has further strengthened its patriarchal violence and exclusion of marginal groups."[23] Ultimately, the PMP organizers had to reckon with the fact that working within the master's house could only achieve limited outcomes, which would not dismantle patriarchy. Here it is worth quoting Abu-Dayyeh again:

> The PMP experience proved that there would never be enough readiness for us to go through the kinds of heated debates experienced and questions raised. There will always be opposition parties who will take advantage of a situation to promote themselves politically by exploiting social issues and the status of women, the easiest and most convenient platform on which they can wage their battle. It became clear through the PMP experiences that such political manoeuvring compromises honesty, integrity, and genuine commitment to human rights principles. Therefore, women leaders particularly, and all social actors, should be prepared to withstand vicious attack and remain steadfast. To do so, one must not underestimate the level of the backlash, including deeply personal attacks, but be unequivocally rooted in one's own value system, with no illusions about who are allies in the struggle and who are not.[24]

In many ways, Maha Abu-Dayyeh's vision and ambition stand as perfect illustrations of the limits to women's accomplishments when working within a colonial, patriarchal system. Despite being immensely qualified, and fully committed, Abu-Dayyeh and her team could not overcome the traps built into the Oslo Accords, which had always been destined to cement occupation and the patriarchal system it upheld.

The Institute of Women's Studies

While the organizers of the Palestinian Model Parliament sought to legislate women's rights through the Palestinian Authority's Palestinian Legislative Council, another group of women was busy launching the Institute of Women's Studies at Birzeit University, the academic hub that had brought so many Palestinian feminists together. The founders included Eileen Kuttab, Islah Jad, Rema Hammami, Rita Giacaman, Lamis Abu Nahleh, Ilham Abu Ghazaleh, Lisa Taraki (Afghan born, married to George Giacaman, a Palestinian she met while both were students in the US, and living in Palestine since the 1970s), as well as Penny Johnson, wife of Raja Shehadeh, the lawyer, writer, and cofounder of Al-Haq. Founded in 1994, and continuing the legacy of Palestinian women's activism, the institute was the Arab world's first such academic center and was grounded in a more pragmatic vision, namely "the production of in-depth research that speaks to the Palestinian reality in its colonial specificity."[25] This recognition of the "colonial specificity" of Palestine inspired research that addressed the material and contemporary conditions of Palestinian women, rather than those one could aspire to, in a democratic future that would somehow emerge from the Oslo Accords.

Unlike the Model Parliament, which eventually fizzled away despite extensive preparation, the Birzeit Institute of Women's Studies has grown steadily and is today recognized as a critically important center for both organizing and research. Activists as well as scholars look forward to its annual conference, and Palestinian feminists in particular appreciate the political home it offers them, where their experiences are centered and their voices upheld.

The institute offers classes at the undergraduate level in disciplines such as sociology, political science, and literature, among others, that highlight Palestinian women's agency while engaging the complex circumstances challenging them. It is also prolific, producing research highly critical of both the Palestinian Authority and the various NGOs that had descended upon Palestinian society. A 1996 publication coauthored by Rita Giacaman, Islah Jad, and Penny Johnson, for example, blasts the Palestinian Authority, accusing it of nepotism instead of meritocracy and pointing out how the PA's social programs only considered women as men's relatives—the wives or mothers of fighters and martyrs—despite ample knowledge and documentation of women's direct contributions to the Palestinian national struggle.[26] Another 1996 publication, by Lisa Taraki, expressed dismay at an NGO's plans to build assisted living homes for elderly Palestinians, observing that it should be obvious to anyone in Palestine that the overwhelming majority of Palestinian families would never place an elder in such a home.[27] These two studies, like many of the working papers and findings of the Institute for Women's Studies, were published in Arabic and thus clearly addressed to Palestinian society.

Indeed, a critical difference between the institute and the various NGOs that had descended upon Palestine is how grounded the institute was in the daily lived reality of Palestinian society. Its analysis of gender looks at the specific colonial context of occupied Palestine, and how occupation exacerbates gender roles.

Similarly, the institute's annual conferences always focus on the lived experiences of Palestinian women under colonialism, with panels on gender in a colonial context, women's decreased employment opportunities under occupation, the formation of masculinity in the colonial context, and other such issues pertinent to the lives of Palestinian women, rather than to some imaginary family that would send their grandmother to a nursing home.

Ultimately, the Birzeit Institute of Women's Studies is proof that amid the discontent, the disappointment, and the repressed aspirations, Palestinian women throughout the homeland are still denouncing oppression, still organizing, and still centering the important issues—safety, care, education, nurturing, self-sovereignty—without which no society can thrive. Today, the institute offers a graduate degree in women's studies and produces some of the most relevant research about gendered aspects of Palestinian society under occupation, addressing the harsh reality of women's lives at the intersection of multiple vectors of oppression. It is one of the most respected academic centers in the region and, in true feminist practice, does not shy away from activism. The institute's homepage states:

> The Institute aims to raise social justice and gender justice issues in Palestinian society in dialogue with social, political, and feminist movements, thus seeking to link knowledge with practice through the production of in-depth research that speaks to Palestinian reality in its colonial specificity.[28]

Hope is an imperative, the backbone of our *sumoud*. And change and progress are most often dialectical, seldom linear. The failure of the PMP to legislate women's equality may have stalled the organizers' advances, but it did not alter their commitment to gender and national liberation. Additionally, the PMP, no longer mobilizing primarily in the streets, created a space within Palestine's new status as a nation-building society to engage in discussions of citizens' rights and expose the flaws of the patchwork of laws inherited from centuries of Ottoman and British rules and combined with religious Personal Status Law. The PMP introduced to the national discourse the argument that women deserved equal rights on the basis of their equal participation in the national struggle.

At the same time as the WCLAC was catalyzing a popular discussion of hitherto-taboo issues, the Birzeit Institute of Women's Studies was engaging in feminist praxis—critical research intended to challenge oppression, not merely write and teach about it. And while the institute denounced but could not end the occupation, or the PA's nepotism, it remains an effective hub for critical education and organizing, a much-needed catalyst of feminist agency in an increasingly oppressive environment.

Even as Palestinian women were repeatedly sidelined by politicians during the Oslo years, they were fomenters of an important national conversation. Nahda Sh'hada writes:

> Anyone living in Palestine between 1995–1998 would have been struck by the passion its people showed in discussing every law submitted to the legislative council; by the huge number of workshops devoted solely to debating proposed legislation; by the regular media coverage of activities related to debates of law. This process

> has created symbols of what constitutes the ideal citizen, and has interpreted those symbols, placing them within a specific political and institutional context.[29]

That "ideal citizen" is a woman persevering, despite numerous setbacks, and striving to transform her society for the better.

7

Whose Feminism? Defining Who We Are, Not Who We Are Not

When the history of Palestinian liberation is written, I want at least a footnote to say that queers were part of the struggle.

—Anonymous Palestinian member of Queers Undermining Israeli Terrorism (quitpalestine.org)

Do what anti-colonial queers have done for decades, reclaim the narrative, and set the terms of the conversation, this time about Palestine.

—"A Liberatory Demand from Queers in Palestine" (*Mizna* journal, November 7, 2023)

The doldrums of the "Oslo years" came to an end with the eruption, in September 2000, of the al-Aqsa Intifada, also known as the Second Intifada, when Palestinians rose up yet again against Israel's brutal military occupation. The immediate spark for this uprising was former Likud Prime Minister and then–Israeli Opposition leader Ariel Sharon's storming of the al-Aqsa compound in East Jerusalem, with a 1,000-strong militarized entourage, on September 28, 2000. Sharon was particularly disliked among Palestinians as he had been found directly responsible for the 1982 massacres in the Sabra and Shatila refugee camps in Lebanon, the anniversary of which they had just commemorated. In addition to being known as "the butcher of Sabra and Shatila," Sharon had also earned the nickname of "the bulldozer" for ordering Palestinian home demolitions and encouraging Israeli settlements deep within the West Bank. Between 1993 and 2000, the number of illegal Israeli settlers there had doubled from 200,000 to 400,000, and it was clear that the new settlements, as well as the expansion of modest outposts into multifamily compounds, were designed to ensure that there would be no viable Palestinian state, even though, according to the Oslo Accords, an independent Palestinian state was to have been formally announced by May 1999. Meanwhile, the settlements themselves were connected thanks to a network of highways dissecting the West Bank, on which only Israelis could drive, while Palestinian towns were being cut off from each other to accommodate settler transportation. Tensions were heightened by the failure of the July 2000 Camp David talks, in which PA President Yasser Arafat and Israeli Prime Minister Ehud Barak had failed to agree on the status of Jerusalem, territorial contiguity, and the Right of Return for Palestinian refugees—critically important issues that had been strategically left out of the Oslo Accords. And the outrage was palpable when Palestinians found out that Arafat, at the Camp David summit, had been asked to give up both East Jerusalem and the Right of Return. Palestinians, then, had reached boiling point yet again, and Sharon's provocative visit to al-Aqsa turned up the fire.

Like the First Intifada, the 2000 Palestinian popular uprising started out with nonviolent demonstrations, civil disobedience, and stone throwing. As always, Israel's immediate response was excessive violence, as Israeli authorities retaliated with rubber-coated bullets and live ammunition, escalating a few days later with military incursions with armored tanks into heavily populated residential areas. In fact, most analysts agree that Israel's highly militarized response was designed to drag Palestinians into military confrontation, which would distract from the ongoing settlement expansion. And inevitably, the level of Israeli aggression led to Palestinians responding through armed struggle, including occasional suicide bombings, which always made global headline news. Yet despite its representation in the Western media as a predominantly violent uprising, the Second Intifada also featured significant nonviolent resistance as Palestinians continued to organize rallies and protests against the Israeli settlements, the demolition of Palestinian homes, as well as the construction of the Apartheid Wall. And the discussions around personal issues remained animated, even as, or possibly because, personal circumstances were worsening, with the economy taking a deep dive. This is because Israel was attempting to break the Palestinian will to resist through economic pressure in the form of frequent curfews, and overall restriction of movement. Consequently, Palestinian per capita income fell by approximately 50 percent from the onset of the Second Intifada to early 2003. Still, as during the First Intifada, the preexisting system of neighborhood-based self-reliance and mutual aid helped sustain popular resistance.

However, unlike the First Intifada, which had catapulted them into leadership positions, this time, Palestinian women found themselves at a severe disadvantage. Palestinian women had already lost social ground since the return of Arafat and the emergence of a conservative Islamist movement, and now, in addition to increasing poverty and the shifting terrain due to Israel's aggression, they were also negatively impacted by the political rivalry between the Palestinian Authority and Hamas. Specifically, the cohesion experienced during the First Intifada, which had begun in the Gaza Strip and spread to the West Bank, with effective and quasi-seamless coordination between the two swaths of occupied territories, was now frayed as a result of Israel's extreme restriction of Palestinian movement between the West Bank and Gaza Strip. Moreover, women were gradually aligning themselves with one political party or another. And as we saw earlier, in the increasingly militarized context, these political factions—both the very paternalistic Fatah movement representing the Palestinian Authority and the Islamic Movement/Hamas, which had formed during the First Intifada and grown significantly during the Oslo years—viewed women first and foremost as the "nurturers of society," rather than leaders and comrades. Even the General Union of Palestinian Women was dominated, post-Oslo, by women who had returned from the diaspora—primarily in neighboring Arab countries—and did not recognize the leadership of the many Palestinian women who had organized during the First Intifada. Additionally, while the GUPW was supposedly independent of the PA, its staff were paid by the latter and had to work within the restrictions imposed by that institution.

Periods of political turmoil and military conflict generally translate into two divergent paths. One is a consolidation of conservatism, especially when gender dynamics were already fraught, with unresolved imbalance. Thus we can witness an intensification of patriarchy, as men from the subjugated group attempt to assert some power over anyone they deem inferior, when that power is taken away from them by the oppressor.[1] Sadly, examples of such regression abound around the world in conflict areas, or even in countries with socioeconomic upheaval without excessive militarization. The second is an opening of hitherto-uncharted social vistas, as the upheaval demands greater overall flexibility. A simple example is young, unmarried women having to spend the night away from their home if they are turned away at a checkpoint, unable to reach home safely or before curfew—something that would be unacceptable in times of peace but is understood as a necessary safety measure when a sniper may kill you as you attempt to go home. Another example would be young women enrolled in university who end up renting an apartment close to their campus instead of commuting daily from the family home. In the context of the Second Intifada, the founding of not one, but two, queer Palestinian organizations was certainly a major social breakthrough.[2] The terrain had been prepared by the recent flurry of national debates around gender issues, and the moment was right, as Palestinian queers felt the need to exit the Zionist organizations that had hitherto housed them and participate fully in the liberation struggle.

"Western Values"

Among the many accusations conservative Palestinians lobbed at the women who continued to organize during the Oslo years was that they were brainwashed by Western feminists and were seeking to impose "Western values" on Palestinian society. This accusation conveniently erased decades of Palestinian women's anticolonial activism that had begun under the British Mandate and was very pointedly aimed at ridding the nation of "the West" and its imperial plans. Indeed, we remember Matiel Mogannam's observation, during the British Mandate, that Britain is the "principal enemy of the Palestinian Arabs."[3] The 1936–39 rebellion, in which many women participated by smuggling food and weapons to the fighters and selling their jewelry to fund the purchase of ammunition, was against Britain, the paragon of Western imperialism at the time. And Palestinians, both men and women, knew it was European Zionism, and "the West," that aspired to colonize Palestine. Palestinian women seeking their homeland's liberation were fighting Western values and plans, not being brainwashed by them.

Besides, anyone looking objectively at Western countries' actions, rather than their propaganda, would immediately notice that "Western values" do not promote equality; if that were so, there would be no long-drawn-out struggles within those countries themselves to end sexual violence, the gender wage gap, homophobia and transphobia, or racism and xenophobia. Nor would there be, in countries devastated by Western intervention, an earnest desire to overthrow Western influence. A decolonized mind recognizes the impulse toward freedom, without attributing it to the oppressor who stole that freedom in the first place.

With regard to feminism specifically, while Palestinian feminists were quite cosmopolitan, regularly attending gatherings in various Arab countries, as well as occasionally traveling to Europe or even the US, their analysis and activism was aligned with that of other Arab feminists such as Nawal El Saadawi, Huda al-Shaarawi, Fadwa Tuqan, and Fatima Mernissi, all of whom invariably grappled with issues of national liberation alongside gender issues—and for whom national liberation was liberation from the West. Few, if any, looked up to the likes of Betty Friedan, Gloria Steinem, or Simone de Beauvoir as inspirations; they had their own fierce role models. Moreover, the very idea of "the West" is an imperial concept steeped in Orientalism and therefore hostile to Arab countries. Without the East, or the "Orient," as Edward Said so forcefully argued in *Orientalism*, there would be no "West." And the Orient, according to the West, is populated by evil, vile, lecherous men, and submissive women. Palestinian women, attached to their homeland, their culture, and their male kin and determined to liberate their country while further empowering themselves, did not embrace such a worldview. Palestinian women, then, were not only impervious to Western brainwashing generally; they were also at odds with Western feminists, whose Orientalist perspective framed them as devoid of agency, and who invariably sought to "save" them from what they viewed as an oppressive culture, while showing no interest in freeing them from a brutal occupation. Palestinian women's feminism was Indigenous and anticolonial. For decades, they had long fought on these two fronts, and by the 1990s, they had fostered a vibrant national discourse that eventually made it possible for queer groups to join the conversation.

Palestinian queers were also fighting their own battles within Israel, with Israel's queer communities, with "the West" generally, and with the Western queer discourse and its priorities. As Lynn Darwish and Haneen Maikey put it: "If LGBT Activism is Western, then so is Feminism."[4] Darwish and Maikey were speaking out of conviction that feminism never was exclusively Western and, thus, that neither should queer activism be associated with "the West."

No Palestinians in Israel's "Gay Haven"

In the mid-1980s, as Ghadir Shafie, a Palestinian born and raised in Akka, was questioning her sexuality, she had nowhere to turn to—no community elders to look up to, no support group that would tell her she was no anomalous freak. School counselors and psychologists were of no help: They readily discussed many issues considered controversial, such as child marriage, domestic violence, and drug abuse, but never sexuality. She called an Israeli hotline, and the responder suggested she move from her predominantly Palestinian town to Tel Aviv, where she could "live freely as a lesbian."[5]

Shafie was still a teenager at the time, but the lure of Tel Aviv as a gay haven had been planted, and shortly after graduating high school, she applied to and was accepted at Tel Aviv University. In a process of gentrification not unlike other cities around the world,

Tel Aviv was, in the 1980s and 1990s, gradually becoming more inclusive as gay Israelis, either individually or as couples, moved there and were met with support from local businesses. At first, most were male soldiers who went there on vacation from mandatory military service, and who so enjoyed the sandy beaches and overall tolerant culture that they relocated there when their tour of duty was over. Even today, Tel Aviv remains a predominantly male gay escapist city, ranking among the cities with the highest numbers of bars per capita in the world.

Shafie's first few months there were both exhilarating and deeply painful, as the "haven" she had moved to enthusiastically welcomed her as a lesbian but rejected her as Palestinian. "The move to Tel Aviv was overwhelming," she recalls.

> There, I thought, I would explore my sexuality and live freely, without having to hide, to be closeted, to cease to exist in so many ways. I was introduced to early 90s gay life in Tel Aviv through its vibrant bars and late-night gay parties, and made many gay Israeli friends.

However, while her new Israeli friends embraced her as gay, they were pressuring her to "closet" her Palestinian identity, saying she could "pass" for non-Arab and should avail herself of that fortunate opportunity. They even suggested she drop her Arab name, which didn't quite "pass." "It didn't take long to realize that they were friendly to me as a lesbian while constantly trying to conceal, even suppress, my Palestinian identity," Shafie noted.[6]

Shafie describes the Tel Aviv scene as "politically neutered," unlayered, accepting of a queer Palestinian's sexuality but rejecting their attachment to their cultural and national identity.

> I went home, feeling disgusted at the thought of being "renamed" by colonial oppressors to better fit their definition of the lesbian category of identity, and not offend their racial sensibilities. I had been a Palestinian Arab my entire life, who simply happened to question her sexuality. I had come to Tel Aviv to be who I was, but

> it became clear to me that I was welcome there as a "lesbian," not as a Palestinian. In their world of alleged "freedoms" and rights, there was no place for my Palestinian-ness. I had to choose between being "gay" and being Palestinian, but giving up a part of myself was impossible to bear. I had never experienced such rejection, and the thought of this exclusion made me sick of the Israeli LGBT scene.[7]

This reductionism, the refusal to acknowledge and accommodate multilayered identities, serves to reinforce the binary worldview of colonizers, whereas engagement with multiple jeopardies is a foundational concept in Third World feminisms and women of color feminisms. In the US, it would be the equivalent of white feminists telling a woman of color not to bring up race when discussing gender-specific issues such as access to health care and reproductive rights—as if white women and women of color faced the same challenges with regards to these issues in a white supremacist country. Queer Palestinian citizens of Israel could not discount the asymmetry between their circumstances and those of Jewish Israeli queers. In addition to approximately 100 laws that discriminate against them, Palestinian communities in Israel receive significantly less funding, sometimes only one-tenth of what Israelis receive, for education, infrastructure, and public services. Palestinian queers are not spared that discrimination. In the West Bank and Gaza Strip, they are not spared home demolitions, checkpoints, curfews, or military assaults. For those of us in the Diaspora, queer identity is not sufficient grounds for us to be allowed the Right of Return. As Sa'ed Atshan notes in his book *Queer Palestine and the Empire of Critique*, "Queer Palestinians face the same sets of conditions as straight Palestinians living under Israeli occupation."[8]

Of course, this Zionist reductionism—lesbian, but not Palestinian—is also a settler colonial move to disappear the native, revealing Tel Aviv's allegiance to the settler colonial state rather than to a lateral, transnational solidarity grounded in the understanding that the ethnonationalist state is an oppressor. This is despite Tel Aviv's intentional distancing from Israel, which is overwhelmingly homophobic, and which ranks very low globally among desirable countries to visit. This strategic escape from political reality is necessary to attract gay tourism, which contributes significantly to the city's economy. Of her interactions with Israeli queers, Shafie says, "You have to check your identity at the door, and they tell you: you can't talk about Palestine or liberation or occupation here, you can only talk about lesbian rights."[9]

At the end of the academic year, Ghadir Shafie left Tel Aviv, dejected with the pressure to closet herself: to come out *only* as lesbian, but to keep her nationality a secret. She was both: a lesbian and a Palestinian, and she determined to always twin these two issues, organizing for liberation not just as a queer individual but also, and equally, as a Palestinian. Home to her would always be Palestine, and Palestinian culture—a grounding attachment that Israeli queers rejected. "The moment we represent ourselves as gay Palestinians and speak about politics, it's the end of the story. They want us to be the victims of our own society, and they want to be the saviours."[10] She did not need to be "saved" by Western or Israeli queers—if anything, she felt the need to be saved from them. She recalls:

> Very often in the West you hear that they say they want to "save" Palestinian queer people from the homophobic society, from the conservative society, from the backward family and we usually say, thanks but no thanks. We don't need to be saved as queers, we have managed to raise the bar with our own community, within the Palestinian feminist movement, within the Palestinian National movement. We have managed to create a discourse that includes all our struggles, that unites queer, feminist struggle and resistance to all forms of oppression.[11]

With other Palestinian lesbians, Shafie determined to carve a space for herself within Palestinian culture and society, away from the colonizer's attempt to save her from her full identity.

In stark contrast to the "politically neutered" discourse of Israel's queer scene, by the 1990s, and thanks in no small part to the long legacy of Palestinian feminists demanding full social and political liberation, Palestine was brimming with vibrant debates around gender issues. Palestinian feminists had never separated their plight as women from the larger context of living under colonial rule and occupation. Palestinian feminism, then, with its attention to complex personal lives rather than selectively gay-friendly but anti-Palestinian Tel Aviv, would become Shafie's ideological and political home. Back in her hometown of Akka, Shafie started communicating online with other Palestinian lesbians, sharing her experience, and creating community.

From Whispers to Voices: Aswat

Not long after Shafie had left Tel Aviv, Rauda Morcos unexpectedly found herself with much time on her hands, having lost her job after granting an interview about her poetry to the Israeli newspaper *Yedioth Ahronoth*. Born in Kafr Yasif, a mere eleven kilometers from Shafie's hometown, Morcos had also grown up a Palestinian citizen of Israel, subjected to the anti-Palestinian racism of Zionists. Morcos, an established poet in her twenties, had mentioned her sexuality in the interview, which the journalist promised not to reveal. But when the conversation was published, it was under a blaring headline identifying her as a "Lesbian Poet." This was not inconsequential. Morcos was physically assaulted, her car was vandalized multiple times, and, more importantly, she lost her job as a youth educator, because homophobia is such that queers are frequently presumed to prey on children. She turned to the only support network available to her: a telephone and email forum where she had engaged with other Palestinian lesbians, many of whom had shared their experiences, fears, love stories, and disillusionment with Israel's queer scene. These women connected through their voices, or *aswat*.

Like Shafie, Morcos felt the need to have a space to be in community with her peers, other Palestinians in Israel, away from Israeli-dominated groups. For years, she volunteered as the organizer of the forum, and in 2003, Aswat, "the Arab Israeli Center for Gender and Sexual Freedoms," officially opened in Haifa, with the twenty-nine-year-old Morcos as its inaugural director. By that time, even though Palestinian society had been debating various gender issues for years, same-sex love remained a taboo subject. Morcos felt it important to broach the topic openly, rather than in the most restricted spaces. Her task was to add to the layers of discussions of social liberation in Palestine by introducing the subject of queer liberation. Confronted with a choice between bringing the issue of Palestinian identity into Zionist spaces, or queer identities into Palestinian feminism, Morcos did not hesitate.

The terrain was not easy. She was introducing one more vector of oppression, and the need to address it, to communities that were already suffering at the most basic levels. "For the West Bankers and Gaza Strip people, before even starting to deal with women's rights and gay rights, the first thing is human rights and the Israeli occupation," Morcos commented in a retrospective lecture, noting the reality of the macro environment being the foremost concern of Palestinian society. But she persevered: "So for me, putting the issue of homosexuality on the Palestinian societal agenda was a huge step and a huge challenge. With my personal struggle and the collective struggle of Aswat, we have really succeeded to put that issue [there]."[12]

Morcos and Shafie saw eye to eye on the need to always take the larger context into account as they advocated for sexual rights, as they understood that to be "free" as queers remains meaningless if they are not free as Palestinian women: The three aspects of their multidimensional identities, being queer, Palestinian, and women, were inseparable. Their queerness did not occur in a vacuum, and their struggle could only be intersectional. As Shafie put it: "To talk about sexual rights on its own will not work in Palestine. You have to intersect it with the feminist and national struggle."[13] Still, as Palestinian citizens of Israel concerned with the challenges of queer Palestinians throughout historic Palestine, the Aswat organizers were dealing with the Israeli-imposed fragmentation of our people, which made it impossible for LGBTQI+ Palestinians in the West Bank and Gaza Strip to access the organization's office in Haifa. Nevertheless, the very presence of such an office, with its insistence on its Palestinian identity, facilitated discussions of Palestinian same-sex love in the West Bank and Gaza Strip. Now, they could define themselves and name their needs and priorities.

Beyond borders, too, Aswat played a significant international role, reaching out to Palestinians in the far Diaspora, as well as non-Palestinian anti-Zionist queers globally. These communities could now communicate with and learn from Palestinian queers in Israel without an Israeli intermediary who would, by virtue of the larger power dynamics in Israeli society, always be in a position of power over Palestinian queers.

When Morcos stepped down as the director of Aswat in 2007, after having seen the group transform from whispered conversations in virtual space to loud and articulate voices for complete liberation, Ghadir Shafie was a ready and equally qualified successor.

alQaws

In 2020, in a tribute to Haneen Maikey, who was stepping down after leading them for twenty years, the staff of alQaws wrote: "The political identity of alQaws has also become an essential part of our work. We are an unwaveringly political grassroots organization, standing in direct opposition to patriarchy, colonialism, and capitalism."[14]

Maikey's legacy is impressive indeed. In 2007, and despite the still-formidable taboo against queerness in Palestinian society, she founded the first queer Palestinian organization in Jerusalem, which she directed until 2020. Like Shafie, Maikey had first discussed sexuality issues within a Zionist organization and felt the need to sever this dependency by creating a politicized, anticolonial, Palestinian queer space where the intersectionality and complexity of Palestinian queer lives could be discussed in a wholesome way, rather than an arbitrarily fragmented and censored one. And like Shafie and Morcos, she had felt a need to ground Palestinian sexual rights within the Palestinian national struggle discourse, away from the "politically neutered" Israeli queer discourse.

Born in 1979, Maikey was in her early twenties when she was hired in 2001 as the Palestinian outreach coordinator at the Jerusalem Open House for Pride and Tolerance, an Israeli institution that, despite its best intentions, fell short of grasping the fact that their slogan, "Born to be free," occasionally born aloft at Jerusalem Pride parades or displayed as a banner on their website, clearly does not extend to freedom from colonialism.[15] The lack of attention to political dynamics at the Open House is best expressed in the words of Hagai El-Ad, the center's director from 2000 to 2006, who boasts:

> At the Open House we believe that gays and lesbians share something in common that bonds them together and transcends national identities. Our shared experiences of homophobia provide us with a commonality that is different than other attempts at Arab-Israeli co-existence.[16]

I am reluctant to sound overly critical of El-Ad, a human rights activist who later served as director of the Association for Civil Rights in Israel before moving on to become director general of B'Tselem from 2014 to 2023. El-Ad has participated in Palestinian-led protests against illegal Israeli settlements, been arrested for trying to prevent evictions in Sheikh Jarrah, and more recently argued that Israel is practicing apartheid. Nevertheless, his belief, in 2006, that queers share something that "transcends national identities" reveals a naivete that Palestinian queers bristled against. Maikey's recollection of the Jerusalem Open House was that it was "an apolitical organisation, an apolitical space, and actually an apolitical start for Al-Qaws."[17]

Yet politics matter. This is because while "the personal is political" is supposedly a feminist mantra, "the political is personal" is the Palestinian feminist and queer reality, as well as a significant part of the challenges of the lives of all Palestinians, whether living as second-class citizens or under military occupation in our own homeland, or in the Diaspora. We have seen how, in the eyes of most male politicians, Palestinian women, like women everywhere, are viewed primarily as nurturers, wives, mothers, and agents of social reproduction. Even when their agency during militarized conflict is acknowledged, it is considered a temporary accommodation to the circumstances, rather than a permanent status. Similarly, Palestinian queers, like queers everywhere, experience homophobia and transphobia in most social circles, having only a few restricted places where they can be fully at ease with all aspects of their identity. Palestinian queers, however, endure especially oppressive circumstances, as they also fight Israel's exploitation of homophobia, whereby Israel threatens to disclose their sexuality to their conservative parents if they do not collaborate with its intelligence services by becoming informants. This practice stands in stark contrast to Israel's claim to be gay friendly, showing instead that Israel does not distinguish in its oppression of all Palestinians, by any and all means possible, including through the exploitation of their vulnerability. Thus, being queer in Palestine frequently comes with the stigma that accompanies this identity in most societies, as well as the suspicion that they are not to be trusted politically. In a context where one's very survival often depends on community support, collective care systems, and mutual aid, a lack of these can mean the difference between life and death. And despite the resilience of Palestinians, the social fabric that has long sustained us was eroding under Israel's repeated attacks and the significant challenges of living under an increasingly violent occupation. Palestinian queers, then, rather than finding a haven in Israel, were further endangered by it.

For alQaws, this needed to change.

Maikey and her staff have recently come under some criticism from fellow queers for placing the anticolonial struggle among their top priorities—something that alQaws does not deny.[18] For Maikey, insufficient attention to the anticolonial struggle erases the lived experience of Israel's violence against queer Palestinians. Instead, alQaws argues there is "no pink door in the apartheid wall" that would spare Palestinians from the overall oppressive structures of Israeli domination, just because they are gay. They point to the fact that Israeli soldiers have never stopped to ask any Palestinian in the West Bank if they are gay before shooting them, detaining them at checkpoints, demolishing their homes, or stealing their land. Israel consistently criticizes Hamas for persecuting gays in the Gaza Strip yet has never offered these individuals asylum, preferring instead to use their vulnerability both to entrap them and to further villainize Hamas. In its cyclical genocidal assaults on the Gaza Strip, it does not spare queers. And while Tel Aviv occasionally offers respite to queer Palestinians escaping the West Bank or, less frequently, the Gaza Strip, Israel does not grant them citizenship, as letting them move to and establish residency in the 1948 territories would be considered a precedent for the Right of Return. Of course, no Diaspora Palestinian, queer or straight, is granted the Right of Return just for being gay. Minimizing or marginalizing the harshness of the colonial condition under which Palestinian queers live, then, serves Israel's desire to present itself as a haven for this community, safer than their own Palestinian society, when Israel is violating their rights everywhere, every day.

Besides insisting on always accounting for the macro environment of Israeli occupation, alQaws's analysis was truly radical, seeking to transform society rather than simply giving queers greater access to some of its privileges. While acknowledging that the term "queer" is Western and, unlike "homosexual," does not have an Arabic equivalent, Maikey explains that they prefer it to "LGBTQI+" because it is at once more inclusive and more overtly political.[19] Maikey made it clear on numerous occasions that the organization's goals did not include "representing the Palestinian LGBTQ community," which remained nonhomogeneous. Her understanding of "queer" was faithful to the original impulse behind that reclaimed term, referring to a community that did not seek "acceptance" into normative society or "equality" with the privileges offered in a patriarchal system.

On the ground, alQaws ran a hotline to address the concerns of the Palestinian queer community, but it also set out to serve this community while addressing all aspects of their oppression and engaging in political as well as social resistance. And as they were pawns in Israel's propaganda machine, they decided to attack that machine by fighting pinkwashing and joining the 2005 Palestine-led call for BDS, the Boycott, Divestment, and Sanctions movement that had launched in 2005 and advocated an economic, cultural, and academic boycott of Israeli institutions that do not denounce Israel's illegal occupation; divestment from companies that profit from the violation of the human rights of Palestinians; and imposing sanctions on Israel until it abides by international law.

Pinkwashing

No overview of Palestinian queer activism would be complete without a discussion of Israel's pinkwashing campaign, and the global response to it that Palestinian queers were instrumental in orchestrating. Briefly, Israel's pinkwashing campaign is that country's attempt to distract from its long record of human rights violations by presenting itself as a liberal, LGBTQI+-friendly country, thus deflecting from its reality as a hawkish illegal occupier. Israel's nation branding focuses on winning over liberals abroad, particularly in the US and Western European countries, which provide it with the political immunity to carry on its violations of international law. Liberals make up the primary target audience for Israel's propaganda because it is otherwise confident in the staunch support of conservatives. It is important here to distinguish between liberals and genuine progressives, who would not support an ethnonationalist state that violates the human rights of the people it has dispossessed and seeks to establish the supremacy of one ethnic or religious group over any other. In order to appeal to liberals, then, Israel touts the fact that it is gay friendly, priding itself, for example, on the fact that openly gay and trans Israelis can serve in the army. Here, again, the distinction between liberals and progressives is important: Liberals can live with being complicit in what they condemn, while progressives would not support the military, even if it is gay friendly, and would still recognize the Israeli army for the brutal occupation force that it is. Israel also advertises the fact that it recognizes gay marriage (even though it does not allow such marriages to be officiated in Israel, so gay Israelis need to get married elsewhere) and has antidiscrimination laws protecting LGBTQI+ individuals in employment and public services. Again, this appeals to liberals rather than to progressive queers, who are not necessarily pro-marriage, even as they understand that this institution comes with numerous social and financial privileges. And while Israel protects gays from discrimination, it has approximately 100 laws discriminating against non-Jews, even if they happen to be gay.

Launched in the early 2000s, the pinkwashing campaign is an integral and significant part of Israel's propaganda campaign, which seeks to redress Israel's tarnished image without actually changing the practices that led to that country's very low global ranking for human rights. Other examples of Israel's propaganda campaigns are redwashing (a term coined after "red Indians"), its portrayal of all Jews, and only Jews, as the Indigenous people of the land; and greenwashing, its portrayal of its policies as environmentally friendly, "making the desert bloom," even as it is busy uprooting ancient trees and making entire swaths of land uninhabitable. Specifically, by the 2000s, Israel was no longer viewed by most nations as a fledgling nation surrounded by bloodthirsty hordes of barbarians intent on destroying it out of sheer hatred of Jews. Instead, an increasing number of people globally saw Israel as a powerful expansionist country with the military power to crush its neighbors, and the chutzpah to act in flagrant violation of international law and the human rights of the people whose land it illegally occupied, knowing it is exempt from accountability because of the political immunity offered by the US, its staunchest ally.

Palestinian queers were in the best position to expose this rebranding that completely misrepresented Israel's practices, and Aswat and alQaws set out to do just that. Whenever global allies asked members of the organization about homophobia in Palestinian society, they would respond with the need to look at the macro environment of occupation, second-class citizenship, and a denial of their Right of Return, all imposed by Israel and overwhelmingly aggravating whatever oppression Palestinian queers experienced at the micro level. They insisted that to live freely as queers, they must be able to live freely as Palestinians, and Israel is denying them that freedom. And in 2005, when the Palestinian-led call for BDS was issued, Aswat and alQaws joined forces with the newly formed Palestinian Queers for BDS (PQBDS) to play a prominent role in the global campaign for solidarity with Palestine.

PQBDS

The Second Intifada was still raging across the country when, on October 12, 2004, PA President Yasser Arafat fell ill with nausea, vomiting, abdominal pain, and diarrhea. The symptoms worsened very fast, and on October 29, he was transported to a hospital in France. By then, in addition to the initial symptoms, he had also developed liver and kidney failure. He lapsed into a coma on November 3 and was pronounced dead on November 11, 2004. The team of medical experts who had treated him at the French hospital ruled out many likely and less likely reasons for his demise but failed to determine a cause of death, noting instead a "mystery blood disorder." Arafat's wife Suha, the only person with the legal right to do so, did not request an autopsy at the time of death. Years later, however, she agreed to have Arafat's body exhumed, and laboratory tests revealed unusual quantities of polonium 210, both in the samples of his body that were tested and on personal belongings like his toothbrush and *kuffiyeh*. Polonium 210 is a highly radioactive poison that has been used in political assassinations. Its production requires nuclear capabilities, and only a handful of countries, including Israel, the US, and Russia, are known to possess any.

While Arafat's death remains shrouded in mystery, it did not come as a surprise, as he had many foes, not least the Israeli government, who held him responsible for the Second Intifada. And shortly after Arafat's death, the Second Intifada did indeed come to an end. Just like the First Intifada, this came through an "agreement" between politicians that fell way short of addressing Israel's long-standing oppression of the Palestinian people. The Sharm el-Sheikh summit of February 2005 brought together the rulers of the two countries that had signed peace agreements with Israel, namely Egyptian President Hosni Mubarak and Jordanian King Abdullah the Second, along with Ariel Sharon (known as the "butcher" or "bulldozer"), who was by then Israel's prime minister, and PA President Mahmoud Abbas. Abbas had just been elected as Arafat's successor, and this was his opportunity to make a name for himself and establish a "legacy" as a peacemaker. By then, Israel had killed close to 5,000 Palestinians during military confrontations and significantly expanded the checkpoints restricting Palestinian freedom of movement, while continuing to expand on settlement construction.

As Palestinians grappled once again with the reality that politicians will not help them achieve liberation, they turned to the grassroots again, calling upon global solidarity in their struggle to overthrow the oppressor. In July 2005, over 150 civil society organizations representing sectors of the Palestinian people in all parts of the homeland and diaspora issued the call for Boycott, Divestment, and Sanctions on Israel. Inspired by the global campaign that had contributed to ending apartheid in South Africa in the previous century, the BDS movement called on people of conscience everywhere to engage in

> non-violent punitive measures until Israel meets its obligation to recognize the Palestinian people's inalienable right to self-determination and fully complies with the precepts of international law by:
>
> 1. Ending its occupation and colonization of all Arab lands and dismantling the Wall;
> 2. Recognizing the fundamental rights of the Arab-Palestinian citizens of Israel to full equality; and
> 3. Respecting, protecting, and promoting the rights of Palestinian refugees to return to their homes and properties as stipulated in UN resolution 194.

Meanwhile Israel had ramped up its propaganda yet again, and this was a battlefront Palestinian queers were well positioned to engage. Among the important initiatives launched collaboratively by alQaws, Aswat, and the newly formed PQBDS was the mobilization of queers both in Palestine and globally to articulate a contextualized anticolonial discourse, accompanied by practical steps against

Israel. This activism not only exposed Israel's lies; it also served to counter the image of Palestinian queers as informants and collaborators, as they were now seen to be fully active in leadership positions in anti-Zionist campaigns for national liberation.

Here it must be noted that Israel does not only exploit the circumstances of queer Palestinians for its intelligence gathering. It has also coerced sick people in need of cancer treatment, for example, whether for themselves or more frequently for their loved ones, into giving out information in return for being granted passage to a health center. Israel also takes advantage of married individuals having affairs, threatening to reveal their secret to their spouse if they do not give out information. However, as a result of homophobia, a married man having an affair, or a mother pleading for her sick child to be allowed to leave the West Bank for medical treatment, would not generally be suspected of collaborating with Israel, whereas a gay person may be, just for being homosexual. With catchy slogans like "There's no pink door in the apartheid wall," or "No pride in apartheid," backed by solid analysis, Palestinian queers and their allies were also instrumental in disseminating the apartheid analogy, exposing Israel's discriminatory practices against Palestinians and dealing blow after blow to that country's pretense of being a vibrant democracy. As Shafie put it: "Perhaps the biggest change that Al Qaws has led was to challenge the stereotypical images of the 'gay' Palestinian—produced over decades of sexual taboo and exploited many times for political ends that serve the imperialist interests of the Israeli state. The primary change in the image was from that of a victim—the victim of society, family and institutions, to a new image as an individual and activist with agency and control over themselves, their peers and their society."[20]

Major Campaigns

Because the BDS campaign relies on support from non-Palestinians, a coalition formed by Aswat, alQaws, and PQBDS and hereafter referred to collectively as PQBDS called on international queer communities to endorse the 2005 call for BDS and, specifically, to boycott cultural events that promoted Israel's propaganda. And these were many. Sa'ed Atshan writes that Palestinian queer activism was most dynamic from 2000 to 2012, and that it has plateaued since then. Yet while it may be true that we are not seeing any major *new* queer campaigns since 2012, the energy behind all the queer organizing that occurred during those dozen years has not waned, and many initiatives, such as disruptions at Pride events, denunciations of pinkwashing events ("pinkwatching"), and the organizing of alternative, anti-pinkwashing queer venues, have become regular occurrences. Below are only a handful of the many queer actions for Palestinian liberation that occurred in the opening years of the twenty-first century.

QUIT!: Outside the Frame

The San Francisco, California–based Queers Undermining Israeli Terrorism (QUIT!), formed in 2000, was a natural ally to Palestinian queers. QUIT!'s political analysis aligns perfectly with that of Aswat, as they argue that "our struggle is for liberation, not equality, in this or any oppressive society." In a direct response to homonationalism, with its celebration of queers serving in the Israeli army, they explain: "We don't seek to be soldiers of imperialism, not in the US and not in Israel." And just as that of Aswat and alQaws, QUIT!'s understanding of the queer struggle is intersectional, fighting for liberation from all oppressive structures simultaneously: "We see all fights for liberation as our fight, and we see our fight as queers as part of all liberation struggles. We do not want to assimilate in this oppressive and unequal society, we want to radically transform it."[21] Since its inception, QUIT! has been active in opposing pinkwashing, and in 2007 it called on Frameline, which hosts the San Francisco International LGBT Film Festival, the largest queer cultural event in the world, to end its partnership with the Israeli consulate. Frameline declined. QUIT! persevered for five years, with many public intellectuals calling on them to sever that partnership, and when they could not prevail, QUIT! launched its own queer film festival, Outside the Frame, which featured filmmakers who had withdrawn their films from Frameline. Outside the Frame was followed in 2021 by what is now an annual international film festival, Queer Cinema for Palestine, with sponsorship and entries from over 250 groups in over thirty countries. Queer Cinema for Palestine has issued a pledge for filmmakers not to show their films at TLVFest, the annual LGBTQI+ themed film festival held in Tel Aviv, and so far 300 artists have signed the pledge.

IGLYO out of Israel

When the International Gay and Lesbian Youth Organization announced it would hold its 2011 general assembly in Tel Aviv, with sponsorship from Israel, PQBDS reached out to the organization's board urging them not to be complicit in pinkwashing. Founded in 1984, IGLYO is the largest international queer youth organization, with over 125 member organizations from forty countries. When IGLYO's leadership dismissed the Palestinian queer groups' request, PQBDS issued a joint call to the IGLYO member organizations to boycott the assembly should the umbrella organization refuse to change the location. The response was overwhelming, as a number of member organizations announced they would not attend the general assembly, in solidarity with Palestine. These included such organizations as the UK-based National Union of Students–LGBTQ and the International Lesbian and Gay Cultural Network, as well as national ones such as Lebanon's Helem (Arabic for "Dream," also an acronym that translates to "Protection of Lebanese LGBTQI"); Turkey's Kaos Gay and Lesbian Cultural Research and Solidarity Association (the oldest and largest gay and lesbian association in the country, whose name, like "Qaws" in Arabic, means "rainbow") and Pembe Hayat (the first transgender rights association in the country); as well as Belong To, an Irish LGBT youth organization. Eventually, citing "much debate on the proposed location of the GA by IGLYO Member Organizations and also by LGBTQ and human rights allies," as well as "recent legal changes in Israel," the board of IGLYO decided to change location. PQBDS welcomed the decision, issuing a statement reiterating the fact that Israel oppresses queer Palestinians and calling on allies to respect the BDS call. The statement read, in part:

> All Palestinians—queer and straight—must deal with the effects of Israel's apartheid system, illegal wall, colonial settlements, and military occupation. Furthermore, Palestinians in Gaza live under a medieval and illegal siege, and in the largest open-air prison in the world. Like all Palestinian citizens of Israel, queers are subject to institutionalized discrimination in all walks of life, and Palestinian refugees are denied their basic, UN-sanctioned right of return.

US Social Forum

If Palestinians are known for our *sumoud*, Zionist organizations are known for their dogged determination to infiltrate liberal spaces. The US Social Forum, an offshoot of the World Social Forum that was held in Brazil in 2001, is one of the largest gatherings of social justice activists, leftist groups, antiwar activists, prison abolitionists, and other progressives in the US. It was first held in Atlanta, Georgia, in 2007, and the 2010 gathering was scheduled for June 22–26 in Detroit, Michigan. Prior to the event, the hype around this gathering was growing by the minute. Detroit is known as a progressive, resilient city that rose from recession despite structural oppression; participants would have the opportunity to learn from its many local community-led initiatives, listen to revolutionary grassroots organizing icon Grace Lee Boggs, and choose from over 1,000 cultural events and workshops to attend. Twenty thousand people registered, and finally, just one week from the beginning of the actual event, the program was published.

Much to the horror of Palestinian queers, the program listed a workshop called "LGBTQI Liberation in the Middle East," facilitated by StandWithUs—an Israel advocacy organization that aligns with the far right and hounds activists for Palestinian rights. As soon as the program was published, queer Arabs reached out to the organizers explaining that this was unacceptable, as it violates the antiracist, antiviolence guidelines of the gathering. Palestinians had already been misrepresented at the 2007 forum, and Social Forum organizers had pledged not to let this happen again. Yet now they had accepted a proposal for a workshop about Palestinian queers facilitated by a belligerent Zionist organization.

From Turtle Island to Palestine, Palestinian queers and their allies communicated their objections to the organizers, and PQBDS sent a letter explaining that "StandWithUs has no connection with the LGBT movement in the Middle East apart from ties to Zionist Israeli LGBT organizations, yet it claims to speak for and about our movements. It has no credibility in our region." The letter added that "as organizations working in and from the Middle East, we condemn its attempt to use us, our struggles, our lives, and our experiences as a platform for pro-Israeli propaganda."[22] Progressive as many of the Social Forum organizers were, they were very reluctant to cancel this workshop, which they had accepted, they later told PQBDS, because they had been too overwhelmed with proposals to vet them and simply accepted every single one. But Palestinian queers and our allies persevered, some of us while on our way to the forum. With the time difference between Palestine and Michigan, messages were coming round the clock, the actual scheduled time of the pinkwashing workshop was drawing uncomfortably near, and the forum organizers were not budging. The organizers even explained that the reason the SWU workshop would not be canceled was because if it were, there could potentially be costly consequences to other presenters at the forum, since the Zionist organization might influence foundations to withhold funding from other groups facilitating workshops there. In other words, the Social Forum organizers were willing to throw Palestinian queers under the bus to avoid a potential loss of funding to other organizations. And they expected Palestinian queers to accept this sacrifice, for the sake of not jeopardizing the Zionist funding of other groups. This was a deal with the devil, and PQBDS got busy flyering, planning disruptions, protests, and an improvised workshop just outside the room where StandWithUs was scheduled to hold its workshop.

Then, at the very last minute, the organizers agreed to the demand to cancel the workshop. PQBDS had prevailed at the largest gathering of progressive organizers in the US and educated thousands of them about pinkwashing.[23]

QuAIA: "No Pride in Apartheid"

In spring 2005, the Arab Students Collective at the University of Toronto, Canada, put together an ambitious "Israeli Apartheid Week," with displays, panels, cultural events, and workshops raising awareness of Israel's regime of occupation, settler colonialism, and apartheid rule, as well as Palestinian culture, resilience, and resistance. The event was such a success, with rooms filled at capacity and significant media coverage, that in 2006 a number of colleges across Canada held similar weeks, and within a few years, over 200 cities worldwide were organizing their own Israeli Apartheid Week, which has become a key component of the international BDS campaign.

One of the presentations at the 2008 Israeli Apartheid Week was on pinkwashing, and audience members who had long suspected something was awry with Israel's gay-friendly image were now sufficiently informed to form a new group, Queers Against Israeli Apartheid. Just as QUIT! had hit the ground running, QuAIA disrupted that year's Toronto Pride parade with a clear message: "No Pride in Apartheid." The disruption caused a major uproar in the city, catalyzing a much-needed multiyear conversation around Israel's practices. Eventually, in 2015, QuAIA Toronto folded, after having disrupted marches every year since its formation. Yet, just as Israeli Apartheid Week had started as one event at one university and is now a global annual forum, so QuAIA had engendered numerous chapters in various cities that continue to disrupt Pride marches and Israeli-sponsored pinkwashing events.

The domino effect was taking hold. A Palestinian member of QUIT! had written, "When the history of Palestinian liberation is written, I want at least a footnote to say that queers were part of the struggle." But queers will never be just a footnote in the Palestinian struggle for liberation. What a handful of Palestinian feminists living in the belly of the beast launched in 2000, with the formation of Aswat and alQaws, has blossomed into a global movement. And it is no exaggeration to say Palestinian queers have written entire chapters, exposing one of the greatest propaganda machines in history and completely changing the global discourse about what it means to be feminist, queer, and Palestinian.

8

Our Feminism: Tal'at and the Palestinian Feminist Collective

We aspire to build a different world, for our emancipation is hinged on the shattering of capitalism, colonialism, and patriarchy all at once.

—Tal'at feminist movement (in Hala Marshould and Riya Alsana, "Tal'at, a Feminist Movement That Is Redefining Liberation and Reimagining Palestine," *Mondoweiss*, February 25, 2020)

We are re-imagining and re-creating a world free from systems of gendered, racial and economic exploitation that commodify human life and land. Ours is a vision for a radically different future based on life-affirming interconnectedness, empowering the working classes, and love for each other, land, life and the planet itself.

—The Palestinian Feminist Collective, "Pledge That Palestine Is a Feminist Issue," 2021

Israa Ghrayeb's screams could be heard from outside her Bethlehem hospital room, punctuated by what sounded like heavy blows. A nurse recorded them but did not intervene. Someone, most likely the nurse who recorded them, uploaded them to the internet, where they can still be found today. I listened to them yet again as I sat down to write this chapter; they are haunting. Besides the nurse who recorded them, numerous medical staff also heard and later documented the screams. They go on, and on.

No one intervened.

Israa, a twenty-one-year-old makeup artist, had been hospitalized on August 10, 2019, with a broken spine and bruises on her arms and torso, which medical staff identified as likely signs of domestic abuse. Her family claimed she was mentally unstable, "possessed" by "bad spirits," and that she had fallen from the balcony at their home. They were not questioned about the fall, or the bruises. From her hospital bed, Israa posted on social media that she would need to cancel her August and September appointments to undergo surgery for her broken spine, and that she would inform her followers of when she could resume work. She was an "influencer" with 12,000 followers on Instagram. Mostly, she posted photos of her makeup artistry. Less frequently, she would post selfies, something her family disapproved of, finding it dishonorable. Shortly before her hospitalization with a broken spine, Israa had posted a photo of herself with her fiancé, the man to whom she was to be officially engaged the next day, whom her family had approved of. Still, for her controlling family, this post of the happy couple was beyond the pale.

Israa was discharged after initial treatment. On August 22, she was admitted to the same hospital again. This time, however, her life had been snuffed out. She had died of "severe respiratory failure."[1] On September 2, protests erupted in Ramallah and Bethlehem under the hashtag #WeAreAllIsraa, demanding a full investigation into her death. That investigation, which went beyond a mere postmortem, revealed that she had been psychologically abused, and that her family had tried to "exorcise" the spirits they claimed possessed her. The autopsy uncovered extensive beating that had occurred over weeks, possibly months. The West Bank's chief prosecutor charged three male relatives with her murder, saying Israa's death was a result of respiratory complications due to "abuse and torture."

Israa Ghrayeb's was the eighteenth femicide in 2019, according to the Women's Centre for Legal Aid and Counselling.[2] The center had documented twenty-three such murders in the West Bank and Gaza Strip in 2018, thirteen in the West Bank, and ten in Gaza. Most had been written off as "accidents," or "falls," as Ghrayeb's family had claimed. But the recording of her screams, while it failed to save her life, had shaken Palestinian society to the core. Thousands of outraged women and men, young and old, took to the streets in what was the launch of a new grassroots Palestinian group, Tal'at, which articulated a feminist analysis of this scourge, while both the WCLAC and the General Union of Palestinian Women demanded that a draft 2004 law intended to protect women from domestic violence be finally enacted. A few months later, in early 2020, Tal'at reported a total of thirty-four cases of femicide in 2019, the year of Ghrayeb's murder.[3]

Tal'at, Arabic for "stepping out," is etymologically derived from the root word for "rising." It has the feminine plural declension. *Tal'at*, then, means women rising, stepping out. Tal'at's slogan, "No free homeland without free women," articulated the intersectional understanding of liberation that had characterized Palestinian feminism for over a century, as it addresses the convergence of social and political liberation, a cohesive struggle for self-determination. And Tal'at's Indigenous feminism is expressed in their choice of the word "homeland" (*watan* in Arabic, not *bilad*, which translates as "country"), which asserts belonging while erasing the borders and fragmentation imposed by the colonizer. The slogan is also a clear rejection of the "first things first" approach of other postcolonial struggles, which prioritized national liberation and ultimately failed to tend to critical social issues that had been supposedly postponed till "later."

In their initial statements and press releases, Tal'at locate their feminism within contemporaneous revolutionary Arab feminisms such as the Lebanese and Iraqi, noting that women there were occupying squares, smashing banks, and agitating for the rights of Syrian and Palestinian refugees. They were looking at the immediate historical context of the Arab Spring uprisings around them, which women had been instrumental in mobilizing from Libya to Bahrain. They knew, as did most Arab feminists, that it was twenty-five-year-old Asmaa Mahfouz who had called on tens of thousands of Egyptians to take to the streets in the protest that launched that country's surge against President Hosni Mubarak. Had Tal'at looked a little further into the past, they would of course have mentioned Algeria's women, who were full participants in their country's national liberation struggle, or Egypt's feminists, many of whom assumed leadership roles during the 1919 revolution against the British, using nationalism to advance a feminist agenda. As a predominantly youth group, Tal'at's members had not experienced the First Intifada, led by women, but they had certainly heard about it and knew of the betrayal Palestinian women had experienced when that struggle was ended with the establishment of the Palestinian Authority.

Tal'at's analysis is grounded in the complex reality of life under occupation, the only life most of its young members had ever known, always pointing to the macro context of settler colonialism in their analysis of patriarchal violence. They write:

> Our movement is shaped by our lived experience of more than seven decades of Israeli settler-colonial violence. As a people, we are stripped of our most basic rights and needs while crippling our collective development and resistance. This reality compels us to analyze experiences of violence—in their varied forms—as social and political matters that must be dealt with at their root and collectively, as a society.[4]

Even as the group came together to protest femicide, the killing of Palestinian women by their male relatives, Tal'at explain that Israel is enabling Palestinian abuse. They point to the fact that inside the 1948 territories, police officers often return runaway Palestinian women to the very individuals they suspect are abusing these women, under the guise of "intra-community matters." And in the West Bank and Gaza Strip, they explain that the crushing weight of occupation creates the circumstances of domestic violence. Pointing to the systematic, engineered impoverishment of Palestinian society, they write: "This all culminates in a multilayered system of violence where power relations, in their gendered, economic, social and political forms, are intensified and reproduced, directly impact[ing] on intra-community social formations."[5]

All Forms of Violence

Young women posting on social media were not the only Palestinians being attacked by relatives who disapproved of their lifestyle. In July 2019, only weeks before Israa Ghrayeb's murder, a transgender Palestinian youth from Tamra, in northern Israel, was stabbed outside an LGBTQI+ shelter in Tel Aviv. The sixteen-year-old suffered serious chest and leg injuries, which necessitated surgery. As in Ghrayeb's case, a close relative—the teen's own brother—was the prime suspect.

Shortly after this attack, close to a thousand LGBTQI+ folks and allies held a protest rally in Tel Aviv under the banner "Fighting for Our Lives," denouncing violence against transgender individuals. Separately, some 200 queer Palestinians held another rally in Haifa. That protest was organized by alQaws, Aswat, and Adalah (the Legal Center for Arab Minority Rights in Israel), along with other allied queer groups. The flyers advertising the protest, as well as many of the signs carried there, were in Arabic, pointing to the need for Palestinian society to address these issues. Signs read "The stabbing of queers begins with the denial of their existence," as well as "Disrespecting trans people is also stabbing them"—both references to the stabbing of the transgender Palestinian youth by his own brother. But the analysis also included the Israeli occupation, with signs such as "Queers against normalization and pinkwashing," a direct reference to Zionist practices.

Following the protest, alQaws planned a series of discussions in various Palestinian communities throughout the West Bank, to break through the silence around homophobia and transphobia. The group also announced they would hold a "queer camp" at the end of August 2019 to provide a space for LGBTQI+ Palestinians to share their experiences. But the supposed "traditional values" reared their ugly head again, as the PA police spokesperson, Louai Irzeqat, issued a statement condemning the planned discussions and banning all events organized by alQaws, claiming the group's activities go against "traditional Palestinian values" and accusing its staff of being "foreign agents."[6] AlQaws were not intimidated, and they responded to the PA by suggesting their opponents focus on fighting the real threats to Palestinian society:

> We believe that the police and Palestinian society at large should focus on combatting the occupation and other forms of violence that tear apart the sensitive fabric of our society and values, instead of prosecuting activists who work tirelessly to end all forms of violence.[7]

The PA's policing of queer activism was part of its campaign to repress various rights-based organizations and movements, in order to appear as the sole and effective protector of Palestinian society, even as it continued to cater primarily to Israeli security concerns. Its ban on alQaws's activities also (inadvertently) played into Israel's pinkwashing propaganda, as Israel could now rightly claim that the PA officially rejects and bans all queer activism, thus helping make Israel appear to be the haven for gay Palestinians that country claimed to be. Palestinian feminists understood that, growing even more resentful of the PA. Falastine Saleh, a queer activist based in Ramallah, noted that "since its inception, Israel has been the number one oppressor of Palestinians of all political, sexual, and social backgrounds," before asking, "Doesn't the PA have more important things to worry about? Like … I don't know … maybe the Israeli occupation?"[8] By then, Palestinian discontent with the PA was pervasive across the West Bank, as the ironically named "authority" had proven utterly corrupt, inept, and fully subservient to Israel. A new sign began to appear at the West Bank protests: *Irhal*, meaning "Leave," the demand being made by the people rising against tyrants throughout the Arab world.

Duplicating the Master's Tools

By 2020, Mahmoud Abbas had become ever more servile to Israel: His term had expired in 2009, yet he was still president of the Palestinian Authority and remained confident he would not be effectively challenged by Israel so long as his government functioned as a subcontractor to the occupation. And subcontract it did. First and foremost, the PA coordinated with Israeli forces to "maintain order," which meant repressing popular rebellion against Israel's occupation. The PA's police force, financed as it was by the US and European Union, was primarily concerned with protecting Israel's security, not international law or human rights, even as Israel continued to illegally occupy the West Bank, expanding illegal settlements there, with Israeli occupation soldiers protecting the illegal settlers. And as with playing into Israel's hand by suppressing queer organizing and activism, subcontracting the occupation also helped Israel's image, as the occupying force which controlled the land, borders, economy, and infrastructure in the West Bank and Gaza Strip was not seen as the only power suppressing Palestinians. Abbas was wielding the master's tools, enjoying the trappings of nominal power, even though his own power was conditional upon subservience, and nefarious to his people. He had been "authorized" to control, not liberate.

Indeed, the PA was such a good student of Israel's repressive measures that Palestinian prisoners recall that when they were being tortured in Palestinian prisoners, their Palestinian guards switched to Hebrew as they barked orders at them.[9] Palestinian police had also learned Israeli security forces' dirty tricks. For example, PA officers started attacking Palestinian women for their opposition to the PA's assassination of Nizar Banat, an opponent of Abbas's corrupt regime. Banat, a vocal critic of the PA, had been arrested in his home on June 24, 2021, and pronounced dead only hours later, beaten to death by Palestinian security forces. When protests erupted after his murder, the PA arrested protestors using the same techniques as those of the Israeli army, which included intelligence gathering that relies on exploiting the details of private lives as bait to silence dissent. Specifically, the PA police officers arrested Palestinian women, stealing their mobile phones and threatening to publish their private messages and photos if they failed to comply with PA security demands—directly mimicking Israeli security officers' threats to out Palestinian queers, or anyone vulnerable to doxxing, by exposing their private messages.

Meanwhile, the PA's understanding of gender mainstreaming, a long-standing demand of feminist groups, was limited to its attempt to increase the number of women police officers from 5 to 10 percent of the force.[10] But greater representation of women in a corrupt, masculinist, violent, and quasi-mercenary institution does not feminize that institution. Indeed, the Israeli army, which proudly boast of its embrace of gay and trans soldiers, is a prime example of gender diversity at the service of a patriarchal master. And the PA was growing ever more violent in its attempt to subdue the Palestinian people it was meant to serve, even as they grew more discontent with life under a seemingly endless and unchallenged occupation. Little was done toward implementation of the 1994 Declaration of Principles on Palestinian Women's Rights, which calls for equality between men and women in all fields—political, civil, economic, social, and cultural—as well as a change in the Personal Status Law, which favored men over women. A more recent, 2011 draft code was similarly ignored. And gender violence was widespread, both within the household and in the streets—the latter primarily at checkpoints, where occupation soldiers humiliated women or prevented them from reaching medical facilities, even when pregnant and visibly in labor. A report cowritten by WCLAC and al-Muntada—the Palestinian NGO Forum to Combat Violence Against Women (a coalition of seventeen Palestinian women's and human rights groups) points specifically to the archaic legal system that offers women and girls little if any protection from gender-based violence—archaic by virtue of its being a relic of former powers that controlled the area, and which cannot be fully updated in the absence of a sovereign state's legislative body.[11] The report notes:

> Palestine has developed a unified draft Penal Code in 2011 which is still pending and was not yet passed. The current Penal laws that are in force are the Jordanian Penal Code No. (16) of 1960, and the Palestinian Penal Code No. (74) of 1936 in the Gaza Strip.[12]

The report also points the finger at prevailing patriarchal attitudes within Palestinian society, aggravated by the Israeli occupation, as it documents that femicides rise significantly during Israeli-imposed curfews and lockdowns. Specifically, in 2019, the report notes:

> 29 per cent of currently or ever married women in Palestine had experienced some form of violence (such as psychological, physical, sexual, social or economic violence) by their husbands in the past twelve months. The prevalence was significantly higher in Gaza (38 per cent) than in the West Bank (24 per cent).[13]

While femicides, just like rape, are globally underreported, with the former frequently being written off as suicide, the report points to an alarming proportion of female to male suicides in Palestine:

> In its 2018 report, WCLAC addressed this issue through analyzing the comparatives of some statistical reports. The Public Prosecution, for example, noted in its report of 2018 that the total number of attempted suicide and commission of suicide cases was (236); indicating that (196) cases were committed by "adults," while (37) cases were committed by children.

What is striking in these figures is that the rate of suicide or attempted suicides indicate much higher rates among females than among males.

> The percentage of females in the adults category was twice as high than males with 71 per cent versus 29 per cent. In the case of children, the percentage was even much higher among females than in males reaching to 95 per cent of the cases.[14]

These high rates also raise many questions about the motives behind committing or attempting suicide among females, and whether those were really "suicide" cases or, rather, "push to commit suicide"—meaning family pressures imposed on girls to kill themselves by forcing them to drink poison, hang themselves, throw themselves from the roof of their homes, and so on.

If these are indeed suicides, Palestine would be the only country in the world where more females than males commit suicide, begging the question as to why that is the case. If they are the result of a "push to commit suicide," one again must ask why women, even young girls, are pressured to end their lives.

Gaza

The entire Gaza Strip measures less than 1.5 percent of historic Palestine, and 80 percent of its inhabitants are refugees from other parts of the country. That in itself is violence. The influx of refugees, first in 1948, then again in 1967, has made it one of the most densely populated areas in the world, with multiple generations of dispossessed Palestinians living in dismal conditions in refugee camps, sometimes only a few kilometers from their ancestral village. Again, this is protracted violence. But Gaza was to be subjected to hitherto-unthinkable levels of savagery after Hamas started governing the territory following its victory in the 2006 elections, leading an enraged Israel to impose a strict blockade that deprived the Strip of food, medicine, hygiene products, utilities, and other basic necessities. Ironically, Israel had welcomed and supported the formation of Hamas in 1987, viewing it as a less significant threat to Zionism than Marxism, the dominant ideology of the other Palestinian political groups.

The 2006 elections were only the second since the Palestinian Authority had been formed in the wake of the Oslo Accords, and Hamas, the Islamic Resistance Movement that had formed during the First Intifada, offered an alternative to the utter moral bankruptcy and corruptness of Fatah, the political group that dominated the PA. First and foremost was the widespread popular resentment of the PA's failure to achieve any progress in peace negotiations, even though the Oslo Accords had stipulated Israeli withdrawal from the West Bank and Gaza Strip, with Palestinian self-governance as a first step toward the establishment of a Palestinian state. Instead, Israel's illegal settlements had expanded in both the West Bank and Gaza Strip, with Israel diverting natural resources to these and appropriating more Palestinian lands to build bypass roads for the settlers. In 2005, Israel "disengaged" from Gaza by removing all 9,000 Israeli settlers and the soldiers needed to protect them, as well as dismantling all twenty-one settlements, but was still occupying the territory, albeit without "boots on the ground," as it continued to have active control over its borders and air space. Then came the nepotism, corruption, and growing authoritarianism of Mahmoud Abbas, who demanded the Palestinian people's respect when he could not earn it, even as he was mocked by Israel and the US. The overall resentment was aggravated by the tanking economy, the lack of reliable basic services such as electricity, water, and internet, and the checkpoints that turned a simple errand into an unpredictable and risk-laden journey.

With its rigorous discipline, demonstrated commitment to serving the people, and defiant determination to free the homeland, Hamas offered a stark contrast. An offshoot of the Muslim Brotherhood, it initially focused on providing the social services that the government could not or would not provide. For example, as the Palestinian economy was collapsing, Hamas was assisting schools, hospitals, orphanages, and struggling families, as well as running social programs for youth. In Qalqiliya, where Hamas had won the June 2005 municipal elections, the Hamas city council paid off the city's debt, raised salaries, and worked on road repairs. Fatah, on the other hand, frequently delayed salary disbursement. With a leadership cadre of brilliant strategists, Hamas capitalized on the widespread Palestinian discontent with Fatah and the PA, the *irhal* sentiment Palestinians of all walks of life were feeling toward their nominal president. It ran a successful campaign downplaying its own agenda, which was somewhat more conservative than that of a significant proportion of the Palestinian people, and won the elections with nearly 78 percent of the 1.3 million eligible voters casting ballots. The so-called Quartet (US, Russia, UN, and EU) conditioned future foreign assistance to the PA on the new government's commitment to nonviolence, recognition of the State of Israel, and acceptance of previous agreements—conditions which Hamas rejected. PA

President Abbas, who was also chairman of Fatah, tried to form a unity government, but the long-festering feud between Hamas and Fatah erupted into open confrontation, following which Hamas took control of the Gaza Strip, while the PA's authority became limited to the West Bank, and even there, only to those areas over which the Oslo Accords granted it control. A new era had begun.

Hamas's victory in the 2006 elections was pyrrhic in many ways. It cemented the division between the West Bank and Gaza Strip, now under different Palestinian governments, thus aggravating the fragmentation of the Palestinian people and leading to extreme isolation of Palestinians in the Gaza Strip, which Israel soon subjected to a strict blockade, translating into a rapid deterioration of the living conditions of Palestinians there. And it established a strict Islamist rule, which reflected to some degree the people's growing religiosity, yet which many Palestinians bristled under, as they had hitherto lived a somewhat secular, if conservative, lifestyle.

Most discussions of the Gaza Strip in the Global North refer to that area as "Hamas ruled," as if that were illegal or criminal, when Hamas had won the 2006 legislative elections that third-party observers unanimously agreed were fair. And as with much of the Global North analysis of the region, the focus is on the micro level, rather than that macro level: the fact that while Gaza is internally ruled by Hamas, it is still occupied by Israel, still subjected to Israel's illegal control of its maritime, air, and land borders. And it is the illegal Israeli blockade of Gaza, not "Hamas rule," that impoverished the area, depriving its inhabitants of basic necessities and killing tens of thousands in four wars between 2008 and 2021.

In 2007, Israel blocked all entry and exit points into Gaza, restricting the delivery of fuel, medicine, and food, even limiting the fishing zone that would have allowed people to catch their dinner at sea. The blockade led to a significant impoverishment of the population: Between 2005 and 2022, the unemployment rate more than doubled to become one of the highest in the world, simultaneously leading to an increase in violence within the household. Basic food items became a luxury, as Israel limited food delivery trucks to a trickle compared to what Gaza needs. Daily life was severely impacted by the impossibility of repairing the buildings, schools, hospitals, factories, water desalination facilities, and other social infrastructure destroyed by the four wars Israel had so far waged on the blockaded strip. Tens of thousands of Palestinians had been injured during these wars, with limited to no access to adequate medical care. Consequently, patients who could have survived their injuries often died or lost a limb for lack of treatment. Cancer rates also rose as a result of exposure to hazardous chemicals, and patients could not leave the blockaded strip for treatment abroad.

With the restrictions on fishing, a region that once boasted a unique, spice-rich, fragrant cuisine became primarily vegetarian, not by choice. And while Palestinians overall are a tech-savvy people, if only out of necessity—especially in Gaza, where the internet is their only window to the world outside their blockaded enclave—they could not take on remote online jobs, as Israel only allowed sluggish 2G connections in Gaza. Within years of the blockade, it was commonplace to refer to Gaza as "the world's largest open-air prison." Less commonplace in mainstream discourse but widely accepted in the discourse of Palestinians and their allies was the term "genocide," with all the somber gravity of this crime against humanity. As early as 2010, Palestinian public intellectual Nadia Hijab, cofounder of al-Shabaka, the Palestinian Policy Network, had written an essay entitled "When Does It Become Genocide?" that concludes with the following ominous call to action:

> It is hard to conceive of a better description of what is going on in Gaza. All UN member states have the duty to prevent and stop acts of genocide. What is needed is a country brave enough to take the lead, before it is too late.[15]

From Pain to Hope

Twelve years into the blockade of Gaza, and within mere months of the formation of Tal'at, the COVID-19 pandemic reached Palestine, further aggravating the critical situation in the occupied territories.

Palestinians found themselves defenseless against the pandemic, as Israel continued to control all of Palestine's borders, denying them lifesaving vaccines while potentially infected Israeli soldiers and settlers continued to come and go in the West Bank. Meanwhile, the blockaded Gaza Strip, infamous as one of the most densely populated areas in the world, was a petri dish of infection. By December 2020, Israel was hailed as the country that had to date achieved the highest vaccination coverage in proportion to its population size, even as it still denied vaccines to Palestinians in the West Bank and Gaza Strip. Human rights organizations and global medical NGOs described Israel's policies as "medical apartheid," an egregious continuation of Israel's violation of international law mandating that it provide for the welfare of people under its occupation.[16] By the summer of 2021, Israel offered the Palestinian Ministry of Health a vaccine swap deal, whereby Israel would give some vaccines to the West Bank and receive an equal number of vaccines from the PA at a later date, when the PA received vaccines from the Pfizer company. The Palestinian Ministry of Health refused the deal, as the vaccines Israel was offering were so close to expiration that they could not all have been administered before they expired. And still that country was hailed in the West as a beacon of democracy.

The Palestinian people had no one to turn to. By then, Donald Trump had been elected US president, and on January 28, 2020, he announced a plan he entitled "Peace to Prosperity," drafted by his son-in-law Jared Kushner, who lacked any diplomatic experience but had deep business and personal ties with Israel, including Israel's Prime Minister Benjamin Netanyahu. The plan, formulated without any consultation with Palestinians, completely favored Israel, allowing it de facto control over East Jerusalem and parts of the West Bank. Trump also stated that the settlements, which violate international law, were not illegal, and he put conditions on the Palestinian refugees' right of return, even though this right is recognized under international law. Prior to that, in 2018, he had moved the US embassy to Jerusalem, thus reversing decades of US policy, which had kept the US embassy in Tel Aviv in compliance with the international consensus that Jerusalem's status should be resolved through negotiations between Israelis and Palestinians. Even PA President Mahmoud Abbas, Israel's subcontractor in the West Bank, rejected the plan, declaring he would not be known as the man who sold Jerusalem.[17]

Palestinians knew they had to continue building the alternative society they hoped to live in, which no politician, no human rights organization, would offer them. And once again, Palestinian feminists—Palestinian queer feminists, to be precise—took the lead. In July 2020, Tal'at joined alQaws and Aswat as Palestinian queers and their allies took to the streets to chant for freedom from violence, with a slogan that expressed their determination to change society, to recenter joy and loving: *Min al-alam ila al-amal*, meaning "From pain to hope." The rally, organized as "a rallying cry for queer liberation," was an opening for marginalized Palestinians to rage against the many factors of oppression they endured from their own society, as well as due to life under settler colonialism and occupation.[18] Palestinian queers' insistence on rising above the arbitrary colonial borders between Palestinian areas colonized in 1948 and those colonized in 1967, and the divisions further imposed between the latter that fragmented the homeland into the Gaza Strip, the West Bank, and 1948 Israel, is seen by feminist analysts as the foundation of the May 2021 Unity Intifada, which saw Palestinians rise up across the historic homeland, and our Diaspora, against home demolitions and land theft in Jerusalem.

AlQaws wrote in a press release:

> We rage against the patriarchal violence exerted on our bodies in our streets and in our homes. We rage against structures of familial control over our desires and gender expression. We rage against the oppressive norms that dictate our collective shame around gender and sexuality. We rage against our marginalization and erasure by colonial narratives. In doing so, we raise the rallying cry for our own liberation—and the liberation of all Palestinians.

Prior to these protests, Tal'at had allied itself with alQaws and Aswat to include queer experiences in its analysis of violence and liberation, and to denounce the prioritization of "geographical liberation," explaining that it evolved to challenge this reality by asserting that "our liberation struggle must be based on centering the experiences of those socially, politically and economically marginalized and by practicing active solidarity with all those who endure the savagery of the current system."[19] Tal'at's defiance, its youthful energy, and its encompassing analysis mobilized Palestinian feminists around the globe and, along with the Palestinian Youth Movement, was the direct impetus behind the formation, in North America, of the Palestinian Feminist Collective, officially launched in March 2021.

The Palestinian Feminist Collective

Unlike Tal'at, which came together out of emergency, the formation of the Palestinian Feminist Collective (PFC) was anything but spontaneous, as its founding members diligently pondered who to invite to join the collective and carefully debated the nuances of every word in the "pledge" it circulated as its calling card, aware that they were crafting a new yet critically needed vocabulary in hostile territory.[20] For while most Diaspora Palestinians living in settler countries on Turtle Island think of ourselves as "in the belly of the beast," we are, in fact, also in the brain of the monster, where the discourse on Israel is forged by propaganda experts and imposed on North American journalists and academics with greater pressure than in Israel itself. The North American terrain, then, was where discursive change had to take place, before policies could translate into improved circumstances on the ground.

In true collective spirit, the PFC members are not named, preferring to speak as a chorus, as they explain:

> We are an intergenerational collective of activists, organizers, practitioners, creators, thinkers, artists, scholars, healers, water and land protectors, life-givers, and life-sustainers. We are committed to achieving Palestinian social and political liberation by confronting

systemic gendered, sexual, and colonial violence, oppression, and dispossession.[21]

The "pledge," a call to solidarity, is worth reprinting in its entirety:

> This Women's History Month, we, the undersigned, join the Palestinian Feminist Collective, a U.S. based network of Palestinian and Arab women and feminists, in affirming Palestine as a feminist issue. Alongside the PFC, we build upon the history of Palestinian women and their co-strugglers who have worked to end multiple forms of oppression. We reject all appropriations of feminist and queer rights discourses that are used to dehumanize Palestinians, justify ongoing Zionist settler-colonization of their homeland, and repress their political activism. In doing so, we commit to resisting gendered and sexual violence, settler colonialism, capitalist exploitation, land degradation and oppression in Palestine, on Turtle Island, and globally.
>
> For decades, Palestinian feminists have resisted Israel's masculinist and militarized siege of Palestinian land and life. Since its inception, the Zionist settler colonial project has hinged on the expulsion of Palestinians from their homes and land, creating generations of landless Palestinian refugees. Zionist violence continues to dominate Palestinian lives in intimate ways. Throughout the homeland, Israel demolishes Palestinian homes, subjects Palestinian prisoners of conscience to systematic sexual and physical abuse and torture, and polices Palestinian bodies, sexualities, reproductive rights, and family life. Palestinians continue to affirm life in the face of the enduring Nakba (catastrophe) which takes place through deadly closure in the Gaza Strip, military occupation in the West Bank, legal designations of second-class citizenship in the settler state, exile in refugee camps and across the shatat (global diaspora), and denial of the right to return home.
>
> We uphold the legacies of solidarity between Palestinian, Black, Indigenous, Third World feminist, working class, and queer communities who have struggled side-by-side within larger anti-colonial, anti-capitalist, and anti-racist movements in the US and globally. This stands in contrast to liberal feminist traditions in the U.S.

that continue to weaponize feminist discourses against Palestinians and other marginalized communities by failing to confront the structural forms of gendered and sexual violence inherent to settler/colonialism, imperialist wars, racial capitalism, and global white supremacy. Liberal and Zionist feminisms rely on Orientalist discourses to silence and undermine the collective aspirations of Palestinian women and their co-strugglers, contributing to intensified political repression that criminalizes free speech on Palestine and Palestinian liberation.

In the interest of advancing *a truly intersectional and decolonial feminist vision* for the United States, Palestine and our world, we hereby pledge to:

1. Embrace and advocate for Palestinian liberation as a critical feminist issue;
2. Support Palestinian rights to free speech and political organizing everywhere;
3. Reject the conflation of anti-Zionism with anti-Semitism, in particular the legal enforcement of the International Holocaust Remembrance Alliance's (IHRA) definition of anti-Semitism;
4. Heed the call of Palestinian civil society for Boycott, Divestment, and Sanctions;
5. Divest from militarism and invest in justice and community on Turtle Island;
6. Call for an end to US political, military, and economic support to Israel, and to all military, security, and policing collaborations.

Our commitment to the liberation of Palestinian lands and people is rooted in love, which is at the heart of all projects of decolonization. Our values grow out of embodied cultural wisdom and justice to transform our communities. We are committed to ending the greed, domination, and fragmentation so deeply entrenched in capitalism, colonial extraction, and US empire. We are re-imagining and re-creating a world free from systems of gendered, racial and economic exploitation that commodify human life and land. Ours is a vision for a radically different future based on life-affirming interconnectedness, empowering the working classes, and love for

> each other, land, life and the planet itself. For these reasons, *we pledge, today and everyday, to recognize Palestine as a Feminist Issue* and to uphold this commitment in our daily lives and organizing praxis.[22]

The pledge was published on March 15, 2021, to mark International Women's Month, asking allies to adopt Palestinian liberation as a critical feminist issue. The pledge very rapidly garnered hundreds of individual signatures: over 2,700 in under forty-eight hours, and over 150 organizational endorsements within that same time period. The signatures rushed in from North America, where the pledge was launched, as well as Palestine, but also, within what felt like minutes, from numerous other countries including Australia, Argentina, Kenya, South Africa, Sweden, Germany, Ireland, Brazil, the Czech Republic ... Clearly the Palestinian feminist call was resonating with people around the globe, even as global powers remained staunchly on the side of the oppressor.

The pledge opens with a recognition of "the history of Palestinian women and their co-strugglers who have worked to end multiple forms of oppression," before asking endorsers to commit to six concrete steps and commitments. The pledge, then, called upon progressives to act, and organize, rather than pay lip service to Palestinian liberation. As it was posted on the social media account of the Palestinian Youth Movement, which cofounded the PFC, the pledge catalyzed many important discussions about the struggle of Palestinian women, and the term "feminism" itself.

The debate around the term "feminism" is understandable considering that one impetus for the pledge, as explained in a Palestinian Youth Movement moderator's comment, is mainstream Western feminism's utter disregard for the plight of the Palestinian people generally, including Palestinian women, and queers, whose lives are intimately impacted by Zionism. This is articulated in the pledge itself and has been amply documented for decades. As a Palestinian feminist organizer on Turtle Island myself, I have experienced many of the challenges Diaspora Palestinian activists and our allies have faced as we have engaged with other feminists and "progressives" in the Global North—groups and individuals we thought would have appreciated the intersections with our circumstances, but who nevertheless failed to recognize the plight of the Palestinians as a gross injustice and a violation of a people's human rights.[23] I have also argued that the greater oppressors of Palestinian women are Israel and Zionism, rather than Palestinian men, since it is Israel, not Palestinian men, who denies Palestinian women their freedom of movement, their right to an education, their right to live anywhere they want in their homeland. It is Israel, the illegal occupying power, not Palestinian men and Palestinian patriarchy, who denies Palestinian women reproductive justice, access to medical treatment, even access to sufficient food and clean water.[24]

Nevertheless, in the US as in many Western countries, Palestinian feminists and their allies remained marginalized from mainstream feminism, with its normalization of Zionism, revealing a willful blindness to the macro environment of state violence. This was evident with the 2017 Women's March, a large national coalition that came together to protest the election of Donald Trump out of a justified fear that his administration would severely curtail women's and queer rights. Palestinian American antiracist organizer Linda Sarsour, one of the leaders of the march, addressed the large crowd in Washington, DC, as a "proudly Muslim American, proudly Palestinian American," explaining to the millions who were listening that what they were protesting on that day, namely Trump's racist and sexist agenda, had been her community's lived experience for many years. Sarsour openly supported and promoted the Boycott, Divestment, and Sanctions movement to hold Israel accountable for its crimes and was an outspoken critic of that country, arguing that one cannot be progressive on all issues except for Palestine. Not surprisingly, she was accused of antisemitism because of her criticism of Israel and eventually had to step down from the leadership of the Women's March. Sarsour's experience is only one of hundreds of thousands of such incidents where, when Palestinians and their allies refuse to normalize Zionism and insist that it is incompatible with feminism, they find themselves alienated and pushed out of liberal "feminist" spaces.

Ultimately, even though this may not have been its intention, the PFC pledge was about reclaiming, not redefining, the term "feminism," as Palestinians and our allies affirm, yet again, that one cannot be a feminist while supporting gendered violence, settler colonialism, Indigenous dispossession, and apartheid. Unlike what detractors have posted, feminism is not only "compatible" with Palestinian culture; it has long characterized Palestinian women's struggles.

Demanding a New Analysis

With its insistence that Palestine is a feminist issue, the Palestinian Feminist Collective went against decades of Zionist propaganda, and the Global North colonial feminism that upheld it while looking away from Palestinian women's circumstances.

The PFC analysis foregrounds Zionist settler colonialism as inherently a project of gendered and sexual violence. It explains that since Israel views Palestinians as a "demographic threat," it has always sought to control Palestinian life and life-giving. Hence it is important to understand the long history of Zionist rape and sexual assault of Palestinians, from the onset of our dispossession to the present—not as anomalies, a few bad apples or the actions of undisciplined fighters, but as state-sanctioned policies foundational to settler colonialism. This explains the rapes committed by Zionist militias in 1948 to terrorize the defenseless Palestinians into leaving their villages: They were campaigns of sexual violence and sexual terrorism, in the service of ethnic cleansing. It explains the sexualized torture, rape, or threats of rape of Palestinian prisoners, a long-standing practice the extent of which is only now coming to light, even as Palestinians themselves have always been aware of it, as evidenced by the currency of the expression *al-ard qabla al-'ard*, or "land before honor." It explains the fact that Israeli Knesset members believe Palestinian women should be killed because they give birth to Palestinian babies. In 2014, for example, then–Israeli Justice Minister Ayelet Shaked posted on social media a quote from Israeli writer Uri Elitzur calling for the wholesale killing of all Palestinians, including "the mothers of martyrs," as war strategy:

> Behind every terrorist stand dozens of men and women, without whom he could not engage in terrorism. They are all enemy combatants, and their blood shall be on all their heads. Now this also includes the mothers of the martyrs, who send them to hell with flowers and kisses. They should follow their sons, nothing would be more just. They should go, as should the physical homes in which they raised the snakes. Otherwise, more little snakes will be raised there.[25]

And of course it explains the amply documented sexual abuse and rape of Palestinian prisoners—men, women, and children—in Israeli prisons, discussed further in the next chapter. However, none of this explains why Western feminists refuse to see Zionism as incompatible with feminism. Yet, as PFC member Loubna Qutami put it,

> When Palestinians (men and women and gender non-conforming peoples) experience sexualized torture, rape, castration under interrogation—certainly that is a human rights violation; but it is also gendered and sexual assault. Thus Palestinian liberation must certainly be embraced by anyone who believes they are a feminist, otherwise feminism is hollow of any attention to material realities.[26]

In the North American context where few actually know Palestine and its struggles, and where we are primarily defined by language—the Orientalist, racist language of the mainstream discourse and media—semantics are important, and the discussions of Palestinian, Indigenous, and Third World feminism as a liberatory practice were not "strictly academic." But the PFC's vision went beyond semantics, beyond reclaiming the term "feminism" and exposing the bankruptcy of imperial feminism, into cross-movement building and organizing. Thus it was important for the PFC to explain that because Palestine is a feminist issue and gender violence is an inherent part of Zionism, anyone claiming to be a feminist should organize for Palestinian liberation.

Many of the founding members of the collective were seasoned organizers with a solid transnational anticolonial analysis, and they immediately set to work at cross-movement building with potential allies in labor, health care, abolitionist, and other progressive causes. In June 2021, with an update that August, the PFC published *Freedom Within Reach*, an action toolkit with a wealth of useful resources, pointing to actions supporters can take, groups they can ally with, talking points they can use in discussions about Palestine. The toolkit offers

> resources to empower us all to continue to mobilize, to speak out, to take action, to fight back against repression campaigns, to center Palestinian voices, and to shift the narrative toward achieving Palestinian liberation. Our goal is ultimately to end international state and institutional complicity in Palestinian subjugation and to highlight the lessons that Palestinians can teach us in this moment.[27]

There was much work to be done, and the Palestinian Feminist Collective was ready.

9

Genocide Is a Feminist Issue

> *We bear witness to the reproductive genocide taking place in Palestine by the Israeli regime. We bear witness to traumatized mothers who have to deliver their babies without anesthesia, with doctors using the flashlights of their phones to conduct the operations due to being cut off from electricity by the occupation forces ... We see women having miscarriages, stillbirths, and early deliveries as a result of stress, trauma, and fear, and babies prematurely dying after birth due to the lack of fuel and electricity necessary to maintain their incubators.*
>
> —Palestinian Feminist Collective, "Pledge That Palestine Is a Feminist Issue," 2021

At dawn on October 7, 2023, Hamas fighters fired a powerful barrage of rockets into southern Israel, creating a cover for militants to breach a section of the high-tech border fence that had been strangulating the Gaza Strip for over sixteen years. Over two thousand Hamas fighters entered Israel on foot, on motorcycles, in a tank, even using paragliders. They were followed by a second wave of several hundred Palestinian civilians, who took the opportunity to walk into Israel for the first time since they had been imprisoned in the Gaza enclave for sixteen years. Hamas and the Palestinian civilians attacked the residents of two kibbutzim as well as concert-goers at a nearby rave. Hamas militants also kidnapped 251 Israelis and foreign nationals residing in Israel, taking them hostage back to Gaza, in hopes of negotiating a Palestinian prisoner release. The fighting between Hamas and Israeli soldiers lasted into the night, and by the time the Palestinian militants had returned to Gaza, an estimated 1,195 Israelis had been killed and another 3,000 injured, some by their own military. Determining an exact figure for the number of Hamas fighters and other Palestinians killed that day is challenging, with estimates ranging from 500 to 1,000. Israel's response to the breach was swift and, as always, indiscriminate and disproportionate. In fact, by October 8, 2023, Israel was turning the Gaza Strip from an open-air prison into an extermination camp.[1]

After fifty-six years of occupation, including the sixteen years of siege during which Israel had waged four major military assaults on Gaza, killing thousands of Palestinians, no mental contortionist could convincingly argue that the attack was unprovoked. Still, many supposed pundits tried. Chronology and context never mattered to Zionists when it came to blaming Hamas, or any Palestinian, for any violence in historic Palestine: To them, Israeli actions are always "responses," never offenses. The Zionist starting point is always the latest act of Palestinian resistance, not what Palestinians are resisting. Still, the scope of the Hamas attack was certainly unprecedented and sent Israel and Zionists reeling. By then, Hamas had been thoroughly vilified in the West, and stories about the atrocities inflicted by Hamas fighters on Israelis circulated like wildfire, unquestioned in the Western media. Yossi Landau, a senior medical official with ZAKA, an Israeli volunteer civilian emergency search and rescue organization, told American media he had personally seen Israeli children and adults beheaded by Hamas fighters in Kfar Aza kibbutz, and that at one point he had carried the headless corpses of three babies in his own arms. Landau added that he saw a pregnant woman whose fetus had been pulled out of her, giving the precise address: "Unit 426" in an apartment complex in one of the kibbutzim: "It was full of blood," he said. "When we turned her over, we saw that the abdomen was open. A knife was next to her, and we saw the fetus attached by the umbilical cord, and she had been shot from behind."[2]

Israeli military spokesperson Libby Weiss also told US media outlets that Israeli soldiers arriving on the scene reported finding "beheaded children of varying ages, ranging from babies to slightly older children," as well as adults who had been dismembered.[3] In the US, hundreds of influential entertainment industry figures, from Amy Schumer to Jerry Seinfeld, signed an open letter condemning the attack, with many using their social platforms to repeat the accusations against Hamas, frequently embellishing them with even more gruesome details. *Stranger Things* actor Noah Schnapp, for example, posted on Instagram to his 25 million followers: "40 babies beheaded and burned alive in front of their parents by Hamas."[4] Not to be outdone, at a meeting with leaders of US Jewish organizations at the White House, then–US President Joe Biden said, "I've been doing this a long time. I never really thought that I would see, have confirmed pictures of terrorists beheading children."[5] "Confirmed pictures" means photographs that have been verified by photo forensic experts as authentic and unadulterated.

The claims were unfounded. Within hours, official Israeli spokespeople were denying them, saying not one single baby had been beheaded, even though some had been killed in the fighting. As to the video of the eviscerated pregnant woman, it was found to have been produced by a Mexican cartel in 2018.[6] Landau must have watched it, or merely heard about it at some point, and thought it appropriate to claim he actually witnessed the atrocity, committed by Hamas fighters on that fateful October day. Or maybe he had some vague recollection of the stories of the evisceration, by Zionist fighters, of pregnant Palestinian women during the 1948 massacres and decided they were so horrible he should blame a similar crime on Hamas.

It is said every accusation is a confession.

The White House also retracted Biden's statement, saying, "The president based his comments about the alleged atrocities on the claims from Netanyahu's spokesman and media reports from Israel." Biden himself, however, never walked back his statement and in fact repeated the accusations at a reelection campaign rally in December 2023, as he stated:

> I saw some of the photographs when I was there—tying a mother and her daughter together on a rope and then pouring kerosene on them and then burning them, beheading infants, doing things that are just inhuman—totally, completely inhuman.[7]

Biden clearly did not care that the allegations had been denied, the accusers discredited, the existence of the photos retracted, or the fact that the reports of the horrors he was citing had been disavowed by the Israeli government itself: A disconnect from reality is an essential aspect of being an Israel apologist, and Biden is an avowed Zionist.

Along with the beheading of babies, another set of nightmarish allegations was circulating: that Hamas militants had raped Israeli women and girls. The primary source for these allegations was also the ZAKA organization, whose spokesperson, Yossi Landau, was proven to have lied about seeing forty beheaded babies and an eviscerated pregnant woman, yet the rape allegations were taken at face value in the Global North. And even when ZAKA volunteer Chaim Otzmagin, the other "witness" to the supposed atrocities, also retracted his own claim of having seen what he had described as evidence of rape, no Israeli official denied the sexual assault allegations.[8]

It is said every accusation is a confession.

Sexual violence is almost always present in situations of armed conflict, and some instances of rape are indeed likely to have taken place on October 7, 2023. It is also the case that depicting one's perceived enemy as a sexual predator is a long-standing strategy to distract from, or justify, one's own violence. This is all the more true across racial lines, where the oversexualized "predator" is viewed as violating sexual, racial, and national lines, rendering the alleged crime even more heinous and necessitating a collective response from the violated community. And in the context of Hamas and Israel, the rape accusations carried within them the deep-seated racism that had earlier characterized the rape accusations in the segregated US South—Blacks were threatening white purity and had to be lynched. Here, the accusation was that Hamas fighters—Muslim, bearded, Arab men, "diabolical," as some reports called them—had raped Jewish women, sullied the bearers of God's chosen people. The rape allegations were thus weaponized to justify the ferocity of Israel's assault.

Worse yet, on December 28, 2023, the *New York Times* published "Screams Without Words," an article the newspaper's editors claim was a thorough investigation into the October 7 attacks, which argues that Hamas militants had engaged in a "systematic pattern" of gang rape, assault, and mutilation of Israeli women. The editors also claimed that the reporters had interviewed 150 people, including witnesses, medical personnel, soldiers, and rape counselors, before writing the article. Yet as with the stories of the beheaded babies, within days, the veracity of the claim of a "systematic pattern of gang rapes" masterminded by Hamas leaders and perpetrated by Hamas militants—as distinct from possible individual opportunistic instances of sexual assault—was questioned by journalism experts. Within weeks, over sixty media experts were denouncing the shoddy journalism of the writers of "Screams Without Words," as they made their assertions while failing to produce a single shred of evidence, without finding a single survivor, and without fact-checking any of the secondhand reports they had heard. But the rape allegations did not go away, as they provided Zionists with the venom they needed to justify Israel's accelerated genocide of the Palestinian people in the Gaza Strip.

As if there could ever be any justification for genocide.

And even though no true feminist ever denied that isolated cases of rape may have occurred on October 7, 2023, numerous high-profile Zionists expressed outrage at the fact that the allegations of a "systematic pattern of gang rapes" were being questioned. In a video message to an Israeli-led assembly at the United Nations, former US presidential candidate Hillary Clinton said, "It is outrageous that some who claim to stand for justice are closing their eyes and their hearts to the victims of Hamas." Similarly, author and technology executive Sheryl Sandberg, addressing the same assembly at the UN headquarters in New York, slammed the organization for its silence on the alleged rapes. Sandberg also wrote a column in which she argued that the silence on the alleged mass rapes "is deafening," urging her readers to "denounce these rapes in every conversation, at every rally, and on signs held on every street corner." Gilad Erdan, the Israeli ambassador to the UN, repeated the accusation: "These were not sick, spur of the moment decisions to mutilate Israeli women and girls," Erdan said. "This was premeditated, this was planned, this was instructed."[9] Kamala Harris, who was US vice president at the time, volunteered that "in the days after October 7," she had seen "images of bloodied Israeli women abducted. Then it came to light that Hamas committed rape and gang rape at the Nova Music Festival."[10] Essayist and poet Katha Pollitt also described the response to the gang rape allegations as a "deafening silence."[11] "#MeToo Except if you're a Jew" trended on social media, alleging that Jewish Israeli rape victims were not being believed—even though none had actually come forward. Even if one were to believe the Zionist assertion that every single Israeli rape victim had been killed, no autopsy of any woman suspected of having been assaulted revealed that such a crime had been committed.

Israel's Record, 1948–Present

Importantly, the United Nations, which Clinton and Sandberg were taking to task, had offered to conduct an investigation into the alleged rapes by Hamas. Israel declined, as that offer included the UN looking into alleged sexual atrocities committed by Israeli guards in Israeli prisons—a condition Israel rejected. Yet these atrocities, the Israeli state–sanctioned sexual torture of Palestinians, were no mere allegations: Many had been entered into official records dating back to the very foundation of the Zionist state. And the hordes of Zionists who decried the questioning of allegations of mass gang rapes by Hamas militants of Israeli women had nothing to say about the amply documented reports of Israeli soldiers and police officers' rape of Palestinian men, women, and children. For example, none of the Zionist feminists spoke out against the gang rape by Israeli soldiers of a blindfolded, handcuffed Palestinian prisoner, which had been caught on tape and leaked on the internet—a documented instance, not an allegation. Israelis were outraged at the leak, not at the monstrous act, and the whistleblower was imprisoned, while the rapists became popular heroes. None denounced the numerous social media posts by Israeli soldiers displaying Palestinian women's intimate wear as trophies, after destroying their house—a clear act of sexual violence that would undoubtedly have been understood as a moral violation if perpetrated by anyone else. None expressed either horror or sympathy at the fact that Palestinian women were giving birth in unsanitary conditions, without anesthesia, and that newborn babies were dying for lack of prenatal care.

For Palestinians, it was not a question of being believed: The veracity of our horror stories was not in question, while the genocide was livestreamed into people's living rooms and onto their cell phones around the globe. News of babies decomposing in incubators had made global headlines, as had the kidnapping and execution of medical staff, and the fact that hospitals were being directly targeted. Rather, it was a matter of whether the world *cared* about Palestinian misery, Palestinian torture. Scores of Palestinian survivors had overcome the greatest violations of their body and spirit to come forward and talk about their rape. The stories were absolutely horrifying: Prisoners were being sodomized with rifles, with hot iron rods, bottles, broom sticks, even with trained dogs. Many were gang raped daily, over many days. Many did not survive their assault, but the autopsies told their stories. Again, these were not mere allegations; they were documented facts.[12] Israeli prisons, as novelist susan abulhawa described them, had turned into "sexual torture camps."[13]

Moreover, the sexual abuse of Palestinians had been taking place for decades because, as a settler colonial ideology, Zionism has always relied on sexual violence in its ethnic cleansing of Palestine. In her extensive research on violence against women in conflict zones, Palestinian scholar Nadera Shalhoub-Kevorkian has examined the "severe effect of militarization and violence on women's everyday lives, their bodies and survival strategies."[14] She has interviewed many Palestinian families who said they fled their homes in 1948 out of fear of rape—offenses committed by Zionist fighters as part of efforts to terrorize Palestinians into leaving. Indeed, many towns and villages were thus ethnically cleansed before May 15, 1948.

Israeli historian Benny Morris also lists numerous acts of rape of Palestinian women by Zionist forces throughout 1948. He writes:

> In Acre four soldiers raped a girl and murdered her and her father. In Jaffa, soldiers of the Kiryati Brigade raped one girl and tried to rape several more. At Hunin, which is in the Galilee, two girls were raped and then murdered. There were one or two cases of rape at Tantura, south of Haifa. There was one case of rape at Qula, in the center of the country. At the village of Abu Shusha, near Kibbutz Gezer [in the Ramle area] there were four female prisoners, one of whom was raped a number of times. And there were other cases. Usually more than one soldier was involved. Usually there were one or two Palestinian girls. In a large proportion of the cases the event ended with murder. Because neither the victims nor the rapists liked to report these events, we have to assume that the dozen cases of rape that were reported, which I found, are not the whole story. They are just the tip of the iceberg.[15]

Another of the early documented instances of Israeli state-sanctioned sexual violence happened in 1949, when a platoon of Israeli soldiers kidnapped a young Bedouin girl, described as "in her mid-teens." When their commanding officer gave them the choice between using her as kitchen staff or a sex slave, they opted for the latter. They cut her hair and washed it with kerosene, so she would be "clean for f–ing," then gang raped her so violently that on the next morning the officer in charge, Second Lieutenant Moshe, "saw fit to remove her from the world."[16] Moshe entered the incident in his log, as did Israel's first prime minister, David Ben-Gurion, whose diary contains many other reports of the rape and gang rape of Palestinian women and girls in 1948 and 1949. These reports, many of which go into graphic details, are cited in many Palestinian and Israeli historians' scholarship.

While it is safe to assume that there were many instances of rape that were not reported, there is also evidence that government officials were quite aware of the fact that Israeli soldiers were engaging in sexual assault. Aharon Zisling, Israel's agriculture minister in 1948, declared in a Knesset meeting that he deemed the rape of Palestinians acceptable. "Let us say that instances of rape occurred in Ramle. I can forgive instances of rape, but I will not forgive other acts," Zisling is quoted as saying in minutes of a July 1948 meeting that were disclosed due to a technical glitch.[17] Israeli sources are thus replete with details of the sexual violence Israeli forces committed against Palestinians throughout the inception of the Zionist state. The veracity of the many reports of rape is not in question.

A Long Record of Abuses

Nor were these rapes just a "phase" the new country was going through. Rather, they are a permanent feature of the state. Settler colonialism necessitates the destruction of the Indigenous family, and the pulverization of communal bonds—a devastation wrought through sexual violence, which became policy. It is not mere coincidence that rape was pervasive in the residential schools on Turtle Island, for example; it was the colonizer's weapon of choice to "kill the Indian" after having stolen the land. In Israel, reports by various human rights groups show the continuity of officially sanctioned torture, frequently sexual, by Israeli soldiers and police officers of Palestinian civilians rounded up for administrative detention, from 1948 into the present. By September 2008, Amnesty International submitted a report to the International Committee Against Torture documenting the pervasiveness of torture and sexual assault of Palestinian men, women, and children in Israeli prisons.[18] A few years later, in April 2021, Human Rights Watch published a report, *A Threshold Crossed: Israeli Authorities and the Crimes of Apartheid and Persecution*, averring that Israel is engaging in the crime of apartheid and making "excessive use of torture" of Palestinians in administrative detention.[19] In November 2023, Amnesty International published another report, *Horrifying Cases of Torture and Degrading Treatment of Palestinian Prisoners*, on the same topic.[20] In August 2024, Israeli human rights organization B'Tselem published a report, *Welcome to Hell: The Israeli Prison System as a Network of Torture Camps*, documenting some of the torture, including sexual violence and gang rape, of Palestinians in Israeli prisons.[21] As the report makes clear, rape, or the threat of rape, is often used during interrogation to coerce Palestinians to confess to crimes they did not commit.

It is said every accusation is a confession.

Israel's dirty secret was out, and there could no longer be any denying that Israeli gender violence against Palestinians is rampant, especially throughout its prison system. As Khitam Saafin, president of the Union of Palestinian Women's Committees, who spent three months in administrative detention, put it: "It's not something that's done by an individual soldier who decided to humiliate or mistreat [the prisoners], it's part of the process, part of the policy, in order to affect the entire society and put it under pressure." A female soldier is supposed to be present during interrogation, but that is not always the case. Besides, female Israeli soldiers are no less violent than their male counterparts and often feel they have to gain the "respect" of their male counterparts by being overtly violent. The Jerusalem Fund for Education and Community Development, a US-based nonprofit organization focused on education and policy analysis, notes that the

> sexual harassment and violence against Palestinian women is tactically used as institutionalized maltreatment by the Israeli regime. Although women face the brunt of this systematic treatment, Palestinian men are similarly humiliated in a sexualized way in efforts to break up and traumatize families.[22]

Indeed, in the aftermath of October 7, 2023, reports started coming out of the rape of Palestinian men, many of whom were coming forward with their experiences, overcoming all social taboos to denounce the cruelty they had been subjected to. And it was also becoming public knowledge that some never survived the sexual violence. On November 17, 2024, for example, reports emerged that Dr. Adnan al-Bursh, head of orthopedic surgery at Gaza's al-Shifa hospital, had been raped to death.[23] He and other doctors, nurses, and medical staff had been working at al-Awda Hospital in northern Gaza when they were rounded up and taken away by Israeli soldiers for "national security reasons." From there, Dr. al-Bursh was transferred to Sde Teiman detention camp. Four months later, al-Bursh was dragged and dumped into the prison yard, naked from the waist down, bleeding, unable to stand. He died moments later. He had been gang raped to death by Israeli soldiers.

Al-Bursh was one of the over three hundred medical staff arrested in Gaza since October 7. Many of them have reported cruel treatment, torture, and sexual violence, including rape. A Human Rights Watch report published on August 26, 2024, details some of the abuse they endured, including a detainee who was "bleeding from his bottom" as "three soldiers took turns raping him with an M16 [assault rifle]."[24] A March 2025 report by the UN noted: "Israel has increasingly employed sexual, reproductive and other forms of gender-based violence against Palestinians as part of a broader effort to undermine their right to self-determination."[25] Also in March 2025, the Independent International Commission of Inquiry on the Occupied Palestinian Territory, including East Jerusalem, and Israel, published *More Than a Human Can Bear*, a report examining "the sharp increase in sexual and gender-based violence perpetrated by members of the Israeli Security Forces and settlers online and in person across the Occupied Palestinian Territory, including rape and other forms of sexual violence."[26] The report also examines "how sexual and gender-based violence has taken different forms when committed against male and female members of the Palestinian community in order to dominate, oppress and destroy the Palestinian people in whole or in part." To be sure, this is a direct reference to the UN definition of genocide, which states that "deliberately inflicting on [a] group conditions of life calculated to bring about its physical destruction in whole or in part" is a defining criterion of this crime against humanity. There could be no more doubt about the fact that Israel was using rape as a weapon of genocide.

Shut Down Colonial Feminism

Israel's sexual violence was only one facet of its savagery after October 7, 2023. The manufactured famine was another, made even more criminal by the massacres at food distribution sites. The world saw hundreds of weary, emaciated Palestinians killed while waiting to receive flour. We saw exhausted Palestinians barely able to walk being gunned down as they were forced to relocate yet again, to supposedly safe spaces that proved even more treacherous than those they had just left. We saw their anxious faces as they dug through the rubble with their bare hands to reach the wounded trapped under chunks of broken concrete. We have seen thousands of children losing their limbs, undergoing amputations without anesthesia. We watched as five-year-old Hind Rajab was executed by snipers in an Israel tank who shot a total of 355 bullets in the direction of the car she was in, even as she hesitated to speak to an operator on a rescue line because she was bleeding from her mouth and was concerned she would stain her dress, making for more work for her mother. We saw Israeli soldiers kidnapping Palestinian doctors and murdering Palestinian journalists.

Every accusation is a confession.

The Zionist weaponization of the Hamas rape allegations makes sense in light of the many reports exposing Israel's record of human rights abuses and the atrocities it was committing. And just as Israel had long used pinkwashing to distract from its violations of international law, so now it was using "woman washing," the allegations of a systemic pattern of violence by Hamas against Israeli women, to distract from its own record of sexual torture of Palestinians. The timing of the allegations was optimal, as there had been much discussion in the Global North, since the 2017 Women's March, of the incompatibility of Zionism with feminism, putting Zionist feminists on the defensive as they maintained that they could reconcile Zionism—an exclusionary ideology whose reification hinges on genocide—with feminism. For years now, especially in the US, there had been a national discussion, including in the *New York Times* and on social media, about the tension between these two. Long before "Screams Without Words," Emily Shire, editor of *Bustle* magazine, had published an op-ed in the *Times* asking if there was room for Zionists in the feminist movement. She concludes her essay: "I will remain a proud feminist, but I see no reason I should have to sacrifice my Zionism for the sake of my feminism."

Other Zionists had picked up Shire's observation, saying they had felt excluded from feminist communities because of their Zionism. The defensiveness of Zionist feminists was the reason a new group appeared on the scene, the Zioness Movement, with its slogan, "Unabashedly progressive, unapologetically Zionist." That slogan was itself a response to Linda Sarsour's speech at the 2017 Women's March on Washington, which she opened with "I stand here before you unapologetically Muslim American, unapologetically Palestinian American." But the contradiction at the very core of supposedly progressive Zionism was evident when it was found out that the Lawfare Project, a well-heeled right-wing pro-Israel organization that litigates against anti-Zionism, BDS actions, and anti-Israel actions in general, had incubated and funded the Zioness Movement, which claimed to be a grassroots organization. The Lawfare Project, which offers pro bono services to litigants, has been accused of chilling free speech because of its involvement in suing students and faculty who are critical of Israel. It is also known to have put pressure on universities against hosting certain events or speakers known to hold views critical of Israel. Still, the discussion around how Zionism could be reconciled with progressive values would not die down. And the tide had certainly turned: In my own Introduction to Women's Studies classes, where we open with a collective attempt at crafting our own definition of "feminism," I have an exercise where the students list five ideologies that cannot be reconciled with "feminism." Over the years, students had volunteered patriarchy, misogyny, and inequality, but more recently, they cited racism, colonialism, and Zionism.

As report after report came out documenting Israel's sexual violence against Palestinians, Palestinian feminists could not help but notice the silence of Global North feminists around these blood-curdling atrocities. And the Palestinian Feminist Collective determined to take colonial feminism to task, exposing the hypocrisy of claiming to care for "women and children" while tolerating both sexual violence and reproductive genocide—so long as the perpetrator was Israel. Within weeks of Israel's accelerated genocide, on November 25, 2023, on the occasion of the International Day for the Elimination of Violence Against Women, the PFC published their "Shut Down Colonial Feminism" statement, which explains that "in Palestine, the Zionist settler-colonial project is driven by a demographic anxiety that constructs Palestinian women's bodies, sexualities, and reproductive capacities as security threats. Palestinian mothers are coded as 'problems' and are systematically denied reproductive justice and security." The PFC was thus highlighting the very gendered aspect of Israel's policies—viewing women's bodies as a demographic threat to be neutered for the sake of Zionist settler colonialism. The PFC was also foregrounding the greater context of violence that Israel imposes on the Palestinian people. The statement opens with the PFC's definition of colonial feminism: "By colonial feminism, we refer to Western and colonial discourses and policies that deploy the language of liberating women to justify invasions, genocides, military occupations, resource extractions, and labor exploitations." The PFC then explains:

> Gender and sexual violence is indispensable to settler colonialism and its intent to eliminate Indigenous peoples, steal their lands, and repress their resistance. In Palestine, the Zionist settler-colonial project is driven by a demographic anxiety that constructs Palestinian women's bodies, sexualities, and reproductive capacities as security threats. Palestinian mothers are coded as "problems" and are systematically denied reproductive justice and security.

The PFC goes on to document some of the horrors endured by Palestinian women in the few weeks since October 7, 2023, listing the fact that 50,000 women were pregnant on that day, with 150 expected to give birth every day, including by cesarean sections, without anesthesia or painkillers and in harrowing conditions. The

PFC also wrote that Israel was targeting Palestinian masculinities by threatening to out queers if they do not become informants on their own communities in Gaza. The statement ends with a call to action, urging supporters to speak out against colonial feminists whenever they appear in the media, the workplace, or the classroom, to organize teach-ins on colonial feminism, and to uplift the "Say No to Genocide" campaign by the PFC and INCITE! Feminists of Color Against Violence.[27]

A few weeks later, and three months into the accelerated genocide, the PFC issued another statement entitled "The PFC Condemns the Reproductive Genocide in Gaza," which again addressed the gendered aspect of Israel's assault on Palestinian life. The PFC defines reproductive genocide thus:

> Reproductive genocide refers to the policies, discourses, and practices that delimit, restrict, target, or diminish the life-giving capacities, choices, access, short-term health, long-term health, and life chances of communities made vulnerable by systemic military violence and occupation, besiegement, settler colonialism, and/or imperial warfare.[28]

The situation was dystopian, and deteriorating by the day, as Israel bombed homes, schools, safe shelters, and hospitals. Women were giving birth amid an apocalyptic war, in the absence of medical care, food, and water, and lacking hygiene products, which were deliberately blocked from entering the Gaza Strip by Israel. Many were already suffering from a lack of micronutrients due to the extremely limited diet available in Gaza prior to October 7, 2023, with an estimated 50 percent of Gaza's pregnant women suffering from anemia. Women and girls who could afford the exorbitant price resorted to taking birth control pills to stop their menstruation cycles, for lack of sanitary pads, and many shaved their heads because they could not shampoo their hair. The lack of clean water and food meant mothers could not breastfeed their newborn infants. And the overall lack of any safety, including for hospitals, meant that newborns were left to die in incubators. By September 2025, Israel had killed one Palestinian child every hour since October 7, 2023. Also by September 2025, it was estimated that ten Palestinian children per day were losing one or more limbs, creating a generation of amputees. Tens of thousands had lost one or both parents, and some had lost their entire extended families, making for the largest orphan crisis in modern history.

While everyone in the Gaza Strip was living in extremely unsafe conditions, gender-based violence also soared with the repeated displacement and the breakdown of social protection, leaving women and girls increasingly exposed to intimate partner violence, sexual abuse, and child marriage. According to the Women's Affairs Center, which operates shelters in Gaza City, many shelters across the Strip shut down due to the unsafe conditions, while others were operating at limited capacity, often exceeded. The center's Hana Zant also explained that women were at a disadvantage at food distribution centers, since families were registered under the husband's name before October 7, 2023, making it impossible for women to obtain food if the husband had been killed since then, as family records were not being updated during the intensified genocide. Similarly, if a family had been separated, with the husband in a different town or country, the woman could not obtain food for her children, as she was not officially recognized as "head of household."[29] By August 2025, famine was widespread across the region; 135 children had starved to death, and around 132,000 children under the age of five were at risk of death from acute malnutrition.[30] Two-thirds of all women in Gaza suffered severe depression, and over half had recurrent nightmares and anxiety resulting from the relentless hunger and abject living conditions.

In the aftermath of the October 7 attacks, Israel's unadulterated evil was on full display around the world. The genocide was livestreamed, around the clock, month after month after month, with massacres at aid distribution centers, massacres at hospitals, massacres at so-called safe zones, to which weary Palestinians had been forced to relocate yet again. The relentless assault on all Palestinian life encapsulates what Palestinians have known all along: that our very existence is viewed as a threat to Israel, regardless of whether we are students, homemakers, dreamers, poets, cooks, militants, or "womenandchildren." Israel had deemed us all a demographic threat as early as 1948, and there have always been Israeli leaders and thinkers who thought it an unfortunate mistake that we were not "finished" in 1948. Israel has used sexual violence to "finish" us since its inception.

Ultimately, it was no longer possible for anyone to call themselves a feminist and not denounce the horror. In the aftermath of October 7, it became obvious that any outrage at the allegations of Hamas militants' rape of Israeli women that is not accompanied by outrage at and denunciations of the amply documented Israeli sexual violence against Palestinian men, women, and children stems not from feminism, but from racism.

Israel's genocide of the Palestinian people started long before October 7, 2023. It started long before Hamas was formed in 1987. And it was never about Hamas. Instead, it has always been about Palestine as a people, a culture, a nation, and how our existence threatens the Zionist settler colonial project. And resistance to genocide is necessarily fertile, life giving, and life sustaining.

Resistance is feminist.

Epilogue

I never thought I would need to write a chapter about the intensified genocide of my people, and how genocide—the killing of all life associated with a people—is indeed a feminist issue. My plan, as I set down to write *Falastiniyyat*, was to cover the hundred years between 1921—the founding of the Arab Women's Association—and 2021, the formation of the Palestinian Feminist Collective. My intent was to show that Palestinian feminism has always been Indigenous (caring about the land) and decolonial (rejecting the imperial visions for our land) while also understanding that there can be no national liberation, that is, no liberation of the land, without the liberation of all its people. This concept is not recent: Palestinian women were demanding equality with men as early as the 1920s and argued even then that national liberation would be incomplete without women's emancipation from the many restrictions placed upon them by their own society. As members of that society, they seized their agency, making forays into empowerment. Palestinian women's activism for collective liberation continued throughout the decades, from the British Mandate through the First Intifada. When the Oslo Accords put an end to their leadership during that uprising, women were quick to note once again that there would be no national liberation without women's liberation. Queer voices joined that chorus, calling for social and political transformation and the inclusion of Palestinian queers as agents of decolonization. Thus the slogan, in the 2020s, of Tal'at, the Palestinian Youth Movement, and the Palestinian Feminist Collective—that there can be "no political liberation without social liberation"—is a continuation of, rather than a departure from, the two-pronged struggle of Palestinian feminists over the past century. While Palestinian women activists in the early twentieth century did not necessarily view themselves as feminists—indeed, the term had little if any currency anywhere—the social transformation that they brought about, as they rose up against their society's oppression, points toward what is today openly acknowledged as Third World feminism—a worldview that analyzes the interaction of the personal, the political, and the macro-political and seeks collective rather than individual empowerment. This concept was first formulated by Palestine's proto-feminists, and it courses throughout the years of our dispossession, and our *sumoud*.

When the *fellahat* chanted coded songs to warn fighters of the arrival of British colonizers; when Sitt Hind al-Husseini gathered orphaned children after the 1948 Deir Yassin massacre, then opened a girls' school that taught pride in every course offered; when Samiha Khalil devoted her life to the children of fighters killed after 1967, while preserving Palestine's threatened cultural heritage; when the young Jean Makdisi spoke out against Orientalist stereotypes in the Global North while Camille Odeh was organizing with disenfranchised communities in Chicago during the civil rights era; when grassroots "women and children" rose up against Israel's illegal occupation in an intifada that still presents a model of community organizing; when Soraida Hussein first noticed signs of intimate violence and determined to set up a support network for abused women; when alQaws, Aswat, and Tal'at took to the streets of Palestine to denounce not only Israel's occupation but also the nefarious trickle-down effect this had on Palestinian society; and when the Palestinian Feminist Collective took on colonial feminism, condemning Israel's reproductive genocide in Gaza, Palestinian women, the *falastiniyyat* who make us proud, were all saying Palestine is a feminist issue, because racism, settler colonialism, and genocide are feminist issues.

I wrote most of this book in the aftermath of the October 7, 2023, Hamas breach of the apartheid wall choking the Gaza Strip. It is critically important to note that the genocide did not begin on that day; it began in 1948. Israel's violence has been relentless ever since. Not a day has gone by since May 15, 1948, without Israeli violence, without Israel's violation of international law and the human rights of the Palestinians. Not a day has gone by since the onset of al-Nakba without land theft, kidnappings of innocent civilians, and their indefinite imprisonment without charges in prisons that rank among the worst in the entire world, where physical, sexual, and psychological torture are the norm, not the exception. Not a day has gone by since 1967 without soldiers of the Israeli army defending an illegal occupation in savage ways. By October 7, 2023, the most common description of Gaza was "the world's largest open-air prison," as a result of illegal "collective punishment" for a people who had elected political leaders their occupier did not approve of. There were already reports of its being "unlivable," of its water being undrinkable, of its economy being intentionally devastated. And always, there was mention that the population in Gaza was very young. In 2023, 47 percent of the population was under eighteen years of age. Even if voting for Hamas were considered a crime—it is not—on October 7, 2023, 47 percent of the population were not born in 2006, the year of Hamas's election. Moreover, since the voting age is eighteen, anyone who had voted in 2006 would have been at least thirty-five years of age. As a full 75 percent of the population in Gaza was then under the age of twenty-five, the majority of people in Gaza in 2023 had not voted for Hamas—assuming that was the "crime" for which they were being punished.

But it was never about Hamas. The "crime" of my people was not voting for Hamas; our crime was our being Palestinian. And by the logic of settler colonialism, we had to be eliminated. And because settler colonialism is gender violence, not a day has gone by since Israel's foundation without sexual violence, even as this crime has intensified since October 7.

Meanwhile, Palestinian women and queers have been engaged in *lamlama*, the gathering of orphans, of seeds, of the multihued threads of our *thobes*; they have supported each other through mutual aid and genuine philanthropy; they have cared for the larger community as an extension of their family; they have spoken out against restrictive social norms, against occupation, against racism, against war.

Today, with the documented record of Israeli soldiers' depravity and the decades of rape and physical, psychological, and sexual torture committed by Israelis against Palestinians, anyone still interjecting "What about Hamas?" is a shameless, Islamophobic, anti-Palestinian racist. The outrage over the unsubstantiated claims of Hamas militants' rape of Israeli women, when there is silence about the amply documented reports, by the most reliable human rights groups, of the sexual torture of Palestinians by Israeli soldiers, stems not from feminism, but from racism. Ultimately, what the October 7 attacks revealed is the moral bankruptcy of Zionism, as well as that of Zionist and imperial would-be feminists—a bankruptcy Palestinian feminists have been countering for the past century, and which we will continue to expose, until Zionism is completely discredited, Zionist leaders are hounded as the war criminals that they are, and Indigenous life is celebrated.

Healing from our genocide will neither be easy nor fast. And as it is becoming clear to all that the "two-state solution" is little more than a delusion, with Israel intent on stealing ever more Palestinian land, it is imperative that we focus on the nature of the one state that is surfacing yet again, because Palestine has always been indivisible. Dismantling the structural systems of Jewish supremacy and settler colonialism in Palestine will be a protracted endeavor that requires a tenacious determination to retain our culture, our identity, our heritage that would otherwise be dissolved into the morass of a "one state" proposal with little attention to the asymmetrical power dynamics of a century of imperialism. We do not want equality with the settlers. We want decolonization. "Free Palestine" is not a vacuous liberal chant. "Free Palestine" means land back, and our Palestinian Indigeneity upheld.

For over a century, we have proven that we belong in our homes, our streets, our cities as the rightful stewards of our land, its waters, its terraced gardens, its ancient stone houses. Palestinians have given the world the word *intifada*, a shaking off of oppression, as well as *sumoud*, persistence. And one day, the falastiniyyat will celebrate in the streets of our liberated homeland, from the river to the sea.

Min al-nahr lil bahr,
Min al-mayyeh lil mayyeh.

Notes

Introduction

1 Rima Najjar, "Life in Abu Dis Continues Quietly," *Biography* 37, no. 2 (Spring 2014): 637.
2 In Arab culture, a child is considered an orphan if they lose one parent, not necessarily both. I was raised as an orphan by my mother.
3 Award-winning novelist susan abulhawa, for example, lived at Dar al-Tifl for three years, before moving to the United States.
4 See my discussion of Golda Meir in Nada Elia, *Greater Than the Sum of Our Parts: Feminism, Inter/Nationalism, and Palestine* (Pluto Press, 2023), 33–4.
5 Because I am referring to the historic diversity of the Palestinian people, I include the Druze under Islam, since they started out as an offshoot of that religion, even though they now view themselves as a separate faith and are also now considered non-Muslim by Sunni Islam.
6 This is not to deny the existence of colorism and anti-Black racism among Palestinians. Nevertheless, Black Palestinians are not viewed as outsiders.
7 See, for example, Ellen Fleischmann, *The Nation and Its "New" Women: The Palestinian Women's Movement, 1920–1948* (University of California Press, 2003).
8 See, for example, Islah Jad, *Palestinian Women's Activism: Nationalism, Secularism, Islamism* (Syracuse University Press, 2018).
9 Orayb Najjar, *Portraits of Palestinian Women* (University of Utah, 1992).
10 Jehan Helou, *Making Palestine's History: Women's Testimony* (Spokesman's Books, 2022).
11 Most Palestinians do not recognize the Western imperial distinction between "legal dispossession" in 1948, and "illegal" since 1967. We experienced our Nakba, our catastrophe, our dispossession, and the occupation of our homeland, beginning in 1948, not 1967.
12 Whereas "Maskubiyyeh," the Arabic form of "Moscovite," refers to the

entire Russian Quarter, the term is now used primarily for the Israeli detention and torture center in that compound.

13 "Sitt" is an honorific used for women held in high esteem.

1. Emerging

1 Evelyn Shakir, *Bint Arab: Arab and Arab American Women in the United States* (Praeger, 1997), 81.

2 See, for example, Charlotte Karem Albrecht, *Possible Histories: Arab Americans and the Queer Ecology of Peddling* (University of California Press, 2023).

3 Shakir, *Bint Arab*, 82.

4 Zeev Jabotinsky, "The Iron Wall: We and the Arabs," Jabotinsky Institute, en.jabotinsky.org.

5 Matiel Mogannam, *The Arab Woman and the Palestine Problem* (Herbert Joseph, 1937), 69.

6 Heiny Srour's 1984 film *Leila and the Wolves* beautifully recreates rural Palestinian women's activism during the Great Revolt.

7 Mogannam, *The Arab Woman*, 77.

8 Ellen Fleischmann's book *The Nation and Its "New Women: The Palestinian Women's Movement, 1920–1948* (University of California Press, 2003) provides an invaluable detailed overview of the many social and political initiatives undertaken by Palestinian women during the British Mandate. I am indebted to her for much of my own knowledge of women's organizing during that period.

9 Mogannam, *The Arab Woman*, 56.

10 Ibid., 74–5.

11 Ellen Fleischmann, "The Emergence of the Palestinian Women's Movement, 1929–1939," *Journal of Palestine Studies* 29, no. 3 (Spring 2000): 16–32.

12 Mogannam, *The Arab Woman*, 68.

13 Ibid.

14 Ibid., 69.

15 Ibid., 13.

16 Fleischmann, "Emergence of the Palestinian Women's Movement," 72.

17 "Sadhij Nassar," in *Interactive Encyclopedia of the Palestine Question*, palquest.org.

18 Mogannam, *The Arab Woman*, 54.

19 Fleischmann, "Emergence of the Palestinian Women's Movement."

20 Kate Millett, *Sexual Politics: A Surprising Examination of Society's Most Arbitrary Folly* (Doubleday, 1970).

21 Carol Hanisch, "The Personal Is Political: The Women's Liberation Movement Classic with a New Explanatory Introduction," 2006

(1969), carolhanisch.org. This essay is based on a February 1969 memo Hanisch sent to the women's caucus of the Southern Conference Educational Fund, which was later included in Shulamit Firestone and Anne Koedt (eds.), *Notes from the Second Year: Women's Liberation, Major Writings of the Radical Feminists* (Radical Feminism, 1970). The desire to describe these meetings as "political," not "therapy," was itself due to the fact that the need for therapy was overall viewed negatively, as an indicator of personal inadequacy or privileged indulgence.

22 Ibid.

23 Cited in Fleischmann, *The Nation and Its "New" Women*, 108.

24 Ibid., 116.

25 The British Mandate officially began in 1923, lasting until the creation of Israel in 1948. However, Britain had captured Jerusalem from the Ottoman forces in December 1917 and occupied the rest of the country following the defeat of the Turkish forces in September 1918. British rule over Palestine, then, is best understood as lasting from 1918 to 1948.

26 See "The Palestine Mandate," Avalon Project: Documents in Law, History, and Diplomacy, 2008, avalon.law.yale.edu.

27 Rashid Khalidi, "The Palestinians and 1948: The Underlying Causes of Failure," in Eugene Rogan and Avi Schlaim (eds.), *The War for Palestine: Rewriting the History of 1948* (Cambridge University Press, 2007), 12–36.

28 Britain initiated many of the worst practices that Israel continues to this day, namely collective punishment, administrative detention, and destruction of property as retaliation for resistance. In this particular instance, Britain is said to have burnt down seventy houses in Baqa al-Gharbiyya as punishment for the villagers' resistance.

29 Matthew Hughes, "Women, Violence, and the Arab Revolt in Palestine 1936–39," *Journal of Military History* 83 (April 2019): 487–507.

30 Fleischmann, *The Nation and Its New Women*, 54.

31 Ibid., 55.

2. Surviving

1 "Sitt" is an honorific expressing high status or respect for a woman.

2 "Hind al-Husseini," in *Interactive Encyclopedia of the Palestine Question*, palquest.org.

3 The Irgun, founded in 1931, and the Stern Gang, founded in 1940, were extremist Zionist militias that rejected the Haganah's restraint and engaged in numerous violent attacks against Palestinians and assassinated British authorities and UN staff. Britain officially designated them terrorist groups. In 1948, many of their members joined the Israeli military.

4 "Hind Taher al-Husseini," Jerusalem Story, May 10, 2021, jerusalemstory.com.

5 While this passage is cited in many biographies of al-Husseini, I have not been able to locate the primary source.

6 Private video of interview on Al-Qastal network shared by a woman who attended Dar al-Tifl in the 1980s.

7 UN Palestine Commission, "Attack on Deir Yassin (9 April 1948): Letter from United Kingdom," April 20, 1948, un.org.

8 Ilan Pappe, *The Ethnic Cleansing of Palestine* (Oneworld, 2006), 78.

9 Walid Khalidi, *All That Remains* (Institute for Palestine Studies, 2006), 496.

10 Darin J. Sallam, dir., *Farha* (TaleBox, 2021), 92 min.

11 Private video of interview on Al-Qastal network shared by a woman who attended Dar al-Tifl in the 1980s.

12 Dean Spade, *Mutual Aid: Building Solidarity During This Crisis (and the Next)* (Verso, 2020), 7.

13 In Ellen Fleischmann, *The Nation and Its "New" Women: The Palestinian Women's Movement, 1920–1948* (University of California Press, 2003), 43.

14 Private video of interview on Al-Qastal network shared by a woman who attended Dar al-Tifl in the 1980s.

15 Email communication, August 31, 2023.

16 Interview conducted September 21, 2023, in Arabic and translated by the author.

17 "Susan Abulhawa's Statement to the Kalimat Palestinian Literature Festival," US Campaign for the Academic and Cultural Boycott of Israel, usacbi.org.

18 Arnon Golan, "The Battle for Jaffa, 1948," *Middle Eastern Studies* 48, no. 6 (November 2012): 997–1011.

19 For an in-depth look at the Great Revolt of 1936–39, see Palestinian director Annemarie Jacir's *Palestine 36* (Curzon Films, 2025), 119 mins.

20 Janan Abdu, "Nariman Khurshid and the Chrysanthemum Flower Organization" (in Arabic), *Jadaliyyah*, June 3, 2015, jadaliyyah.com, translated by the author.

21 Again, the details of this particular incident differ in different sources, with some saying the young boy was six years old, others ten. There is agreement that Mahiba determined to engage in armed resistance after witnessing his execution.

22 Linah Alsaafin, "Radical Lives: Moheba Khorsheed," Novara Media, November 24, 2014, novaramedia.com.

23 Anita Shapira, *Land and Power: The Zionist Resort to Force, 1881–1948* (Oxford University Press, 1992), 238.

24 "Grievance 27" of the US Declaration of Independence claims that the King of England "has excited domestic Insurrections amongst us, and has endeavoured to bring on the Inhabitants of our Frontiers, the

merciless Indian Savages, whose known Rule of Warfare, is an undistinguished Destruction, of all Ages, Sexes and Conditions."

25 Pappe, *The Ethnic Cleansing of Palestine*, 210.
26 Ibid., 209.
27 Ibid., 210.

3. Sustaining Communities

1 Anne Irfan, "Why Palestinians Are Known as the World's 'Best Educated Refugees,'" *Columbia University Press Blog*, August 23, 2023, cupblog.org.
2 It is important to note that there was an educated urban elite, but not all city residents were necessarily highly educated. My own mother was from a very modest family, and her parents pulled her out of school at the age of twelve because they did not value education much.
3 Edward Said, *Culture and Imperialism* (Vintage, 1993).
4 Ibid., xiii.
5 Cited in Marion Benvenisti, *Sacred Landscape: The Buried History of the Holy Land Since 1948* (University of California Press, 2000).
6 Virginia Tilley, *The One-State Solution: A Breakthrough for Peace in the Israeli-Palestinian Deadlock* (University of Michigan Press, 2005), 190, emphasis added.
7 Benny Brunner, *The Great Book Robbery* (2911 Foundation, Xela Films, and Al Jazeera English, 2012).
8 Dalia Hatuqa, "Israel's Great Book Robbery Unravelled," Al Jazeera, January 29, 2013, aljazeera.com.
9 Adam Horowitz, "The Nakba and the Great Book Robbery of 1948," *Mondoweiss*, October 25, 2010, mondoweiss.net.
10 Quote from his diary, cited in Brunner, *The Great Book Robbery*.
11 Brunner, *The Great Book Robbery*.
12 Fleischmann, *The Nation and Its "New" Women*, 144.
13 See discussion in chapter 1, "Emerging."
14 For more on Zulaykha al-Shihabi's long record of political activism, see "Zulaykha al-Shihabi," Jerusalem Story, May 10, 2021, jerusalemstory.com.
15 "Samiha Khalil," *Interactive Encyclopedia of the Palestine Question*, palquest.org.
16 Wafa Ghnaim, *Tatreez and Tea: Embroidery and Storytelling in the Palestinian Diaspora* (CreateSpace Independent Publishing, 2018).
17 Tahani Rached, dir., *Soraida, A Woman of Palestine* (National Film Board of Canada, 2004), 119 min.
18 See Leanne Mohamad, "Leanne Mohamad—What Is Tatreez?," YouTube, March 31, 2023.

4. Speaking Out

1 Jean Said Makdisi, *Beirut Fragments: A War Memoir* (Persea, 1990), 123.
2 Ibid., 124.
3 I intentionally use "Jew hatred," instead of the more common expression "antisemitic," because the latter is incorrect on a number of levels and erases the majority of Semites, who are predominantly Arabs. Indeed, "semitic" is not an ethnicity but a linguistic group, which includes Arabic, Aramaic, and Maltese, as well as Hebrew and numerous other languages in West Asia and the Horn of Africa. Yet "antisemitism" is rarely, if ever, used to refer to anti-Arab racism. Additionally, the term "antisemitism," incorrectly limited to Jew hatred, has been weaponized over the past few decades to refer to anti-Zionism. Yet there are Jew haters who are Zionists, supporting the establishment of a Jewish state, and the overwhelming majority of anti-Zionists are not motivated by Jew hatred but by a rejection of racism and settler colonialism.
4 Edward Said, *Orientalism* (Pantheon, 1978).
5 Fadwa Tuqan, *A Mountainous Journey: A Poet's Autobiography*, trans. Olive E. Kenny (Graywolf Press, 1990), 157.
6 Ibid., 158.
7 Makdisi, *Beirut Fragments*, 94.
8 Evelyn Shakir, *Bint Arab: Arab and Arab American Women in the United States* (Praeger, 1997), 98.
9 See Joshua Ruebner's *A Tragedy of Catastrophic Proportions: The United States and the Palestinian Nakba, 1947–1949* (forthcoming, 2027).
10 Leon Uris, *Exodus: A Novel of Israel* (Doubleday, 1958).
11 Tuqan, *A Mountainous Journey*, 15.
12 Makdisi, *Beirut Fragments*, 124–5.
13 Ibid., 124.
14 Ibid., 125.
15 See "June 1967 War," *Interactive Encyclopedia of the Palestine Question*, palquest.org.
16 Said, *Orientalism*, 284–5.
17 Ibid., 285.
18 "50 Years On: Reflections from the 1974 AAUG Convention," Center for Arab Narratives, arabnarratives.org.
19 See Janice J. Terry, "The AAUG: An Activist, Academic Organization," *Arab Studies Quarterly* 29, no. 3/4 (2007): 1–5.
20 Ibid.
21 Edward Said, obituary for Ibrahim Abu-Loghd, *Guardian*, June 12, 2001.
22 Ghada Talhami, "AAUG and the Years of Activities," *Arab Studies Quarterly* 40, no. 1 (Winter 2018): 20.

23 Ghada Hashem Talhami, "The Struggle of Palestinian Women: Colonization and Feminist Perspectives," *World Literature Today*, Summer 2021, worldliteraturetoday.org.
24 Quoted in Suraya Khan, "Transnational Alliances: The AAUG's Advocacy for Palestine and the Third World," *Arab Studies Quarterly* 40, no. 1 (Winter 2018): 59.
25 Ibid., 55.
26 Kevin Mattson, *Intellectuals in Action: The Origins of the New Left and Radical Liberalism, 1945–1970* (Penn State University Press, 2002), 9–10.
27 Camille Odeh, "Arab American Activism," *Arab Studies Quarterly* 40, no. 1 (Winter 2018): 23–6.
28 Ibid.
29 Ibid.
30 Camille Odeh's legacy is carried on today by her daughter, Leena Odeh, a lawyer and longtime Chicago community organizer committed to transformative justice.
31 June Jordan, *Civil Wars* (Beacon Press, 1981), 100.
32 See, for example, Marina Magloire, "Moving Towards Life," *Los Angeles Review of Books*, August 7, 2024, lareviewofbooks.org.
33 Evelyn Beck et al., "What Does Zionism Mean?," *Off Our Backs* 12, no. 7 (July 1982): 21.

5. Rising Up

1 Julia Bacha, dir., *Naila and the Uprising* (Just Vision Films, 2017), 76 min.
2 Tahani Rached, dir., *Soraida, A Woman of Palestine* (National Film Board of Canada, 2004), 119 min.
3 Sheren Khalel, "The Women of the Intifadas," Al Jazeera, October 23, 2015.
4 "Soraida Abed Hussein Oral History Content Summary (Document, English)," Women's Learning Partnership, 2012, learningpartnership.org, tracks 1 and 2.
5 Rached, *Soraida*.
6 "Soraida Abed Hussein Oral History Content Summary."
7 The communiqués of the United National Leadership of the Intifada are archived at Birzeit University, the Palestinian Museum Digital Archive, and Al-Quds University Abu Jihad Museum Archives. For a translation of the first communiqué, see "Translation of the First UNLI Bayan of the First Palestinian Intifada," January 8, 1988, Revolutionary Papers, revolutionarypapers.org.
8 Bacha, *Naila and the Uprising*.
9 Ibid.

10 Ibid.
11 Khalel, "The Women of the Intifada."
12 Ibid.
13 Buthina Canaan Khoury, dir., *Women in Struggle* (Majid Productions, 2004), 56 min.
14 Ibid.
15 Edward Said, "The Morning After," *London Review of Books*, October 21, 1993.
16 Bacha, *Naila and the Uprising*.
17 Ibid.

6. Persevering

1 "Maha Abu Dayyeh," Jerusalem Story, July 7, 2022, jerusalemstory.com.
2 In many Arab and Muslim cultures, a person is called by their *kunya*, an honorific meaning a parent, most often of their firstborn son. Mothers go by "Umm," while men go by "Abu," followed by that child's name. In other instances, the kunya can refer to a historic figure. Yasser Arafat was known as "Abu Ammar." The custom is obviously patriarchal, prioritizing boys over their older sisters. But this is in no way unique to Arab culture. English names such as "Jacobson" or "Peterson" indicate paternal lineage, as do Irish and Scottish names, where the "Mc" and "Mac" are followed by a man's name, as in "McDonald" or "McArthur." In Armenian names, the "ian" ending also indicates patrilinear affiliation, so "Kevorkian" is the son of Kevork, "Gregorian" the son of Gregor, and so on.
3 Such factories exist in the West Bank, as well as in Egypt and Jordan, where there are "qualified industrial zones" that can label a product as manufactured in Egypt or Jordan, even though the company is Israeli. They are basically the Arab world's equivalent of the maquiladoras in Latin America and provide a smokescreen for Israeli companies seeking to avoid a boycott of their products.
4 The PLO was formed in 1964 as an umbrella coalition of various Palestinian nationalist groups seeking liberation from Israeli colonialism. Yasser Arafat was its second chairman, ascending to that position in 1969, as the successor to Ahmad al-Shuqairi. The PLO gained prominence after the 1967 war.
5 The *muqataat* (plural of *muqataa*) were militarized forts built throughout Palestine during the British Mandate and used for British administrative offices and housing. In the West Bank and Gaza Strip, most served similar functions under Jordanian rule, from 1948 to 1967, then Israeli rule, from 1967 to 1993. Upon his return to Palestine, Arafat used the main muqataa in Ramallah, and a similar one in Gaza,

as the headquarters of the Palestinian National Authority. Israel later besieged him multiple times in the Ramallah muqataa, where he had taken up residence.

6 Jonathan Cook, "A Gentlemen's Agreement: How Israel Got What It Wanted from Oslo," *Middle East Eye*, September 14, 2018, middleeasteye.net.

7 An English translation of the 1988 Hamas charter is available through the Yale Law Library: "Hamas Covenant 1988," August 18, 1988, Avalon Project: Documents in Law, History and Diplomacy, avalon.law.yale.edu. The 1988 charter was revised in 2017. An English translation is available through *Middle East Eye*: "Hamas in 2017: The Document in Full," *Middle East Eye*, May 2, 2017, middleeasteye.net.

8 See Patrick Wolfe, "Settler Colonialism and the Elimination of the Native," *Journal of Genocide Research* 8, no. 4 (December 2006): 387–409. Wolfe argues that "franchise colonialism seeks to extract resources from the colonized country, whereas settler colonialism seeks to transform that colonized country into a new one, and as such, must first eliminate the native through genocide, assimilation, and removal."

9 See my discussion in *Greater Than the Sum of Our Parts* (Pluto Press, 2023), 78–9.

10 The gendered detrimental effects on society of living in militarized, unsafe, or undignified circumstances is not unique to Palestine, of course, but have acquired specific aspects there due to the protracted Israeli occupation.

11 Islah Jad, "The NGO-isation of Arab Women's Movements," *Institute for Development Studies Bulletin* 35(2004): 34.

12 Ibid., 38.

13 "Statement by Ms. Randa Siniora at UN Security Council Open Debate on Women, Peace and Security," October 25, 2018, NGO Working Group on Women, Peace and Security, womenpeacesecurity.org.

14 Anne-Marie O'Connor, "Honor Killings Rise in Palestinian Territories, Sparking Backlash," *Washington Post*, March 4, 2014.

15 See my discussion in *Greater Than the Sum of Our Parts*, 81–5.

16 Judge Ahmad Al Ashqar, "Murder of Women in Palestine Under the Pretext of Honour," UN Human Rights Office of the High Commissioner, April 2014, ohchr.org.

17 The term "femocrat" originated in Australia in the 1970s and was popularized by Hester Eisentein in her 1996 book *Inside Agitators: Australian Femocrats and the State* (Temple University Press).

18 For a comparative discussion of various feminist analyses of structure and agency, see Amy S. Wharton, "Structure and Agency in Socialist-Feminist Theory," *Gender & Society* 5, no. 3 (1991): 373–89.

19 Very detailed information about the vision behind the PMP, the meticulous planning of the regional parliaments and numerous workshops and seminars, and reflections by the organizers are compiled in a booklet: Maha Abu-Dayyeh et al., *Palestinian Model Parliament: Towards*

Legislation Based on Palestinian Identity, Progressive Ideals, and Just Contents (Women's Centre for Legal Aid and Counselling, 2015), published shortly after Abu-Dayyeh's passing and available at wclac.org.

20 Cited in "Statement by Ms. Randa Siniora," 59.

21 Abu-Dayyeh et al., *Palestinian Model Parliament*, 14.

22 Nahda Sh'hada, "The Palestinian Women's Movement: New Realities/Old Concerns," in Fenneke Reysoo and Christine Verschuur (eds.), *On m'appelle à régner: Mondialisation, pouvoirs et rapports de genre* (Graduate Institute Publications, 2003), 184.

23 Sarah Ihmoud, "Palestinian Feminism: Analytics, Praxes, and Decolonial Futures," *Feminist Anthropology* 3 (2022): 284–98.

24 Abu-Dayyeh et al., *Palestinian Model Parliament*.

25 From the Institute of Women's Studies at Birzeit University website, iws.birzeit.edu.

26 Rita Giacaman, Islah Jad, and Penny Johnson, "For the Common Good? Gender and Social Citizenship in Palestine," *Middle East Report* 198 (Spring 1996), merip.org.

27 Lisa Taraki, "Society and Gender in Palestine: A Critique of International Agencies' Policy Documents" (in Arabic), available at https://iws.birzeit.edu/writable/uploads/articles/1727953072_3156ee9502dd17c5ce6f.pdf.

28 Institute of Women's Studies at Birzeit University website, iws.birzeit.edu.

29 Sh'hada, "The Palestinian Women's Movement," 177–8.

7. Whose Feminism?

1 See Nada Elia, *Greater Than the Sum of Our Parts* (Pluto Press, 2023), 81–5.

2 Sa'ed Atshan provides an extant discussion of Palestinian queer activism between 2000 and 2018 in his book *Queer Palestine and the Empire of Critique* (Stanford University Press, 2020).

3 Cited in Ellen Fleischmann, *The Nation and Its "New" Women: The Palestinian Women's Movement, 1920–1948* (University of California Press, 2003), 116.

4 Lynn Darwish and Haneen Maikey, "From the Belly of Arab Queer Activism: Challenges and Opportunities," *Bekhsoos*, October 12, 2011, bekhsoos.com.

5 Ghadir Shafie, "Pinkwashing, Israel's Intentional Strategy and Internal Agenda," *Kohl Journal* 1, no. 1 (2015): 82–6.

6 Ibid.

7 Ibid.

8 Atshan, *Queer Palestine and the Empire of Critique*, 38.

9 Milena Pafundi, "Solidarity and Feminism in the Midst of Genocide: Interview with a Palestinian Lesbian Activist," *Presentes*, December 14, 2023, agenciaspresents.org.

10 Lubna Masarwa and Chloé Benoist, "LGBTQ Palestinians in Israel: Tahini Firm Stirs Up 'Pinkwashing' Storm over Hotline Donation," *Middle East Eye*, July 22, 2020, middleeasteye.net.

11 Pafundi, "Solidarity and Feminism in the Midst of Genocide."

12 Advocate.com Editors, "Rauda Morcos," *Advocate*, May 8, 2006, advocate.com.

13 IEMed Barcelona, "Queer Activism, Intersectional Feminism and National Struggles in Palestine," lecture by Ghadir Shafie, YouTube, April 23, 2021.

14 alQaws, "From alQaws to Haneen Maikey: We Recognize Your Impact, Appreciate Your Leadership, and We Shall Continue the Struggle," in *Social and Organizational Transformation: A Queer Organizing Milestone in Palestine, 2020 Annual Report* (alQaws, 2021), 35–8, alqaws.org.

15 The Jerusalem Open House for Pride and Tolerance is frequently abbreviated as "Jerusalem Open House" but should not be confused with the organization Jerusalem Open House, which is a conservative, Zionist soup kitchen that provides meals for the city's needy Jewish citizens.

16 Elisa Kukla, "A House Not Totally Divided," *Xtra*, May 15, 2002, xtramagazine.com.

17 "Interview with Haneen Maikey," *Paper* (blog), January 22, 2012, wearethepaperdotorg.wordpress.com.

18 See Atshan, *Queer Palestine and the Empire of Critique*, 10–11.

19 Unlike "homosexual," which has an Arabic equivalent, namely *mithali* (masculine) and *mithaliyya* (feminine), there is no Arabic equivalent for "queer," a term that has been adopted into the Arabic language unchanged. See also Linah Alsaafin, "Though Small, Palestine's Queer Movement Has Big Vision," *Electronic Intifada*, July 12, 2013, electronicintifada.net.

20 IEMed Barcelona, "Queer Activism, Intersectional Feminism and National Struggles."

21 Queers Undermining Israeli Terrorism (QUIT!) website, quitpalestine.org

22 "Arab Queers Say NO to Pinkwashing at the USSF," Palestinian Queers for BDS, June 16, 2010, pqbds.wordpress.com.

23 I have written a blog post about queer activism at the USSF here: Nada Elia, "Reflections from Detroit: Standoff with StandWithUs," *INCITE! Blog*, August 2, 2010, incite-national.org.

8. Our Feminism

1 There are discrepancies in the timeline of Ghrayeb's murder, with some articles reporting she was beaten to death in the hospital, others saying her body was taken lifeless to the hospital after she had been discharged. All agree, however, that she was murdered by her male kin, who tried to pass it off as an accident. There is also complete agreement that no one intervened when she was screaming in her hospital room.
2 "Palestinian 'Honour Killing' Victim Israa Ghrayeb Died After 'Torture, Abuse' by Relatives," *New Arab*, September 13, 2019, newarab.com.
3 Hala Marshould and Riya Alsana, "Tal'at, a Feminist Movement That Is Redefining Liberation and Reimagining Palestine," *Mondoweiss*, February 25, 2020, mondoweiss.net.
4 Ibid.
5 Ibid.
6 alQaws, "AlQaws' Post-Police Statement: The Persecution and Restrictions Continue," October 30, 2019, alqaws.org.
7 Jaclynn Ashley, "PA Rescinds Ban on LGBTQ Group After Protests," *Electronic Intifada*, August 27, 2019, electronicintifada.net.
8 Falastine Saleh, "The PA Scapegoated Our LGBTQ+ Community but It Can't Stop Our Progress," *Middle East Eye*, August 22, 2019, middleeasteye.net.
9 Personal communication with a Palestinian released from a Palestinian jail, who asked to remain anonymous. I have also watched some leaked videos of PA thugs torturing Palestinians, screaming orders at them in Hebrew.
10 "Palestinians to Raise Women's Participation in Security Sector to Double Digits," EU Mission for the Support of Palestinian Police and Rule of Law (EUPOL COPPS), December 5, 2019, eupolcopps.eu.
11 Al-Muntada is Palestinian coalition of seventeen women's and human rights organizations combating violence against women including the following organizations: Bisan Center for Research & Development, Palestinian Working Women Society for Development, Women's Centre for Legal Aid and Counselling (WCLAC), Women's Affairs Technical Committee (WATC), Palestinian Counseling Center, Family Defense Society, Women's Studies Center, Sawa Organization, Young Women's Christian Association of Palestine (YWCA), Palestinian Family Planning and Protection Association, Rural Women's Development Society, Psycho-Social Counselling Center for Women (PSCCW), Health Work Committees, Palestinian Initiative for the Promotion of Global Dialogue and Democracy (Miftah), Stars of Hope Society, QADER for Community Development, and Mother's School Society.
12 Women's Centre for Legal Aid and Counselling (WCLAC) and Palestinian NGO Forum to Combat Violence Against Women (al-Muntada), "Femicide in the Palestinian Society: Report Submitted to Special

Rapporteur on Violence Against Women, Its Causes and Consequences," April 2021, ohchr.org.

13 Ibid., 3.

14 Ibid.

15 Nadia Hijab, "When Does It Become Genocide?," Institute for Palestine Studies, 2010, palestine-studies.org.

16 As the occupying power, Israel is responsible for the safety and welfare of the population in the territories under its control, including the Gaza Strip. These obligations are set out in international humanitarian law, primarily the Hague Conventions and the Fourth Geneva Convention. Israel still occupies the Gaza Strip, even after the withdrawal of its settlers in 2005, because it controls the land, sea, and air borders and exercises key elements of authority over the strip.

17 "Covid: Palestinians Cancel Vaccine Swap Deal with Israel," BBC, June 18, 2021, bbc.com.

18 Walaa Alqaisiya, "The Queer Feminist Roots of Palestine's May Uprising," *LSE Middle East Blog*, February 7, 2022, blog.lse.ac.uk.

19 alQaws, "Queer Palestinians Gather in Haifa Calling for Safety and Liberation," July 29, 2020, alqaws.org.

20 My discussion of the Palestinian Feminist Collective stems from my own involvement with the group as an early collective member and a member of its coordinating committee. This discussion also expands on two short essays I wrote about the formation of the PFC. One appeared as Nada Elia, "Whose Feminism? Palestine's Feminism," *Mondoweiss*, March 19, 2021, mondoweiss.net; the other as Nada Elia, "How Palestine Is a Critical Feminist Issue," *Middle East Eye*, March 25, 2021, middleeasteye.net.

21 PFC website, palestinianfeministcollective.org.

22 Palestinian Feminist Collective, "Pledge That Palestine Is a Feminist Issue," Action Network, March 15, 2021, actionnetwork.org.

23 See Nada Elia, *Justice Is Indivisible: Palestine as a Feminist Issue* (Learning Palestine, 2024 [2017]).

24 See Nada Elia, "The Burden of Representation: When Palestinians Speak Out," in Rabab Abdulhadi, Evelyn Alsultany, and Nadine Naber (eds.), *Arab and Arab-American Feminisms: Gender, Violence, and Belonging* (Syracuse University Press, 2011): 141–58.

25 Ishaan Tharoor, "Israel's New Justice Minister Considers All Palestinians to Be 'the Enemy,'" *Washington Post*, May 7, 2015, washingtonpost .com.

26 Loubna Qutami, "Why Feminism? Why Now? Reflections on the 'Palestine Is a Feminist Issue' Pledge," *Spectre*, May 3, 2021, spectre journal.com.

27 Palestinian Feminist Collective, *Freedom Within Reach: Palestine Action Toolkit* (Palestine Feminist Collective, August 2021), palestinian feministcollective.org.

9. Genocide Is a Feminist Issue

1 This chapter borrows from three articles I wrote in the aftermath of the October 7 attack addressing the allegations of a "pattern of gang rapes" by Hamas militants, and the official reports documenting Israeli sexual violence against Palestinians from the onset of al-Nakba to the present: Nada Elia, "The Continuum of Genocide," *Spectre*, May 1, 2024, spectrejournal.com; Nada Elia, "Weaponizing Rape," *Jadaliyya*, January 19, 2024, jadaliyya.com; Nada Elia, "The Israel Exemption," *Journal of Palestine Studies* 54, no. 2 (2025): 66–74.

2 Nir Hasson and Liza Rozovsky, "Hamas Committed Documented Atrocities. But a Few False Stories Feed the Deniers," *Haaretz*, December 4, 2023, haaretz.com.

3 Holly Williams and Erin Lyall, "Israel Kibbutz the Scene of a Hamas 'Massacre,' First Responders Say: 'The Depravity of It Is Haunting,'" CBS News, October 11, 2023, cbsnews.com.

4 Etan Vlessing, "'Stranger Things' Star Noah Schnapp Tells Instagram Followers 'Choose Humanity over Violence' amid Israel-Hamas War," *Hollywood Reporter*, October 11, 2023, hollywoodreporter.com.

5 Peter Alexander, Summer Concepcion, and Megan Lebowitz, "White House Clarifies Biden's Claim He Saw Photos of Terrorists Beheading Children in Israel-Hamas War," NBC News, October 12, 2013, nbcnews.com.

6 Abira Das, "2018 Mexico Video Falsely Viral as Hamas Killing Pregnant Woman, Unborn Child," Alt News, October 21, 2023, altnews.in.

7 The entire text of his address is available at the Biden White House Archives: "Remarks by President Biden at a Campaign Reception," December 12, 2023, bidenwhitehouse.archives.gov.

8 Tia Goldenberg and Julia Frankel, "How 2 Debunked Accounts of Sexual Violence on Oct. 7 Fueled a Global Dispute over Israel-Hamas War," PBS News, May 22, 2024, pbs.org.

9 Linda Dayan, "Rape as a Weapon of War: Jewish Women Call on UN to Confront Hamas' Sexual Violence," *Haaretz*, December 5, 2023, haaretz.com.

10 Kamala Harris, "Remarks by the Vice President on Conflict-Related Sexual Violence," American Presidency Project, June 17, 2024, presidency.ucsb.edu.

11 Katha Pollitt, "Why Have Feminists Been So Slow to Condemn the Hamas Rapes?," *Nation*, December 15, 2023, thenation.com.

12 See, for example, UN Office of the High Commissioner, "'More Than a Human Can Bear': Israel's Systematic Use of Sexual, Reproductive, and Other Forms of Gender-Based Violence Since October 2023," press release, March 13, 2025, ohchr.org; B'Tselem, *Living Hell: The Israeli Prison System as a Network of Torture Camps* (B'Tselem, 2026), btselem.org.

13 hate5six, "Susan Abulhawa's Response to Zohran Mandani's 'Antisemitism' Accusations," YouTube, March 14, 2026, youtube.com.
14 Nadera Shalhoub-Kevorkian, *Militarization and Violence Against Women in Conflict Zones in the Middle East: A Palestinian Case Study* (Cambridge University Press, 2009), 13.
15 "An Interview with Benny Morris," *CounterPunch*, January 16, 2004, counterpunch.org.
16 Aviv Lavie and Moshe Gorali, "'I Saw Fit to Remove Her from the World,'" *Haaretz*, October 29, 2003, haaretz.com.
17 "Israeli Minister Said He Could 'Forgive Instances of Rape,' 1948 Documents Reveal," *Middle East Eye*, January 6, 2022, middleeasteye .net.
18 Amnesty International, *Israel and the Occupied Palestinian Territories (oPt): Briefing to the Committee Against Torture* (Amnesty International, September 2008), amnesty.org.
19 Omar Shakir, "A Threshold Crossed: Israeli Authorities and the Crimes of Apartheid and Persecution," Human Rights Watch, April 27, 2021, hrw.org. Administrative detention is the Israeli practice, inherited from the British Mandate, of arresting and imprisoning Palestinians for up to six months at a time, renewable indefinitely, without trial and under allegations Israel keeps secret. This makes it practically impossible for their lawyers to mount a defense case.
20 Amnesty International, "Israel/OPT: Horrifying Cases of Torture and Degrading Treatment of Palestinian Detainees amid Spike in Arbitrary Arrests," November 8, 2023, amnesty.org.
21 B'Tselem, *Welcome to Hell: The Israeli Prison System as a Network of Torture Camps* (B'Tselem, August 2024), btselem.org.
22 Dylann N, "Sexual Harassment and Violence Against Palestinian Women in Israeli Prisons," Jerusalem Fund, August 3, 2018, the jerusalemfund.org.
23 *New Arab* staff, "New Report Tells Chilling Details of Israel's Torture, Killing of Gaza Doctor Adnan al-Bursh," *New Arab*, November 15, 2024, newarab.com.
24 Human Rights Watch, "Israel: Palestinian Healthcare Workers Tortured; ICC Prosecutor Should Investigate Attacks on Health Care, Detainee Abuses," August 26, 2024, hrw.org.
25 "Rights Probe Alleges Sexual Violence Against Palestinians by Israeli Forces Used as 'Method of War,'" UN News, March 13, 2025, news .un.org.
26 UN Office of the High Commissioner, "'More Than a Human Can Bear,'" 1.
27 Palestinian Feminist Collective, "Shut Down Colonial Feminism on International Day for the Elimination of Violence Against Women," palestinianfeministcollective.org.
28 Palestinian Feminist Collective, "The Palestinian Feminist Collective

Condemns Reproductive Genocide in Gaza," palestinianfeminist collective.org.

29 Videoconference, September 2025.

30 Save the Children, "Gaza: 20,000 Children Killed in 23 Months of War—More Than One Child Killed Every Hour," September 6, 2025, savethechildren.net.

Index